SEA STORIES

FROM

Searsport to Singapore

"I took my place at the head of the table, surrounded by wet, slimy bodies, and the two Chinamen began to play."

SEA STORIES

FROM

Searsport to Singapore

Selected Works of
LINCOLN COLCORD

Edited by Donald Mortland

NORTH COUNTRY PRESS
Unity, Maine

Library of Congress Cataloging in Publication Data:

Colcord, Lincoln, 1883-1947.
   Sea stories from Searsport to Singapore.

   1. Seafaring life — Literary collections. 2. Sea
stories, American. I. Mortland, Donald. II. Title.
PS3505.02578A6 1987   818'.5209   87-5643
ISBN 0-89621-104-5
ISBN 0-945980-29-9 (formerly ISBN 0-89621-105-3 pbk.)

Book design by Lurelle Cheverie.
Composition by Camden Type 'n Graphics.
Cover design by James B. Murray.

second printing, 1990

Contents

Introduction · · · · · · · · · · · · · · · · · · · 1

FICTION

The Drifting Diamond · · · · · · · · · · · · 17

Servant and Master · · · · · · · · · · · · · 43

Ah-Man: The Story of a Chinese Steward · · · · · · 61

The Game of Life and Death · · · · · · · · · 77

The Leak · · · · · · · · · · · · · · · · · · 99

De Long: A Story of Sunda Straits · · · · · · · · · 115

Carrying Sail · · · · · · · · · · · · · · · · 145

Home · 157

ESSAYS

I Was Born in a Storm at Sea · · · · · · · · · 175

Preface to An Instrument of the Gods · · · · · 191

The Bogie Hole · · · · · · · · · · · · · · · 199

Eastern Names · · · · · · · · · · · · · · · · 203

POETRY

Outward Bound · · · · · · · · · · · · · · · 207

Captain Robert Belknap Goes West · · · · · · · 211

INTRODUCTION

When Lincoln Colcord died in 1947, *Time* magazine noted his passing under "Milestones" and spoke of him as a spinner of sea tales, an authority on nautical lore, and the man who "created a long-remembered sensation in 1929 when he publicly debunked Joan Lowell's best selling autobiographical sea story, *Cradle of the Deep*, as so much romantic fiction and caused the Book-of-the-Month Club to offer refunds on it." With almost any audience today, a speaker draws nothing but a blank with the name Lincoln Colcord—unless, perhaps, he mentions that Colcord wrote the "Stein Song" or speaks of Colcord's contribution to the writing of the English version of Ole Rolvaag's *Giants in the Earth*.

It seems to have been Colcord's fate to be remembered for accomplishments that were really peripheral to his major work as a writer. He took on the task of revealing the truth about *Cradle of the Deep* because he couldn't bear falseness, especially in matters pertaining to ships and the sea. He dashed off the words of the "Stein Song" in a half hour one day when he was in college. *Giants in the Earth* might never have appeared in English if Colcord had not worked with Rolvaag on it, but still the book is Rolvaag's, not Colcord's.

As to "spinner of sea tales" and "authority on nautical lore," the second is accurate, but the first suggests something less than what he was, at his best, as an author.

Lincoln Colcord's life was varied and unconventional, to say the least. He was born in 1883, aboard his father's sailing vessel going around Cape Horn in a gale; his early years at sea and in foreign ports are well portrayed in "I Was Born in a Storm at Sea." His father and mother were both natives of the little town of Searsport, Maine, a village of about 2,000 people on the

1

northern shore of Penobscot Bay, near the mouth of the Penobscot River. At about the time of Colcord's birth, Searsport could
boast that one tenth of all American ships were commanded by
Searsport men. There had been sea captains in the Colcord
family for five generations, and his mother's family, the Sweet-
sers, had a similar record. There were many such families in
Searsport in the last century, seafaring and shipbuilding people,
who married back and forth and built up a tight and prosperous
community, yet never became provincial because the sea was
their window upon the world. So it was in many towns up and
down the Maine coast and its islands.

These Maine seafarers sailed their tall-masted wooden ships
all over the world—to South America, to the West Indies,
around Cape Horn to California and various ports on the west
coasts of both American continents, to England, to Russia, to
Germany, to the East Indies, to China, to Japan, and to the
islands of the south seas and Australia, totally dependent upon
the wind for power. Many times two ships would meet in mid-
Atlantic and find that both captains were from Searsport. It was
not unusual for Searsport captains and their families, upon arriving in Hong Kong or Shanghai or Kobe, Japan, to find several
other Searsport captains and their families upon ships in the
fleet in the harbor—old friends, neighbors, people they had
gone to school with, and even relatives—as well as others from
other Maine towns.

Ships were generally in port in those days much longer than
they are today, and friends would gather on one ship or another
to talk of the world and their adventures and markets and car-
goes—and home. In an article in the *Portland Sunday Telegram* of July 12, 1936, Colcord's sister, Joanna Carver Colcord,
wrote:

> Many a night, under the awning of some ship's deck,
> with the shorelights sending down long taproots of
> flame into the harbor water and the cigar tips glowing
> and fading, the child that was I listened to marvelous
> stories from the world's best raconteurs—seamen—
> and agonized in the vain effort to stay awake to hear
> the end of the last and most enthralling tale.

Colcord seems to have "learned his trade," or part of it, as he and his sister, children from Maine in some Eastern harbor, listened to their elders underneath the awning. In many of his stories he uses a narrator, a fictitious Captain Nichols, who tells the story under the awning aboard his ship, the *Omega,* in some such harbor as Hong Kong or Shanghai or Singapore. (Nichols is often a main character in the story, as he is in Colcord's exotic novel, *The Drifting Diamond.*)

Colcord was a young man when the era of the sailing vessel was drawing to a close, around the turn of the century. "When I grew up there was no sea career for me," he writes. "The day of sailing vessels was done; and I did not give a thought to steam." At the conclusion of his "I Was Born in a Storm at Sea," he describes very beautifully and movingly his feelings about coming ashore for good. He went to the University of Maine and became a civil engineer. As such, he worked briefly in the Maine woods, but the wind in the pine trees made him remember wind in the sails; and the little inland towns, new to him, made him long for letters to tell him what foreign ports his father was visiting and how other relatives and friends were faring. He knew well enough, even then, the sad truth that the days of sail, stretching from his own youth far back into antiquity, were ending. Blessed with a clear and force- ful prose style, he was well equipped to become a chronicler of that age.

He began to write stories of the sea. His first was published in 1908, when he was working in the woods for the Bangor and Aroostook Railroad. He returned to Searsport shortly after that, and in 1910 he married Miss Blanche Nickels, daughter of a Searsport captain and shipbuilder, and a daughter was born to them in 1913. He published his only novel, his masterpiece, I think, *The Drifting Diamond,* in 1912, and a volume of short stories, *The Game of Life and Death,* two years later.

In 1917, abruptly it would seem, he left Searsport and fiction and went with his wife and daughter to Washington, D.C., where he was staff correspondent in the Washington Bureau of the *Philadelphia Public Ledger.* In Washington, he became a friend and confidant of Colonel Edward M. House, who was a friend and confidant of President Woodrow Wilson.

In fact, it was Colonel House who sponsored Colcord for the post with the *Ledger*. In his article on Colcord in the *Dictionary of American Biography*, Walter Muir Whitehill quotes as follows from a letter to Colonel House from H. B. Brougham, publisher of the *Ledger*:

> Colcord is new in this business. If he is a cub he is a lion's cub, and waxing powerful. Since he came here I have watched his course with an amazed admiration which I find it difficult to conceal. He is a man of hungry and indomitable energy and facts are his prey, which he devours and assimilates with a veritable rapacity after the truth. (July 19, 1917)

In 1919, Colcord moved to New York. There he was an associate editor of the *Nation* in 1919 and 1920. For a few years he was writing article after article on political matters, published in the *Nation*, *North American Review*, *Forum*, *Dial*, and *Century*.

Then, in another abrupt turn, he left New York and the *Nation*, stopped publishing political articles, returned to Searsport, and began to write sea stories again. A volume of them appeared in the fall of 1922: *An Instrument of the Gods and Other Stories of the Sea*.

In 1924, his wife died after a long and painful struggle with cancer. This seems to have caused another about face in Colcord's life. He went to Minnesota, this son of the sea and writer of sea stories, where his sister was living, and stayed several years. Here he met Rolvaag and helped him to bring *Giants in the Earth* into print in English in 1927. His association with Rolvaag was a new and important chapter in his life and it provides information revealing Colcord's status as an American writer in the late 1920's.

For instance, in their biography of Rolvaag, Theodore Jorgenson and Nora A. Solum wrote: "Lincoln Colcord was a literary artist of the first water. . . . Rolvaag maintained publicly that on the score of workmanship, no better man than Mr. Colcord was to be found in the United States." Concerning the first meeting of the two men, the biographers wrote: " . . . in Mr. Colcord Rolvaag met the eastern literati of this country: He gained an intimate acquaintance with men of power and became, as it were, an insider. . . . In some degree, the provincialism of the Northfield professor [Rolvaag] gave way to the nationalism and internationalism emanating from New York."

Briefly stated, what Colcord did for Rolvaag was this: he greatly encouraged Rolvaag to press on with plans to bring his book out in English and put him in contact with people in the publishing world in America. Rolvaag had written the book in Norwegian, his native tongue, and had published it in Norway. With the aid of friends, he was translating it into English. Unlike Joseph Conrad, whom Colcord greatly admired, Rolvaag was not master of a polished English prose style. Thus Colcord took the English translation that Rolvaag and his friends provided and, constantly conferring with Rolvaag, rewrote the novel in a style that met his own demanding standards.

Colcord's own reputation as an author was now fairly secure. When his novel, *The Drifting Diamond,* came out in 1912 it was reviewed by *Outlook* twice and by the *New York Times Book Review.* The *Times* reviewer said: "*The Drifting Diamond* is one of the best of its kind. . . . The story . . . [is] told with honesty of style, a convincing plainness of speech. Every step in this adventurous narrative is interesting. . . . It has, too, interesting flashes of Oriental life and character. Lincoln Colcord has told a stirring story and told it well."

His book-length poem, *Vision of War* (1915), had been reviewed in *Nation* and in *Current Opinion.* The reviewer for *Nation* concludes a rather supercilious review by saying: "Mr. Colcord is massive, didactic, utilitarian; author and publisher clearly regard him as the last word in modernism." (Three years later Colcord was an associate editor of *Nation!*)

In *A Short History of American Literature,* published in 1919, Walter C. Bronson discusses William Vaughan Moody, Robert Frost, and Edgar Lee Masters as new American poets, and then, apparently as examples of the very newest, Vachel Lindsay, Conrad Aiken, and Lincoln Colcord, which suggests that in 1919 Colcord seemed to show about the same promise as Aiken and Lindsay.

An editorial comment in *American Magazine* for May, 1915, preceding a letter from Colcord, says in part: "Lincoln Colcord . . . is a wonderful writer [who] knows the sea as few people do." It goes on to say that the following letter "gives some idea not only of how wonderfully he writes whatever he wishes to say, but also how one who loved the old order of things objects to the new."

Thus it was as a writer with considerable reputation and a sound body of publications to his credit that Colcord returned to Searsport in 1930 — for return he did, this time "for good." He had remarried in 1928, but this marriage (to Loomis Logan) was not successful and ended in divorce less than a year later. In 1929 he married a third time, to Miss Frances Brooks, with whom he had a son, Brooks, in 1930. He established his new family in the house built by his father in Searsport, and there he lived and wrote for the last seventeen years of his life, with Penobscot Bay almost literally in his back yard. Here he was truly at home, relaxed, delighted by the scene and the place. Those seventeen years did not contribute greatly to his reputation as a writer (in fact, his reputation waned), but they were not placid years.

A strange thing happened at about this time. One of the several ironies of Colcord's life is that of all his works, the words of the "Stein Song" are probably the least important and least characteristic of his work, and contribute least to his reputation as a serious writer, but have enjoyed by far the greatest popularity, aided, as they were in the late 1920's and early 1930's, by the mellow voice of Rudy Vallee. How all of this came about is a story in itself.

In 1904, Colcord was a twenty-one-year-old upperclassman at the University of Maine. (At that time, the whole university was a rather small institution at Orono.) Other students called him "Doc," and they thought him an ingenious fellow who could do anything if he put his mind to it. His roommate, Adelbert Sprague, was University band leader that year. There was no true campus song, a sorely felt need, which Sprague tried to meet. He had found a military march by E. Fenstad, and he turned to his roommate for the lyrics. Lincoln Colcord went to a piano in the music room and within a half hour was back with the "Stein Song."

For nearly a quarter of a century, nothing of great note happened. The song was popular with students but only gradually became the college's song because some members of the administration found it too Bohemian, especially as Maine was a "dry" state.

Then, in the 1920's, Rudy Vallee, a member of the Class of 1925, rose quickly to great popularity as a singer. (Both radio and phonograph were enjoying the first fine flush of popularity in those days.) One of the songs that he loved to sing was the college song of the University of Maine. In an article that appeared in the *Maine Alumnus*, Fall, 1980, Professor Parker Albee, Jr., wrote:

> Fifty years ago the University of Maine was becoming known around the world with a rapidity enjoyed by no other American university. More precisely, people everywhere were hearing of its shouts that made the rafters ring, its loyal Maine men, its happy hours and careless days. For 1930 was the year that Rudy Vallee '25 was singing the "Stein Song."

The song had become world famous, sung and played from Shanghai to Chicago, Bangkok to Bangor.

Such astonishing popularity attracted the press to the origins of the song. The 1930 Commencement at the University of Maine was carefully covered. Both Adelbert Sprague and Lincoln Colcord, now middle-aged men, were invited. Professor Albee wrote:

> The two friends made their prepared remarks, the band played the song, and the reunion classes sang it as both Paramount and Fox Movietone news-cameras ground away to capture the scene for national coverage.

The press assumed that Colcord was getting rich on the royalties. *The New York Sun* telegrammed him at Searsport to ask about royalties. A writer in *The New Yorker* took the liberty of saying that the authors of the "Stein Song" were sharing ten thousand dollars in royalties.

Actually, Colcord had not received a cent. He had never copyrighted his lyrics and the publishers of the song conveniently overlooked the fact that he had written them. In the spring of 1930, he decided that he ought to have what was rightfully his. Colcord contacted a lawyer, approached the publishers with little

success, sought the advice of Rudy Vallee, who became his ally
and friend. Together they confronted the publishers in their New
York offices; to Vallee's amazement and chagrin, Colcord settled
for a lump sum of three thousand dollars — for the most popular
song in the world!

In an earlier letter to Vallee, there is a clue to the mystery of
Colcord's sudden action. Vallee had written of how hectic his life
had become. Colcord had returned to Searsport that very year
after about fifteen years of what must have been a rather hectic
life in Minneapolis, New York, Washington, and elsewhere,
interrupted only by the four or five agonizing years in Searsport
when his first wife was dying of cancer. Thus he replied in
fatherly, sympathetic tones:

> I feel like answering the last paragraph of your letter
> first; it sounded almost like a cry of pain. Here I sit,
> just above the headwaters of Penobscot Bay, looking
> out over a range of deep blue water and islands covered
> with bright spring green, on one of the most divine
> afternoons God ever dropped on the old world. You
> know what the Maine coast can be in June, when it
> gives half a try. Robins feeding their young under the
> eaves, gulls and fish hawks sailing over the bay, a few
> schooners drifting across the scene, the air warm yet
> fresh and invigorating — and nothing but peace all
> around. No harsh sounds, no harsh people to bother
> with. . . . Peace, and quiet living. Why should we
> strain so hard at the leash? Why should we tie
> ourselves in hard knots and trouble our hearts, when
> nature offers such scenes as this?

He was too eager to return to his peaceful life at Searsport to stay
long in New York in summer, bickering over royalties.

In that year of 1930, the Great Depression, as it was later
called, was just setting in; yet it was Colcord's hour of triumph in
the *Cradle of the Deep* controversy, the "Stein Song" was being
sung all over the country and abroad, and he had a new family.

He had already made many friends of a wide variety of back-
grounds and personalities, Samuel Eliot Morison being one. Add
now Rudy Vallee and Sterling Hayden and Walter Muir White-

hill. Waldo Peirce soon appeared in Searsport, well known artist and friend of Hemingway, later to settle in an old captain's mansion only a block or so up Main Street from Colcord's family home. Just beyond that was his first wife's old home, which had become the summer home of Clifford Carver and his family, of New York City, Carver being the nephew of the first Mrs. Colcord. Colcord's intelligent review of a book by Howard Chappelle gained him another friend.

In 1936, with Carver, Colcord founded the Penobscot Marine Museum in Searsport. In 1942, he became one of the founders of the *American Neptune,* in Salem, Massachusetts.

All through these years, he carried on a flourishing correspondence with friends all over the world, and he wrote scores of book reviews for the New York *Herald Tribune,* usually of books dealing with marine affairs, on which he was a recognized authority.

In those years, the 1930's and early 1940's, I was a boy growing up in Searsport myself. I knew Mr. Colcord only as a rather tall, spare man of somewhat stern countenance whom I frequently saw striding along the sidewalk between his house on East Main Street and the post office. Twice he was a speaker at Searsport High School while I was a student there. (He spoke on weather and what causes storms at sea, as I recall.) Once when my eighth grade teacher took us to the then new Penobscot Marine Museum, Colcord was there and explained to us how to use a sextant.

We seldom saw him in an automobile of any sort, because he never owned one. It is an odd fact that this man who put his hand to the wheel of a ship when he was a boy of ten or twelve never did put his hand to the wheel of an automobile. He never learned to drive. He could guide a ship unerringly all over the waters of the world, but he could not guide a car from his house to the post office. Perhaps it is of a piece with his scorn for steam, for propelling ships by engines. "I gave no thought to steam," he said, and so a career as master mariner was denied him because he was born too late. The world no longer needed men with the skill and knowledge to command sailing ships. (Oddly, his attitude seemed unaffected by the fact that his father, whom he revered, did "go into steam" just before the turn of the century and commanded steamers until his death in Bremerhaven, Germany, in 1913.)

Other glimpses of Colcord appear in the writings of his many
friends, one of whom, and perhaps the youngest, was Sterling
Hayden, writer and movie star. In his book *Wanderer*, Mr.
Hayden tells of how they first met on a little passenger vessel of
which he (Hayden) was mate when he was a very young man and
Colcord was middle aged or more: "He stamps on the deck and
you'd swear he was tempted to smile. His eyes, mouth, and jaws
shine with arrogance. The face is sharp, and handsome, too, in
a jaundiced way as befits a man with his background." The two
men became acquainted during the little trip up the central
Maine coast, shortly after Colcord had returned to Searsport to
stay. The boat anchored at Searsport for the night and Mr.
Hayden spent the evening with the Colcords.

Later, during World War II, Hayden found himself in Maine
and visited the Colcords again. The two men talked of politics.

> I smiled, looking around this room so full of the sea:
> sea books, sea pictures, carved name boards, and
> charts and pamphlets, and I knew there was more sea
> here than in all the ships afloat. . . .

Another quite different friend, Walter Muir Whitehill, writing in 1968, said: "In the years that I knew him, Lincoln Colcord
stuck close to Searsport." After mentioning some exceptions,
such as meeting him in Boston and in Washington, he adds: "But
mostly he stayed in Searsport and the world came to him. Although he has been dead for twenty-one years, I keep stumbling
across traces of his earlier and more active life that he never spoke
of in the years when I knew him." One of these traces appeared
in 1963 when Whitehill gave an address in Minneapolis and was
told by the Governor of Minnesota, Karl F. Rolvaag, of Colcord's
invaluable help to his father in bringing out *Giants in the Earth* in
1927, more than thirty years before!

Whitehill also quotes a letter that Colcord wrote to Colonel
House in 1916, which partially reveals another aspect of Colcord:

> "It's not a bad place [Searsport], much as any others,
> but the secret of our love for it lies in what I have just
> said — we know it intimately. This is the lesson I got
> from Thoreau. Love your own pond. All are beautiful.

Be contented where you are. Content! A lost word in
our America. This restless ambition — I cannot feel
the truth of it. I cannot follow there. I am quite
willing to be out of touch with my times. I would live
as if the times were out of touch with me."

If one wonders why this man of the world repeatedly returned
to Searsport, the answer may be that he had always loved Searsport, as this letter and others attest, and that returning to Searsport was bred in his bones. His ancestors sailed all over the world,
but always returned to Searsport unless they died at sea or in
foreign lands. It was the beloved home port.

This love of Searsport and its environs and particularly his love
of nature ashore are more apparent in his letters to Samuel Eliot
Morison, selections from which were published in the *New England Quarterly* in June and September of 1983. In a letter to
Morison dated May 23, 1923, having returned to Searsport after
wintering with his wife's relatives in New York, Colcord describes nature as he saw it in what must have been a late spring
even for Maine. In part he wrote:

Since our return to Maine, the thermometer has
hardly gone above fifty degrees; day after day of cold
southerly and easterly weather, fog, rain, and always
an overcast sky. . . . I've had a furnace fire every day
since we came — you can't imagine how cold and
damp it is. This is bleak New England, without the
alleviation of joy; yet in spite of the devil I love it. I
love the gray tone of the rain and the fog and the sea,
the green of the fields running down to the dull brown
of the rockweed on the shore. In the woods yellow
birches gleam with a bright inner light in this lowery
weather; and the heavy, rich green of pines and
spruces lends an air of energy and vitality to hillside
pastures sprinkled with boulders. Granite and evergreen are the colors of New England.

The letter continues in this vein for what must have been several
manuscript pages, but it grows more philosophical, too, so that
by the end he is saying:

It is a strange heritage, this capacity of the New Eng-
lander to be happy in his melancholy; to love the fog
and the cold, the overcast sky, the dull water, the grey
and green of the hills. But it is not well to mistake
him. . . . He seems stony and forbidding; but in the
deep, hidden core of his being he is alive with all
power and passion, with all reserves of tenderness and
understanding, with all possibilities of beauty and
love. He belongs to the northern habitat. He is only
waiting for the brief but glorious sun.

It is tempting to guess that in this love of nature and his close
observation of it, Colcord was influenced by his first wife. Her
gravestone, set in what was a far corner of the Nickels Cemetery
in Searsport, near the woods and surrounded by ferns and wild
flowers, is a rough boulder with a plaque affixed which reads as
follows:

Blanche Meade Morgan: wife of Lincoln Colcord.
Died August 24, 1924. A lover of nature.

(The name Morgan, not Nickels, is accounted for by the fact that
she was the adopted daughter of Capt. and Mrs. J.C. Nickels.)
    A lingering question about Colcord's work is why he did not
publish *more* in these later years of his life. One answer seems to
be that he spent so much time in conversation with the many
friends who "stopped by" the house in Searsport or who came to
spend a few days that he just didn't have time to undertake
writing the novel that he planned or the book about the coast of
Maine that he and Morison discussed so enthusiastically. In a
fine biographical essay included in his *Analecta Biographica*, Walter Muir Whitehill says that Colcord was "only in his early fifties"
when he first knew him but he had "retired from the great world
to the quiet coastal town that was the home of his shipmaster
father. . . . To this house there came an extraordinary diversity
of people, among them journalists, seamen, historians, actors,
poets, and painters. In his back yard you might find almost
anyone. Similarly there were few limits to the range of his ideas."
    One wishes that those talks in the Colcord back yard had been
recorded somehow. Both Whitehill and Morison bemoan the

fact that in those later years Colcord was content to express his ideas in the evanescent medium of conversation and put few of them into print except in book reviews and in letters to his friends. After describing Colcord's very major role in founding the *American Neptune* magazine and saying that Colcord has been constantly helpful to the *Neptune* in giving advice and criticism of manuscripts, Whitehill adds: "His own contributions were fewer than I could have wished, for the extent of his correspondence, and the remarkable number of friends who appeared in person in the back yard at Searsport, left him little time for writing. I was one of the many callers who at all seasons were likely to distract him. Whenever I have drawn up beside his gaunt old yellow house, and paused momentarily to look out to a sea whose intense blue was matched by that of the delphiniums in the grass, I have always been visited by a sense of anticipation. . . ."

Samuel Eliot Morison is more emphatic in a letter to Colcord written on January 29, 1937. Morison was trying to persuade Colcord and his family to go on a cruise with him and Mrs. Morison, and apparently Colcord had spoken of his proposed novel as one thing that made him hesitate. Morison wrote:

> As for your novel, that can wait & this can't; but why not write the novel now? The way to write is to sit down and write — stop reading the paper, worrying about politics, writing letters to friends, book reviews, or reading everything that comes out. Just eat, sleep, write, and walk an hour a day.

This seems to provide the best clue for solving the mystery. Colcord and Morison had been close friends since the early 1920's. The Morisons had a summer home on Mt. Desert Island and would pass straight by the "gaunt old yellow house" in going to and from Boston. Thus Morison was often among those in the back yard at Searsport. It was apparently these conversations that led Morison to invent the sobriquet "the Sage of Searsport" for Colcord.

Before leaving the Colcord-Morison letters published in the *New England Quarterly*, I should like to offer two passages that say something about Colcord's style. The editor of the letters, Professor Parker Albee, Jr., makes the following splendid observation: "They [the letters] reveal two distinguished stylists, each a highly sophisticated man of the world who was at the same time fiercely parochial in his affection for New England." One can hardly imagine a more succinct statement about both the styles and the personalities of the two men. In one of the letters, dated 3 August 1923, Morison takes a quick glance at both style and content in Colcord's "I Was Born in a Storm at Sea":

> Both of us read with the greatest interest your autobiography in the American Magazine, and we hope you may continue it. I think it is a really 1st rate bit of writing, & full of wisdom as well. It is so much better ever [sic] than your best stories that I hope you may continue that sort of thing."

Colcord's works illuminate wonderfully that period in Maine history when Maine sea captains sailed their ships on the seven seas and took their families with them. His writings answer all sorts of questions about this life, of which he was a part. Where did they go? — to what ports? How did they live aboard ship? What relationships had they with the crew? How did a boy of fifteen feel about going to sea for his first voyage (as Colcord's own father did and as the central character does in "Home"), and what was it like to come home again for the first time, perhaps several years later? How were the captain's children educated at sea? What pastimes had they? What did they do ashore when they came into foreign ports?

He obeyed, then, the old injunction to write of what one knows well, but he knew a corner of our history that very few other writers ever experienced. His narratives generally proceed like a well run ship, whose commander knows exactly what he is doing and how to do it. His prose style is exemplary, as this volume attests.

Another Maine writer, Sarah Orne Jewett, once wrote concerning the effect of seafaring upon Maine people:

> . . . They have rounded the Cape of Good Hope and braved the angry seas of Cape Horn in small wooden ships; they have brought up their hardy boys and girls on narrow decks; they were among the last of the Northmen's children to go adventuring to unknown shores. . . . The sea captains and the captains' wives

of Maine knew something of the wide world, and never mistook their native parishes for the whole instead of a part thereof; they knew not only Thomaston and Castine and Portland, but London and Bristol and Bordeaux, and the strange-mannered harbors of the China Sea.[1]

Both Colcord's life and his fiction show this to be true. At one time in his life, Colcord became very close to the center of power in this nation. His fictitious Capt. Belknap sees the parallel between managing a ship and governing a nation. His Capt. Nichols has come to understand the Chinese of his day, and he is at home anywhere. The sea gave him this as it had given Colcord, whose works give a world view of things. His people were citizens not only of a little town somewhere on the Maine coast but also citizens of the world.

As Walter Muir Whitehill wrote in the *Dictionary of American Biography*, "Few men have had so varied a career with so little conventional preparation; few have had so wide an influence simply by talking to their friends. He was a man of outstanding vitality and gusto. He met life eagerly, equally alert for the savor of a situation, a bowl of chowder, a bottle of rum, an idea, an anecdote, or a stretch of landscape."

Today his best works are remembered hardly at all, a situation that I hope the publication of this volume will remedy. "Finders keepers, losers weepers," goes the old children's rhyme.[2] It would be sad indeed to lose a novel as good as *The Drifting Diamond* or a poem as powerful as "Captain Robert Belknap Goes West," or any of the other works reprinted here. If this book helps the reading world to "keep" them, then our purpose will be achieved.

DONALD F. MORTLAND
Unity College
Unity, Maine

[1] Sarah Orne Jewett, *The Queen's Twin and Other Tales* (Boston: Houghton, Mifflin and Company, 1900), pp. 1-2.

[2] Here I am indebted to Carlos Baker in his essay "The Function of the Critic," found in *The Art of Prose*, ed. by Paul A. Jorgensen and Frederick B. Shroyer. (New York: Scribners, 1955), p. 217.

THE DRIFTING
DIAMOND

VII

A rumble of thunder interrupted the narrative. Nichols went
to the rail, and glanced up past the edge of the awning. "Typhoon
weather," he commented. "It was just such an air as this—heavy,
thick, still." He paused a moment, thinking. "Yes, I was annoyed
and exasperated with young Lane," he went on. "I wanted to *do*
something about it. Then, quite suddenly, the good old elements
intervened. Noble old elements!—how a breeze of wind will
knock the notions out of a man, how a big wave will strip him to
his essential nakedness! You never can know a man's soul until
you see him at the point of death.

"That noon, just as I was screwing the sun down for the last
time, a tremble went through the ship; her nose lifted about three
inches, and dropped again. All the morning she had been motionless, resting on a calm sea. She nodded slowly, lifted on a
second long swell, then on a third. I looked around:—not a
breath of wind, not a change, not a sign. The three waves were
so low that I could hardly detect them on the still surface of the
water. They had passed evenly, almost imperceptibly, like the
ripples of some deep and hidden disturbance—as if an enormous
fish had crossed our keel a mile below. I stepped to the rail; and
at the same moment, the first of another trio of glassy swells
caught us under the bows. A yard creaked loudly aloft; a low

Editor's note: This selection is an excerpt from Lincoln Colcord's novel,
The Drifting Diamond (New York: The Macmillan Company, 1912),
pp. 63–113.

swishing sound followed the wave along the vessel's side. No change—but for us everything was changed! Perhaps you fellows don't know the sensation, the thrill; perhaps you've never received a message from beyond the horizon, an undulation sent out into still waters from the very heart of elemental wrath. Perhaps you wouldn't have known what it meant—but I did. It meant typhoon!

"I turned to find Lee Fu behind me. He watched the *Omega's* bow rise and fall past the line of the horizon; the swell was still very faint, but regular and long. A sense of motion had come upon the ship; sounds multiplied—unexpected sounds, unnatural sounds. The sails flapped, the spanker tugged at the boom-tackle, the topsail yards squeaked and groaned against the masts, ropes snapped as they tautened.

" 'It is early for typhoons,' said Lee Fu.

" 'Yes!' I answered. 'Too confounded early altogether! I've been through five, and have circumvented half a dozen more; but they were all later in the season. They tell me that an early one, like this, is a law unto itself—you never know what it's going to do next.'

"Lee Fu nodded. 'That is true,' he said. 'I have even seen one travel from west to east.'

" 'Good Lord!' I cried. 'And we're in about the worst place in the whole China Sea. A typhoon coming in through Bashee Channel, now, is liable to turn sharp west just here—or it's liable not to. If we catch the wind from south of west, the center is to the westward of us, and we ought to be all right. I don't believe it would back to the eastward here, Lee Fu, with the shoulder of Luzon to throw it out into the China Sea.'

" 'It would seem not,' he answered. 'At least, Captain Nichols, you have plenty of sea-room.'

"That's the way we talked throughout the afternoon, while we waited for the wind. If this, and if that, and if the other. Theoretically, a circular storm is simple enough; and with sea-room, as Lee Fu said, you can get away from it. When the wind strikes, you can tell by its direction which edge of the storm you're on, and how the center of it bears from you. You also know how that center is travelling—theoretically. A typhoon ought to make a general course towards the north, from northwest to northeast. The good ones do. But there are typhoons that run wild, like a maniac—that charge screaming about the China Sea, smiting this ship, sparing the next, laying waste this village, sheering off from another twenty miles down the coast. And from them there's no escape, except by decree of the god called Chance.

"All that afternoon we waited. Piece by piece we took in the upper sails, although there was as yet no wind. The sky grew coppery, and distant clouds hung like heavy black smoke on the northern horizon. By degrees the sun changed color, and shrank to a fiery ball swimming in the midst of impure vapors—of vapors that crept stealthily above us, enveloping the world. The swell increased, gathered power; it caught the little bark with a swing that had something terrible in it, something purposeful, something that muttered with every lift, 'A little stronger—a little stronger! *Look out!*' I must have walked miles that afternoon—couldn't keep still. The calmness of the sea was a mockery; everywhere I looked, tremendous and awful forces were massing; and there we lay, motionless, prostrate, a speck on a vast lurid ocean, an assemblage of tiny atoms defying the whirlwind, pitting the marvel of thought against the boundless elemental power.

"Lane had been on deck since dinner, watching the weather with the rest of us. The meaning of that wild sky was too plain to be missed, even by a landsman. And then, he couldn't have failed to see the anxiety on our faces, though our technicalities were no doubt beyond his grasp. He seemed very quiet, and asked no questions. The thought came to me, I remember, that at last something had occurred sufficiently important to drive the cursed diamond out of his mind. I must have been preoccupied, to go no deeper into the matter than that. For I knew well enough, if I'd reflected a moment, that apprehension increases love, and that love increases apprehension. Men who have never before cared a hang, will lose their courage when their hearts are involved. They fear for the object of their love, I suppose; at least, that's the sentimental explanation, though I have a feeling there's some selfishness mixed up in it, too.

"We were eating supper, a silent company, when the *Omega* careened sharply. Dishes slid about the table, something fell with a crash in the after cabin; and we needed no shout from on deck to inform us that the wind had struck on the port beam. We rushed out pell-mell. A glance at the compass told me that we'd caught it from due north. We were on the western edge of the typhoon, instead of the eastern, as I'd hoped for; the center was between us and Luzon. Was it moving south across our bow, or coming directly towards us?

"The breeze was fresh, steady, and sweet with the odor of flowers. I sniffed it a while, trying to make up my mind. 'I'm going to run to the southward, before the wind,' I said at last, turning to Lee Fu. 'The storm ought to be travelling west. If it is, we can slip away before it gets here.'

" 'Exactly,' Lee Fu answered. 'I should do the same, Captain Nichols. In a few hours, we will learn more.'

"Lee Fu's knowledge of typhoons is profound; it was a relief to have his support. I at once put her off before the wind, under the two upper-topsails. Night fell swiftly; the darkness was tangible, touching us on either hand. We felt our way about decks, with arms extended like blind men. The wind rose little by little; it moaned overhead through the rigging, it hissed alongside like an attendant brood of serpents. Low sounds came to us out of the heart of the night—faint echoes of thunder, vibrations of distant concussions, wandering down the lanes of the storm. Still that heavenly sweetness hung about us; as if, all unseen, we were sailing between banks of fragrant flowers.

"The glow of the binnacle seemed to be the only light in an immense void. Hour after hour I hung about it, watching for a shift of wind. Eight—nine—ten o'clock, and no change. We'd been holding a south course for four hours then, and must have covered a good forty miles. I took in the fore upper-topsail, hauled up the mainsail, and went below to consult Lee Fu.

"I found him playing solitaire on the chart table. 'I think we'd better haul her up on the starboard tack, and get away to the westward, Lee Fu,' I said. 'East would be better, but we'd be heading towards the land.'

" 'How is the wind?' he asked, holding a card poised above the pile.

" 'Still due north, and blowing on harder every minute. The center is evidently moving along with us, and edging a bit nearer all the time.'

"He placed the card on its proper stack, and looked up. 'It will probably turn and follow us,' he said.

" 'What would you do, then—keep on to the southward?' I demanded. 'That doesn't seem good sense, Lee Fu. We *know* this—and we can't look into the future.'

"He played another card. 'No,' he said. 'Except that if the typhoon is to catch us, it will catch us. Nothing that we do will be of avail.'

"I felt like sweeping his confounded cards on the floor. 'In your opinion, then,' I inquired with some asperity, 'is this particular typhoon booked to catch us? Hang it all, say something definite!'

" 'That, Captain, is beyond my province,' he answered, smiling broadly. 'The thing to do, however, is exactly what you have proposed—stand to the westward.'

"Young Lane had been sitting on one of the side couches, smoking and listening to the conversation. 'What if it does catch us?' he asked suddenly. 'What will happen? Is a typhoon—?'

" 'Mr. Lane, I don't want it to catch us!' I said, considerably out of humor. 'The *Omega* is a small ship, and not as young as she was once. Almost anything might happen, if you come to that.'

"He clutched at his belt, and a deathly pallor spread over his face. 'You don't mean there would be any danger?'

" 'It's dangerous to be alive, Mr. Lane!' I snapped in disgust.

"Lee Fu placed the last card on the table, and showed me four neat packs, each covered by a king. 'I have it!' he exclaimed.

" 'What?' cried Lane, jumping up eagerly, his mind fixed on escape.

" 'The game,' said Lee Fu.

VIII

"To a mere mortal, a philosopher is a trying companion in time of trouble. Lane flushed to the roots of his hair, and turned away. I myself had been touched at Lee Fu's indifference. I knew, however, that the moment he took exception to my course, he'd assume quite a different attitude. No one can be quicker or surer in emergency than Lee Fu. I went on deck, brought the *Omega* up on the starboard tack, and off we dashed in another direction.

"There was something big and glorious, after all, in this skirmish with the elements; the sailor-heart answered to it, the soul of dead sailor-generations awoke at its call. I clung to the weather rail, exulting in the bound of the ship beneath me, in the crash of far-flung water, in the song of straining sails. She swooped bravely as the big swells passed under her; she stood up staunchly to the wind that was now a gale. It seemed as if she, too, had renewed a measure of her youth and fire—had scented the race, as an old horse will, and tossed her head with the spirit that triumphs over time and change. The black night engulfed us, the phosphorescent waves streamed by us, the flower-scented gale careened us; we headed for nothing, we were bound nowhere; we shot like a bolt through the dark, like a bolt fired at random, silent, unswerving, powerful, and showing dim lights that were lost in the amazing gloom. God pity any ship that had stood in our way that night! We were incarnate Fear, loose upon the waters—men in our hollow wooden engine, fleeing madly for the sake of our small but terribly important lives.

"And the typhoon turned, and followed us. Oh, yes!—flee as we would, manoeuver as we would, it leaped along our wake in giant strides, it tracked us like a hound on a fresh trail. Somewhere in the inexorable schedule, it was written that we were to be caught; and from that decree there was no immunity, as Lee Fu had said. The wind held north—due north—and blew on harder yet. At three o'clock it was howling; I took in the main upper-topsail, hauled up the foresail, and a little later took in the main topmast-staysail. It was slow work, on such a night; but my Chinamen behaved splendidly. There was already a heavy sea from the north, kicked up by the wind we had; and underneath that, the big swell rolled in from the northeast. Between the two, the old bark had begun to labor heavily. Too late then to think of running off to the south again; I wouldn't have dared to put her before it. Besides, by the feeling of every fresh gust of wind, I wanted to get her stripped as soon as possible.

"While they were trying to furl the foresail, I felt a touch on my arm. I was standing by the galley door at the time; the sail made a great slatting overhead, and the wind screamed a steady note. Someone was speaking to me—a few words came to my ears. 'Captain Nichols—you—?'

" 'Yes!' I shouted, grabbing the arm that had touched me and followed it in till I found a man's shoulder. 'Who is it?'

" 'It's I—Lane!' the voice yelled. 'My God, sir, this is awful!'

"Holding him by the shoulder, I couldn't see a vague outline—I couldn't see my own arm. How he'd found me, I can't imagine; he must have stumbled on me. 'What do you want?' I shouted. 'What are you doing here?'

" 'I wanted to know—' A fierce squall struck us, the sail thundered, and I lost his voice completely. He pulled himself towards me, and put his mouth close to my ear. 'Is this a typhoon? Is she sinking?' he cried.

"Idiotic landlubber, he'd groped his way on deck in a gale of wind to ask me that! 'You damned fool, go below!' I screamed. 'This is no place for you. You'll be overboard next!' I gave him a push. 'Go below—I'm coming down soon.'

"The moment he'd gone, I reproached myself. It's one thing for a sailor to find his way about decks in the night, and another thing for a landsman. Perhaps Lane had become bewildered, and taken the wrong direction; perhaps he'd lost his footing. A dozen mishaps might have befallen him. I worked myself into a panic over it; and was glad enough, when I was at last able to go below, to find him safe in the cabin.

IX

"As I came down, I saw that Lee Fu and Clewley had resumed their endless cribbage-playing. Young Lane stood in the door of his stateroom, watching them with a sort of fascinated amazement. The cards slid about, and had to be recovered and held in place; the cribbage board was chocked off with thumb-tacks; whenever the ship rolled, the two were obliged to hang onto the table to hold themselves in their chairs. You know how it is at sea—motion is simply an item of environment, and is never allowed to interfere with the habit of life. The expression on Lane's face was amusing. By no possible explanation, could that game of cribbage have seemed anything to him but the shammest of bravado.

" 'Well, gentlemen,' I said, taking off my oilskin coat and throwing it in the corner. 'I think we're ready for it. I've got her down to two lower topsails and a double-reefed spanker. It can blow on any time now.' For my own part, I felt a certain relief in having the thing settled. No more dodging and twisting, no more hesitating over a choice of courses, no alternative left, in fact;

the infernal typhoon had *caught* us, and the matter was in other hands than mine.

" 'Good!' remarked Lee Fu. 'You would be wise to take in your lower topsails also, and your spanker. I recall that the *Omega* rides well under a mizzen topmast-staysail.' He looked up, blinking over his cards. 'I am so sorry, Captain, that my position as a passenger would make it an impertinence for me to assist you on deck.'

" 'Yes, you old reprobate!' I returned. 'You sit down here, snug and dry and warm, and think up work for me, while I'm out in the storm toiling to save your miserable skin. Then when we get in, I suppose you'll tell everyone how you brought the *Omega* through a typhoon!'

"Lee Fu smiled broadly. 'So sorry, Captain.' Suddenly he grew grave. 'Pardon—I forgot. Word came to me some time ago that a man had been washed overboard from the forecastle-head. They were unable to find you in the darkness, and brought the news to me.'

" 'The devil you say!' I exclaimed. 'How—?' I bit the question off just in time—for the answer had flashed upon me. This was no weather to wash men overboard! 'Too bad!' I observed flatly. 'Impossible to do anything, this kind of a night. . . . '

" 'Quite useless,' said Lee Fu, turning back to his cards.

"Clewley and I exchanged glances. So the agent of the Maharajah was gone—and I hadn't even seen him, didn't know who he was, would probably never miss him among my crew! It was difficult to believe that he had ever existed; to Lane he'd been a face at the skylight, to the rest of us nothing but a footfall overhead.

"Just then an unusually heavy sea struck us; the ship gave a jump that knocked me off my balance, and landed me to leeward in Lane's arms. He clutched wildly at the side of the door, his face as white as a sheet. 'What does it mean?' he asked in a hushed voice, holding me fast.

" 'Mean? What?' I demanded.

" 'That—!' he said vaguely, looking up as if he expected to see the top of the cabin fall in. 'Will she stand much of that?' He fairly shook me in the stress of his alarm. 'For God's sake, tell me!' he cried. 'You keep putting me off; and it's all very well for you to play cards, and laugh and talk, and make believe there's nothing serious, but I can feel *that!* I've got some sense of my own—I can see through *you*, too. It's an awful storm, and you're worried.' He drew himself up defiantly, in the manner of one prepared to hear his fate. 'Tell me the truth!' he said.

"I had a great desire to laugh. 'This is really nothing,' I assured him. 'It seems bad to you, no doubt; but we're all sailors, and have seen it blow much harder.'

" 'Nothing!' he cried. 'And one man washed overboard already!'

" 'I mean, it's nothing to what we'll be having twelve hours from now,' I explained, smiling in spite of myself. 'We're in for a bad time of it—no question about that. But you mustn't lose your grip at this stage, Mr. Lane. You may depend upon me to tell you if there's any real danger.'

"He gazed at me with a dumb, troubled look in his eyes. 'I haven't lost my grip,' he said, undecided whether or not to be offended. 'Of course, I don't know—it seems pretty bad.' He turned away, and fumbled with the door knob; there was evidently something on his mind that he had hard work to get out. 'I wouldn't care— You don't think that I'm frightened for *myself*, do you?' he asked, whirling about and facing the three of us.

"Lee Fu laid down his cards. 'On the contrary, Mr. Lane,' he said smoothly, 'we share your feelings. Who could be undisturbed at thought of the Penang Diamond beset by a typhoon?'

" 'That's it—that's just what I mean!' cried the young man, immensely relieved to be understood. 'It's so wonderful, you know. So awful to think of its being in danger—perhaps lost.' He shuddered; I saw his hands close with a convulsive movement. How it had sharpened his sensibilities, this perverted and yet vital experience! The agony of that thought was real to him; he saw the end, felt the loss. 'No, no!' he cried, brushing his hand across his eyes. 'It seems to have weakened me, some way. I know it. Before I owned the diamond, I'd have thought this a good deal of a lark—been interested, you know—enjoyed it. I can't now! It's something here. . . . ' He thumped his breast. 'It hurts, too,' he said.

" 'My dear fellow,' I expostulated, 'you mustn't work yourself up into such a state of anxiety. People who know the sea fairly well, have learned that it's needless to anticipate the turns of the weather. Perhaps we won't get the body of the typhoon at all; it's taken one jump already, and may take another. Besides, what of it if it does catch us? Ships have gone through typhoons ever since the first keel was launched. The only sensible thing to do is not to worry for the present; and on my honor, this is nothing to be alarmed at.'

"He steadied himself to the nearest couch, and sat down. 'I know all that—I believe you,' he said. 'But it doesn't—Captain, you just think—' Words came to him along with the argument. 'Suppose you had something aboard—your wife, or somebody besides yourself—something that you loved. You wouldn't be the same careless man. It makes a great difference. I suppose I sound like a fool—I suppose you're all laughing at me in your sleeves. Well—I don't care. I feel too badly.' He leaned forward, and lowered his voice. 'I think that we're going to be lost, Captain Nichols!' he said.

"'Oh, for heaven's sake don't add premonition!' I begged, chuckling over my 'carelessness'. 'Remember, Mr. Lane, if by any chance your diamond is lost, you'll go along with it.'

"'Yes,' he said hopelessly. 'It isn't that. And it isn't as if the diamond could suffer, or care, either.' His eyes opened wide, staring into unexplored mazes of introspection. At last he shook his head. 'It's a *feeling*,' he said. '. . . . The awfulness of so much beauty being lost to the world!'

"It was an odd glimpse into the construction of a soul. He sat there, twisting his fingers, full of inexplicable sensations—of sensations much more inexplicable to himself than to the rest of us. And behold, it was all about nothing, when you came to think it over! I've heard that said of normal Love, too—that it's all about nothing. These forces that move us, inspire us, transform us—that are the springs of all greatness, of all insignificance, of every act under the sun:—aren't they alike impalpable, undefinable, void, like wind, or the shadow of a cloud? Isn't life itself a terrible hubbub about nothing, a wild chasing of shadows, a blind passage down the wind? The impulses—ambition, hate, love, fear, sorrow—these are the truth, the fact—the only truth we know, the only fact we have to cling to. In Lane's case, he happened to love a diamond; and was accordingly crushed by the 'awfulness of so much beauty being lost to the world!'

"Lee Fu's voice broke the silence. 'Why so much talk of loss?' he asked. 'Granting always that the typhoon may be very severe, may overcome us, and that we may sink, why must the great Penang Diamond sink with us?'

"All of us, I think, looked up in surprise. 'If such an event comes to pass, I don't see how we're going to get around it,' I remarked, after we'd waited some time for him to go on. 'Unfortunately, diamonds won't float.'

" 'I would suggest sealing it up in a bottle,' said Lee Fu. 'It could then be thrown overboard—if occasion demanded. Trust the world to find it some day.'

"Profound idea! Do you know the first thought that flashed into my mind? I wondered if there were a purpose in the suggestion. Yes, that was my clear and rather startling impression; whether I suspected Lee Fu, or Something Else, I couldn't determine. Looking back, it seems as if at that instant I began to see dimly the trend of events—all in a haze, of course, without form or detail, as faint and indistinguishable as the memory of a dream.

"But it was a wise suggestion for the moment; you should have seen Lane grasp at it, like a drowning man at a straw. It solved the immediate problem at once; the diamond was as good as saved. Splendid! Great! He jumped up from the couch as if on springs. Just the thing, wasn't it? Why in the deuce—? So simple, too! Now he must have a bottle. Where could he find a bottle? He stopped in consternation, and turned to me. Suppose there wasn't a bottle? It would have to have a wide mouth. Captain— I ran to the medicine chest, and found a wide-mouthed bottle that had held quinine. Lane produced his diamond, and we gathered round. It wouldn't go in! He gazed at me with a tragic expression; by Jove, I thought he was going to cry. Just then Clewley had an inspiration. 'Try an olive bottle,' he said. I dashed for the pantry, and found there an enormous olive bottle. This I bore back in triumph, and passed to Lee Fu. He drew out a large silk handkerchief, wrapped the diamond in it, and forced the loose bundle through the neck of the bottle. 'Isn't it great!' cried Lane, slapping me on the back. He didn't wait for a reply, but flew to examine the cork. That would never do— hole right through it where the corkscrew— There was a drawerful of corks in the bathroom, and luckily the biggest was just a fit. 'That's the fellow!' exclaimed Lane. 'By George, I feel like another man!'

" 'You will need a paper, an inscription?' queried Lee Fu.

"Jove, yes! A paper—something to let 'em know. What should we say? Should we give any idea of the value? Here, Captain, you write something—write it in ink, you know! So away I went to my desk, and wrote on a sheet of strong linen—it was cross-sectioned with heavy blue lines:— 'Thrown overboard from bark Omega, sinking in a typhoon 150 miles west of Cape Bojeador, September so and so, eighteen hundred so and-so. Return to—' At this point I called Lane. 'Here, Lane, where do you want it returned to?' I asked. 'You'd better put that in. Whoever found it, would feel dreadfully—'

"He snatched up the paper, read it over, and shot a startled glance at me. 'Sinking!' he exclaimed. 'Do you propose to throw it overboard unless we are sinking?' I asked. 'Oh, I thought—' he stammered. 'Let me sit down, please—I'll write in the address.' I made a place for him, and turned my back. He wrote, folded the sheet into a narrow strip, and passed it to Lee Fu. 'Here's the wax,' I said. Lee Fu inserted the paper in the bottle, drove the cork home, and applied the wax while Clewley lit matches for him. Remember, Clewley? My eye fell upon a roll of pink tape in the desk. 'Hold on!' I cried. 'We'll put a strip of this tape through the wax, and tie the ends around the neck of the bottle.' When we'd finished, the diamond was equal to a trip around the world.

"Lane held it up for us to see, and gave a little laugh. 'This event that you're preparing for, doesn't seem to trouble you much,' I observed. His face fell—I feared for a moment that I'd pricked his bubble. But he'd only been struck by another uncertainty. 'It'll float, of course?' he asked. 'It won't—'

" 'Try it in the tub,' I suggested.

"He was off like a shot. 'Wait!' cried Lee Fu. 'Let the wax cool before putting it in water. It might crack.' Lane waved assent over his shoulder. 'I'll be filling the tub,' he shouted. The door slammed behind him, and we heard the sound of running water.

"Then we laughed. And it wasn't so funny, after all; though there were points that bordered on the ludicrous. Our feelings were epitomized by a remark of Clewley's. 'Well, I'll be blowed!' he said. 'A hundred thousand pound sterling in a bottle!'

"The ship gave a savage lurch, and I awoke to the fact that I hadn't thought of my responsibilities for the last half-hour. 'Feel that, Lee Fu!' I cried. 'It's breezing on.' I glanced at the tell-tale compass in the skylight. 'The wind's still due north. What do you think?'

" 'I think that in about twelve hours the center of the typhoon will pass over us,' said Lee Fu without emotion.

"I struggled into my oilskin coat. 'Curse the diamond! Here I've been playing like a silly boy. You fellows keep Lane below, and make him behave himself.'

" 'He shall be our especial charge,' said Lee Fu. 'Presently, I go to assist him at his physical experiments.'

"I left them to their own diversions, and went out into the storm. There I forgot the diamond for a while.

X

"For us who are sailors, the sensations of a landsman at sea are hard to understand. Wind and water are our familiar elements; a ship is our home, the field of our endeavors, the companion of our days. The things of the sea are what we love and know—are often all we know. A seaman lying in his bunk, can tell at once when his ship is carrying too much sail; a feeling is communicated to him, a feeling that's an instinct in the sense that it's the sum and lesson of all past experience. And in a storm, he knows by the laboring of the deck under his feet, exactly how it is with his vessel; he can measure the degree of her effort to a hair. But the poor landsman is separated from this knowledge by a wide and impassable gulf. An ordinary big wave seems monstrous to him, as he compares it with the calm of the day before; and when the masts once lean from the perpendicular, it's as bad as if she'd put her scuppers under. In a storm, he goes through agonies of needless apprehension, as if every wave and every squall were to be his last. Yes, actually!—I've watched 'em. You have no conception of what such a man suffers. His life has been bounded by the firm land—by fields that spread without motion, by hills that stand eternally changeless, by houses that wouldn't dream of leaping across the streets they stand on, by floors that never in the course of their orderly existence have tipped up on one side and down on the other. And here he's cast on a world of waters, bobbing, tossing, floundering, without a fixed object in ship, sea, or sky!

"I've often thought of this in connection with young Lane. He'd faced death that night before it was anywhere near, you see; and when later death hovered over him, I think he didn't quite recognize it until Lee Fu shook my hand. At any rate, he was already prepared; while we had to scramble down from our elevation—down, till we stood beside him, no longer sailors with superior knowledge, but plain men in fear of our lives.

"As soon as I got on deck after that absurd business in the cabin, I made preparations to take in the rest of the sail. But I'd neglected my duty too long. The wind was terrific; it screamed down upon us with a steady, relentless note, with a voice that seemed to be trying to drown every other sound in the world. The lower topsails slat themselves to pieces before we could furl them; in fact, I didn't even send the men aloft. With the whole crew, we managed to get a few gaskets around the spanker and tie it down. Our mizzen topmast-staysail was made with a bonnet along the bottom; this we removed, and set the upper part—a mere rag of a sail. It was enough, though, to keep her head up into the wind.

"Then I waited for the dawn. At five o'clock, there wasn't a glimmer; at six, a gray glow had spread across the water, as if in some way the light came from below the horizon. By seven o'clock we had all the day that we were to see. The scene was appalling. Low black clouds swirled above us, almost brushing the tops of the masts as they passed. They hung so low that we saw them in perspective; they arched over us, they made the world seem smaller and the ocean a confined plane; they drove at us suddenly, enveloped us in gloom, and as suddenly were gone. Out of these clouds the wind was positively amazing. And the sea! Enormous waves lifted us, battered us, shook us, and flung us into chasms fifty feet below, into chasms where the wind died to a breath, cut off by the front of the next wave. Through it all, under it all, you know—in wind, wave, and sky—there was the threat of latent force, the menace of increasing, swelling, exhaustless power, the clear warning of more to come—more to come!

"In the midst of all this, it was a great comfort to know that the plot of two nights before had been settled by Lee Fu. I thought of it a number of times that morning. By Jove, if I'd had incipient mutiny on my hands inside the ship, and a typhoon outside, I don't know what I'd have done. But I had no further fear of the crew. I'd watched them at work since the encounter, noted their unwonted alacrity, and realized the extent of the influence that Lee Fu had over them. They were no longer sailors—they were slaves.

"At breakfast time I went below—my last visit to the cabin for many hours, as it turned out. Lee Fu was reading in the big arm-chair; Lane sat on the couch beside him with his feet braced against the chair leg; Clewley wasn't visible, but came out of his room soon after. I was shocked to feel how much worse the storm was below, than when I'd left the cabin in the night. Down there one could listen, could think, could estimate. I saw that it was already far beyond an ordinary gale.

"Lane jumped up as I entered, and faced me expectantly. Before he'd spoken, I detected a change in his manner. 'Well, Captain,' he inquired, 'what's the news?'

" 'Nothing but breakfast,' I answered, with an attempt at good spirits. 'Has the cook brought it aft yet? I'm as hungry as a bear.'

" 'He came in a moment ago,' said Lee Fu, laying down his book. 'A wave spoiled the coffee, and he has gone to make more.'

" 'Lucky the whole meal didn't go over the lee rail!' I exclaimed. 'How these Chinamen get along the main-deck in weather like this, is a mystery to me. Is your courage holding out, Mr. Lane?'

"Lane gave me a steady look, and laughed. 'Why, very well for a landsman,' he said. 'Captain, is this still "nothing"?'

" 'No, this is "something," all right!' I told him. 'Here's the cook—come on, let's have some chow.'

"Breakfast was a wrestling match; the dishes jumped the rails without an effort, and had to be held in place by main force. Between mouthfuls, we discussed the events of the last few hours. It had been depressing in the cabin, I learned—nothing to talk about, nothing to do but sit and hold on. Suddenly Clewley turned to me. 'Nichols, have you a spare oilskin coat?' he asked.

" 'There are four or five hanging in the bathroom,' I answered. 'What do you want it for?'

" 'Naturally, I want it to put on,' he explained. 'I'm going on deck, Nichols. It isn't pleasant down here. I want to see with my own eyes what's going on.'

" 'It does seem bad below,' I said. 'I noticed it.'

" 'Bad?' he cried. 'It's hellish! I wouldn't stay in this cabin another hour, if you gave me Lane's diamond. I don't mind dying, Nichols, you know, but I'm not going to drown like a rat in a hole!'

" 'Nonsense!' I answered. 'You're talking like a fool.'

" 'You bally ass!' said Clewley scornfully. 'I mean that I'd pass the time better out in the open.'

"Young Lane put down his knife and fork, and looked from Clewley to me. 'I didn't suppose sailors ever felt that way,' he observed.

" 'Good for you, Lane!' I said. 'You're holding your own, and we're losing ground. To tell the truth, things are getting nasty. I know very well that all of you would rather be on deck—and I'd rather have you there. The sou'westers and rubber boots are in a locker under the port couch; you can be fitting yourself out while I do a bit of writing.'

"I'd just finished the entry in my log, and was lighting my pipe for a last smoke, when Lane came into the room and shut the door. He was fully dressed for the deck—rubber boots, sou'wester, and long yellow coat. It seemed to me that the rough clothes had given him a new air, an air of strength and confidence. But a glance into his face showed me that it wasn't the clothes at all. By Jove, the boy had found himself! The weakling, the dupe of diamonds, was gone; there stood a man, broad-shouldered, alert, calm—a man who appeared to be ready to fight for his life, and ready to die.

" 'Captain,' he said, in a tone that was good to hear, 'I've been thinking any amount of things this morning. It has occurred to me that if your crew are really after my diamond they might make an attack in this storm.'

" 'Lord, no!' I exclaimed. It was on the tip of my tongue to tell him the truth; but at that moment a plausible substitute flashed into my mind. 'They're too frightened to do anything like that,' I assured him. 'They're busy praying to their ancestors, and burning joss paper. You should see them.'

" 'I'm glad to hear it,' he said. 'Because, you know, it would be a fine opportunity, if they were clever enough to seize it.'

" 'It's quite impossible,' I answered. 'Don't think of it again. Mr. Lane, let me compliment you on the way you're taking this. I'm extremely sorry to have run you into danger, particularly with your diamond. There *is* some danger, of course—always is with a typhoon. We did what we could; but it's one of those things that can't be avoided.'

"He put his hand on my shoulder. 'My dear Captain,' he said, 'I understand. You aren't hunting for death, any more than the next man. I've thought of that, too, this morning; and I suppose I've been a good deal of an ass—landlubber, I believe you call it. Well, that's over now. We have an even chance, I presume?'

" 'It hasn't come to a question of chances yet,' I put in. 'We have every chance so far.'

"He hesitated, then went on defiantly. 'I still feel the same about the diamond. I don't want it to be lost. If anything happens to us, I'm going to set it adrift. But if we pull through, I don't propose to let your yellow-faced crew take it away from me!'

" 'That's the talk!' I cried. 'Of course we'll pull through. There never was a better sea-boat put together than the old *Omega*. The typhoon will sheer off—we'll have a change soon—I'm sure it won't get much worse.'

XI

"It continued to grow worse; it grew so much worse that a number of times that forenoon I told myself it could grow no more. Now!—my brain would declare—now, it can't blow any harder!—there isn't any more wind left in the sky! And the next minute, '*Whoof!*' would come a squall fiercer than the last, and blow all my convictions, calculations and experiences into a million shreds. But what's the use of describing to you fellows a wind that no stretch of the imagination could conceive? When I tell you that it was solid, like a board—that in those squalls I couldn't have moved my hand to my face—that it blew the sails out of the gaskets, stripped the yards clean save for a few fag-ends of rope and canvas—that it took all the strength of my neck to keep my head upright—when I tell you these things, they sound extraordinary enough, but can't come anywhere near the fact, can't make it seem real. The noise of the wind was deafening, the tremendous liquid power of it was benumbing; I felt exactly as if immersed in the current of a terribly swift river. My body clove a little space for itself; all around me that rushing intangible medium fitted tight, blotting out the rest of the world. I could no more have heard the man at my elbow than I could have heard a man in another planet. Half of the time I kept my eyes shut; they were blown shut, I couldn't open them. All of the time I had to fight for breath; the weight of immeasurable columns of wind rested on my chest; and the atmosphere, too, was charged with water, salt water—was, in fact, a thick mixture of spray and air. That wind was like the wind of the earth's passage through space; it was as if the heavens had really opened, and let down upon us the eternal blast that one thinks of as blowing beyond the clouds.

"We four were in the weather alley-way behind the mizzen rigging; as the typhoon increased, we were obliged to lash ourselves to the shrouds. In those gusts, the ropes cut like knives. The deck was a sluiceway; water spouted completely over us as our bodies stemmed the rush. We were the only souls aft. The helm had been lashed amidships and left to its own devices; the crew were out of sight somewhere, perhaps in the forecastle—I don't know. I didn't once think of them. There were a few hours that I didn't think of any human affairs, didn't see a human being, though Lee Fu and Clewley were lashed less than three feet away on either side of me. I thought only of the ship, the ship. . . . I could feel her!

"Good old ship—noble old ship—wonderful old ship! The message that she sent up to me was altogether too plain. She was fighting, too—fighting hard—fighting for her life, for us who trusted her, for me who loved her. Great massive seas crashed down upon her, engulfed her; she emerged from them struggling, lifted herself as if to get a breath. She strained, twisted, wrenched, leaped high in air, descended with sickening plunges; she seemed like a live thing—one could imagine her snarling and snapping as she wrestled with the waves. God knows how she did it, for the rag of sail was blown away early in the forenoon, but she kept her head into the wind. This was her only hope—our only hope. But after a while, I lost track of her; she was doing things that I didn't understand, things that I'd never before felt a ship do, things that I didn't know a ship *could* do. The storm by this time had grown abnormal, horrible, utterly beyond bounds; it didn't belong any more to the world of healthy wind and wave; it had blown us into some other place, into some sea of demons and sorcery, unknown to man. I felt that the *Omega* couldn't long keep up the battle; it seemed impossible that anything fashioned and constructed by human hands could withstand the fury of that typhoon.

"Lee Fu once said to me, long afterwards:—'Captain Nichols, I have always considered that I died that day. Life since then has been a dream, an unreality, an extension of time.' That's it, exactly! We came so confoundedly close to death, you know, that there might be a question as to our actual survival. For my part, I passed through a number of stages of dissolution. I didn't think of all my misdeeds—that business is a fable, a stock sentimentality of the ages. But I did feel myself slipping farther and farther away from the visible earth, nearer and nearer to some catastrophe, some effacement, some state of nonentity. If the wind had continued without interruption for another hour, I verily believe that I'd have been stifled, crushed out, blown to death, as you might say.

"But along in the middle of the day there came a lull—and suddenly the wind was gone! Yes—it dropped in an instant; if we hadn't been lashed, we would have pitched forward on our faces. Imagine how it would seem to be snatched out of that terrible swift river I spoke of—to have the stunning pressure removed—to be once more in your native element, master of your body and faculties. 'Good God!' I shouted aloud. I could hear myself! I turned—Lane was looking at me—*he'd* heard me. 'What is it' he cried, like a man come out of a trance. His voice sounded thin and faint against the hollow tumult. 'What is it?' he cried again. The question made itself intelligible—I woke up, realized. . . .

" 'The center of the typhoon!' I screamed. 'Quick! Cast off your lashings! Get aft! We'll be caught on the lee side!'

"We freed ourselves, and made our way along the rail. An enormous sea caught us, buried us in green water. When it went off, the rail ended at my hand—beyond, it had been carried away. A moment or two later, we found ourselves hanging on to the wheel and its lashings. The wheel-box had been washed away, I noticed; in a lull, I scrutinized the patent gear carefully, as if fascinated by the sight of the long polished thread. Lee Fu's mouth was within a foot of my ear. 'She will never stand it, Captain,' he said loudly. 'Never!' I cried. 'When the wind strikes, she'll go under.' He nodded towards the compass, still swinging calmly in the binnacle. 'See!' he said. 'She has swung end for end—she is in a whirlpool.' Together we turned and looked forward.

"Few men have seen what we saw, and lived to tell the tale. A circular section had been removed from the body of the typhoon, just as you might cut out the middle of a cheese. All around us, a whirling circumference, we could see the wind tear at the tops of waves less than a quarter of a mile away. The sea in this area was like a maelstrom, like a pool at the base of a gigantic cataract; it seethed and boiled, it tossed upward, as if impelled from beneath. Waves came at us from every quarter; they reared in tall points, in crests of greenish and oily foam; they stumbled, swashed, subsided into themselves with shocks that quaked the deck; they travelled swiftly and marvellously across the open, like ponderous shifting pyramids. Deep holes yawned in the ocean—holes that the ship could have fallen into. She'd topple on the brink, give way beneath us, drop—when suddenly the hole would vanish, and a mighty arm of water would shoot out of the place where it had been. Or two waves would attack her, bow and stern, in opposite direction—would bend her, buckle her, spin her on a pivot through half a circle. She was no longer a ship, to be steered by a rudder, to be handled by sails; she was a bobbing cork, a wallowing log, a piece of flotsam flung about at the will of the waves.

"The sound that accompanied the center of the typhoon was fearful beyond description. Boom!—boom!—boom!—hollow, echoing, splitting, shattering—a sound too unearthly for the language and comprehension of man—a sound that's heard only in nightmares, in the depths of the mind's nethermost hell! Behind the immediate clamor, off in the range of the typhoon, the wind screamed continuously, loud and high, like wild beasts in a jungle.

"I'd been gazing at this scene a moment, when I felt Lee Fu's hand on my arm. 'Good-bye, Captain,' he said. 'It is evident—' The thunder of a wave drowned his voice. It passed, and I heard him again. 'Solve the great mystery!' he was saying.

"I shook his hand. 'Good-bye! Yes—solve something!' It wasn't real, you know; I didn't believe it, didn't quite fathom. . . . As I remember, I had no particular feelings one way or the other; my soul seemed to have drawn apart—to have already taken a step or two away from my body. I turned—found myself face to face with young Lane. 'Good-bye,' I said indifferently—then stopped in surprise.

"He hadn't heard—was looking past me, with an intent and grim expression. I followed his glance, and saw what I at first took to be an apparition. My Chinese crew was coming aft through the port alley-way! They clung to the rail, and crept along it in single file. Their faces were contorted, wild, inhuman, their eyes gleamed, they were naked to the waist. They gibbered together like monkeys. They were almost upon us.

"I started, took a step—a strong hand was laid upon my shoulder. 'What the devil?' I cried. Lee Fu's voice spoke fiercely in my ear:—'Be still! Say nothing!' My eyes wandered to Lane. His face was calm, resolute, even noble. He left the wheel— stood unsupported on the open deck. For that moment the elements seemed to pause, to suspend; the ship rested on an even keel. The first Chinaman had reached the port quarter-bitts. Lane stretched out his arm. 'Stop!' he shouted in a voice of power.

"The yellow forms halted—burst into a frantic chatter. Over my shoulder, Lee Fu uttered a single sharp word. Instantly, they were still. They crowded in a knot about the bitts; their wet arms glistened, held out in supplication. Then I understood! They'd come in search of Lee Fu, the Master—had come for protection, for a word in the hour of death.

"I looked again at Lane. He held a large bottle in his hand. 'Tell them—' he commanded, shaking it at us. A piece of red and white label still stuck to it—the word 'Olives' — Lee Fu's grip tightened on my arm—but I had no desire to interfere. 'Tell them to swim for it!' cried Lane, the light of a great purpose in his eyes.

"Then he threw the diamond with a wide sweep into the sea."

XII

Nichols turned in his chair, and glanced at us quizzically. "Do you know, the moment Lane's diamond crossed the rail I felt that we were saved," he said. "Another enormous sea toppled upon us; I reached out, caught Lane by the middle, and hugged him to the wheel; and while I held my breath under water, I found myself singing, 'We'll weather it now! By Jove, we'll weather it now!' Don't ask me to explain why. I'm very well aware that diamonds have no known effect upon the severity of typhoons. Perhaps it was because I'm a firm believer in the irony of fate. It didn't seem natural that the gods would be willing to allow such a perfectly immense joke to be wasted.

"The wave went off without damage, and a second lull settled upon the ship. Behind me, Lee Fu seemed greatly agitated; he plucked at my coat sleeve, as if to draw me apart. I leaned towards him. 'Nothing is gained, unless the truth be known!' he said in my ear. My mind refused to grasp his drift. 'What——?' 'Before the world, he still possesses the Penang Diamond,' Lee Fu's voice went on. Then, as quickly as he'd thought of the issue, he'd found its solution. 'Ah!' I heard him cry.

"The Chinamen had clung to the bitts and the rail; they were gazing at him with keen, motionless eyes. All at once they commenced a harsh, staccato yelping;—'Hy-ah! Hy-ah!' Their bodies swayed, bowed, writhed. Lee Fu brushed past me. At the movement, they grew silent again, listening, waiting. He spoke rapidly.

" 'The young man has cast the diamond away. This he did to appease the storm. I myself sealed it in a bottle; and you have seen him throw it into the sea. Honor the sacrifice! It was to him more than life.' He held up his hand, and before their eyes pulled a ring from his finger. 'See, here is another diamond—all I have. I offer this also!' He tossed the ring high over their heads. They watched it fall, disappear. . . .

"There was no time for more. An appalling sea descended upon us, with a crash that shook the ship from stem to stern. But the deluge couldn't quench my amazement: by Jove, he'd appealed to a superstition—to the very superstition that I felt! Calm and wonderful man. . . . I remembered that ring—a magnificent stone, worth thousands of dollars. It was the only diamond that I'd ever seen Lee Fu wear. It had gone to strengthen a chance point—in case we were saved!

"It didn't look just then as if we were to be saved. The wind was coming! We saw it the moment we got out heads out of that sea. The awful circular chamber had moved over us, the opposite wall had crowded upon us—the wall of wind and death. It would come from the opposite direction; but the *Omega* had swung until she'd catch it on the same side as before. We had scant time to regain our old places in the mizzen rigging, and lash ourselves there. The Chinamen were with us now—wet, naked bodies, slippery arms. The alley-way was a tangle of ropes, enough for all. An instant did it—the only instant we had. Then the wind struck, the ocean opened, a sea curled to

the height of our main yard—ship and men entered the black
jaws of death, and the waters closed above our heads.

"I have no memory of what comes after; to this day, I can't
conceive how we ever rose from such a wave. It's only by suppo-
sition that I know we did come out of the water—because hours
passed by, and I continued to breathe. But no sensations of the
afternoon remain with me; they were blown away by the wind,
were washed overboard by the incredible sea. By and by, after
long hours, it began to grow dark. I remember thinking that
above all this the sun was still doing its appointed duty, dividing
night from day. Then I realized that some change had taken
place—lifted up my head, looked around me, and suddenly
awoke all-standing from that dream of hell. The wind had
dropped! It had dropped to a brisk gale—the typhoon was over!
The sea still ran high; but it hadn't the old lift, the old power. It
was a dying sea, a dying wind. . . . We lived!

"I twisted around in my lashings, and glanced at Lee Fu. A
thick gloom had fallen; I couldn't see plainly. His body appeared
to droop, his head hung forward inert. A dreadful fear shot
through my heart. But the next moment I made out that he was
asleep! I looked beyond him; Lane and Clewley, too, had lost
themselves. A few of the Chinamen fixed me with beady eyes;
the rest of them had sunk down, had tipped backwards, had
collapsed on the rail—and were sleeping. A deathly somnolence
seemed to have descended on the ship. I felt it, too—it sank into
my muscles, it drenched me like a cool wave. The real waves had
stopped drenching me; I felt that, realized it dimly, and the
knowledge was a pillow of peace for my head. I slept. I leaned my
breast against the sheerpole, and the lashings held me up. Remember, I hadn't closed my eyes for over forty-eight hours; and
the exertion, the fear, the wind. . . . My God, I slept! I was
drunk, I was dead with sleep. I slept dreamlessly, time was nothing—the sun shone on my face, and I awoke. It was morning,
sunrise, the dawn of another day!

"Oh, the sun—! You fellows can't know, can't possibly understand. It rose in a sweet, calm sky—in a sky from which every
trace of anger had been erased. Its level beams overtook us,
warmed us, touched our heavy eyelids, opened our eyes. And we
saw the world again, the sea that still sustained us, the ship that
was still our home. We woke up together, in an instant, it seemed.

Voices broke out, exclamations, questions—everyone was talking at once. I heard young Lane: 'By Jove, I've been asleep—the sun!' Life, life! The wonder and glory of it, the surpassing delight of it, the loveliness, the charm. And he was young besides, you know.

"Suddenly I thought of the diamond. He'd—he'd *thrown it overboard!* Impossible!—impossible! Here was the wind gone, the sea fallen, the sun rising—and the Penang Diamond, its clear blue light hid in the folds of a white silk handkerchief, was afloat somewhere on the illimitable expanse of the China Sea. Instinctively, I looked over the rail; but it wasn't in sight, strange to say. The storm had whisked it away, into those internal regions through which we'd passed. Lane's voice rose again, loud, boyish, exultant. 'My God, Captain, what an escape!' I struggled with my lashings; a knot had jammed in the wet rope. 'Yes—wonderful,' I said. He hadn't thought of his diamond! He'd forgotten that he threw it overboard. Poor chap!—I found myself hoping that the realization would be delayed a little while longer—that he'd be allowed a few moments more of that riotous happiness, before being struck down. A case occurred to me of a man who'd partially lost his memory, who couldn't recall a certain startling train of events. Perhaps young Lane. . . .

"Lee Fu had at last succeeded in freeing himself. He touched me on the shoulder. 'What is that object in the main rigging?' he asked. I followed the direction of his finger, and saw something large and black that swung loose as if suspended by the end. Chinamen began to slink by me, going forward. I captured one of them, and pointed aloft. 'Run up and bring that down,' I said.

"While he was gone, I made a discovery. The forward house had vanished! Forecastle, galley, carpenter's shop, everything within those four walls, had been uprooted and washed away. The big water casks that had stood on either side of the house, were gone; the two boats that had rested on top of it, were gone; and the port bulwarks, from the fore rigging to the break of the poop-deck, were stove out, stripped, picked clean like old bones.

" 'For heaven's sake, look forward!' I cried. 'The whole forward house—'

"I stopped short. The Chinaman had returned from the main rigging, and stood before me holding out a slush bucket. It was one that I myself had rigged as a convenience, with a hook on the bail to hitch over the side of a bo'sun's chair. 'Where did you find that?' I demanded. His face expressed indifference. I had commanded him to fetch it, he answered; it was no fault of his. . . . 'Was *that* in the main rigging?' I cried. He had found it hanging to a ratlin, he told me gravely—had climbed to it and picked it off, as the bo'sun might have taken it down from its place in the locker. I received it helplessly, too thunder-struck to say a word.

" 'Such are the whims of Chance,' commented Lee Fu at my elbow. 'A diamond is lost, a slush bucket is miraculously saved!'

"I cringed within myself. The cat was out of the bag now! Such a raw remark, so unnecessary—so cruel. It didn't seem like Lee Fu. He must have noticed, with his quick sympathies. I felt embarrassed—averted my eyes, toyed with that ridiculous slush bucket, and wished that a tactful word would come to my mind.

"Lane's voice broke in on my solicitude. 'A good stroke, too!' he cried heartily. 'I don't know what a slush bucket is—but it looks useful.' He laughed. 'Where do you suppose the damned bottle went to!' he inquired at large.

"Even then, I didn't gather the true situation. I found myself thinking, 'Good boy—brave boy!' You see, I was determined that Lane should suffer, determined to help him suffer. 'What queer things one does in a moment of danger,' I observed sententiously. 'But you mustn't blame yourself, Mr. Lane. It can't be helped. Perhaps these impulsive things are nearer right.'

"Lane was looking at me with a puzzled expression. 'Why, I never did a more deliberate thing in my life!' he said seriously. 'Blame myself? How can I blame myself when I'm glad of it?'

"My balloon of sympathy fell flat. 'I was afraid—' I began—then discontinued my efforts.

" 'You see,' he went on after a moment, 'that attack opened my eyes. You said they wouldn't try it—you remember? But I had a feeling all the time that they were just waiting for the chance. Think of it, Captain!' he said in a voice of awe. 'We were face to face with Eternity! And those blackguards—they—' He paused, seeking words for an obscure experience. 'I'd been blaming men and circumstances,' he said at last. 'I hadn't admitted that the diamond itself was bad. I don't now—it couldn't be, you know— not actually bad. But I saw what it did to all hearts. *They* weren't any more to blame than I was; because I wanted it, too—wanted to keep it, to fight for it. That's why I threw it overboard. Captain, we should have been thinking of other things.'

"I made no answer. It occurred to me very forcibly that Lane must never know the truth concerning a certain situation."

SERVANT
AND MASTER

I

"Steward!"

"Yes, sir, Cappen."

The little old Chinaman looked up from the brass threshold which he was polishing. Kneeling at the entrance to the forward cabin, with his back toward Captain Sheldon, he peered around his shoulder with a gnome-like movement, his hands pausing on the brass.

Captain Sheldon laid down his book. He pointed an accusing forefinger at the stateroom threshold, which the steward had just finished.

"That's dirty, Wang. You haven't half polished it. What's the matter with you lately?"

"All light, Cappen, all light. Eye gettee old."

He shifted his pan of brick-dust, scuttled across on his knees to the stateroom threshold, and attacked the brass again. With head bent low and hands flying, he worked silently. His back disclosed nothing beyond the familiar mechanical impersonality.

Captain Sheldon watched him with narrowing eyes. He realized that he was beginning to "get down on" the old steward; yet to his mind there was justice in the feeling. Wang wasn't so neat or careful as he used to be. He frowned as he noted the greasy collar of the Chinaman's tunic. A dirty steward! — he always had abhorred the notion. To his strict ideas of nautical propriety, it meant the beginning of a ship's disintegration. The time was not far distant, he saw clearly, when he would have to get rid of old Wang.

He had inherited the steward along with the ship *Retriever* when his father died. "Wang-ti, His Mark," the entry had stood voyage after voyage on the ship's articles; young John Sheldon had grown up taking the venerable Chinaman for granted. He was the "old man's" trusted servant, as much a part of the vessel as her compass or her keel. He took entire charge of the ship's provisioning, as well as of the cabin accessories. He kept the commissary accounts, with never a penny out of the way; his prudence and honesty had saved the ship many a dollar. John often used to hear his father boast that he wouldn't be able to go to sea without Wang-ti.

In his boyhood on shipboard, there had existed a natural intimacy between the captain's son and the factotum of the nautical household. John's mother was dead, he roamed the ship wild from forecastle to lazaret; and Wang had guarded his fortunes with the wise faithfulness that knows how to keep its attentions unobserved. The captain even had permitted his son to sit in the steward's room, watching him smoke a temperate pipeful of opium after the noon dishes were done; this was the measure of his trust in the old Chinaman.

Indeed, John Sheldon, had he been disposed, might have recalled a great deal that went on in Wang's narrow room on the port side of the forward cabin — incidents fraught with deep importance to boyhood. The room was a place of retreat, a zone of freedom. It made little difference whether Wang was there or not; the two understood each other, conversed only in monosyllables, and the Chinaman apparently took no interest in what the boy did. In return, the boy throughout this period never so much as made an inquiry into Wang's life; that matter, too, was taken for granted. Many an afternoon he would lie for hours on the clean, hard bed, his head buried in a book, while the steward sat beside him on a three-legged wooden stool, sewing or figuring his accounts, neither of them speaking a word or glancing at the other. The click of the stone as the Chinaman mixed his ink, the rustle of the pages, and the faint creak of the wooden finish in the cabin, would mingle with the fainter sounds aloft and along decks as the vessel slipped quietly through the water.

But this was long ago, before life had opened, before days of responsibility and authority had overlaid youthful sentiment with a hard veneer of efficiency. The door of that room had closed on John Sheldon for the last time when he had left the ship in New York, a boy of thirteen, to spend a few years at home in school; he was not to share another hour with Wang until the final hour. When next he joined the *Retriever's* company, it was in the capacity of a rousing young second mate of seventeen, broad shouldered and full of confidence, believing that his place in life depended on strength and self-assertion. He picked quarrels with the crew largely for the sake of fighting; he was aggressive and overbearing, as befitted the type of commanding officer which appealed to his imagination. In him, real ability was combined with a physical prowess beyond the ordinary; he failed to meet the reverses which teach a much-needed lesson to men of lesser combative powers, and the years conspired to develop the arbitrary side of his character. As an instance of this unfortunate tendency, he had allowed himself, after rising to the position of first mate on the *Retriever*, to quarrel with his father over some trifling matter of discipline; so that at the end of the voyage he had quit the deck on which he had been brought up, and had shipped away in another vessel.

It was on the voyage immediately following this incident that his father had died suddenly at sea, half way across the Indian Ocean on the passage home. John Sheldon had arrived in New York from the West Coast almost in company with the *Retriever*, brought in by the mate who had taken his place. The first news he heard was that his father had been buried at sea. The ship was owned in the family; it seemed natural, in view of this stroke of destiny, that he should have her as his first command. The officers left, he took possession of the cabin and quarterdeck that had been his father's province for so many years; and Wang continued his duties in the forward cabin as if nothing had happened. The Chinaman had nursed Captain Sheldon when he took to his bed, had found him dying the next morning, had heard his last words, and had laid out his body for burial.

Six years had passed since then. John Sheldon was a dashing young shipmaster of twenty-seven; and now Wang was failing. No doubt about it. The dishes weren't clean any longer; a greasy knife annoyed Captain Sheldon almost as much as an insult. Lately, he had begun to notice a heavy, musty smell as he passed by the pantry door. A dirty steward! — it wasn't to be supported, not on his ship, at any rate.

The Chinaman finished polishing the brasses, gathered up his pan and rags, and started for the forward cabin. Captain Sheldon laid down his book again.

"Steward, have you got a home?"

"Oh, yes, Cappen. My got two piecee house, Hong Kong side."

Wang paused in the doorway, turning half around and steady-ing himself as the ship lurched. His fingers left a smudge on the white paint. As if sensing rather than seeing it, he wiped the place furtively with the corner of his cotton tunic, only spreading the smudge. Captain Sheldon, watching the maneuver, sniffed in disgust, and continued the inquiry.

"Have you got a wife?"

"She dead, seven, eight year."

"Any children?"

"Oh, my got some piecee children, maybe three, four."

"For God's sake, don't you know how many children you've got?"

"Yes, sir, Cappen. Four piecee, all go 'way. Maybe some dead. My no hear."

"Hm-m." The captain knit his brows ponderously, a habit he had acquired in the last few years, and fixed a severe glance on the old Chinaman. "Don't you ever want to go home?"

"Oh, no, Cappen. Why fo' go home? My b'long ship side."

After waiting a moment in silence for further questions, Wang realized that the conversation was not to be concluded this time. He turned slowly and shuffled off through the forward cabin, head bent and eyes peering hard at the floor. Captain Sheldon did not see him stumble heavily against the corner of the settee.

In the protection of the pantry, Wang put down the pan of brick-dust and stood for a long time motionless, holding the dirty rags in the other hand, facing the window above the dresser. He could see the small square of light plainly, but the rest of the room was vague. His tiny, inanimate figure, in the midst of the dim clutter of the room, expressed a weary relaxation; he stood like a man lost in vacant thought.

No one would have suspected the feelings behind the wizened face; Wang's countenance, as he gazed steadfastly at the square of light, was an expressionless blank. He seemed scarcely to breathe; the spark of life seemed to have sunk low within him, to have retreated in fear or impotence. The hand holding the rags paused rigidly, as if petrified in the act of putting down its grimy burden. Had Captain Sheldon come upon him at that moment, he would have ordered him shortly to get busy, begin doing something.

All his thoughts, there in the silence of the pantry, were of loyalty. That uncommunicative intimacy of the past had been fruitful to one, at least, of the parties to the contract. "Young Cappen," who as a boy had been Wang's pride and charge, was his pride and charge still. Had not "Old Cappen," on his deathbed, whispered the final order: "Keep an eye on the boy, Wang. He's stepping high now — but the time may come when he will need you." But of these words, his father's last utterance, "Young Cappen" of course knew nothing. They remained a profound secret between Wang and the dead.

If it were true, Wang recognized in that unwavering gaze, that his days of usefulness were over, he would be no longer able to discharge the obligation. Not that his strength was less; his withered, cord-like sinews ached to scrub and polish, to keep his domain in its old efficient order. But this voyage he hadn't been able to see what needed to be done. He had hardly dared to allow his mind to formulate the explanation. Now he must face it. He was going blind.

He comprehended fully the meaning of the recent conversation in the after cabin. The pain that held him inert and motionless was half of love and half of fear. Perhaps, he tried to tell himself, "Young Cappen" was safely launched on the sea of life now; perhaps he no longer had need of an old man's service. Yet, in the same moment of thought, Wang knew that this was not the fact. The knowledge filled him with a desperate tenacity; until fate actually laid him low, he could not submit to the turn of fortune. Old and wise in life, he realized that "Young Cappen's" hardest lessons still lay ahead of him. He must serve as long as he was able.

That night over the supper table, Captain Sheldon opened a biscuit; there was a dead cockroach in it. His knife had cut it in halves. He threw the biscuit down in disgust. Wang always made the cabin bread. . . . Well, why didn't the old fool take it away? He must have seen the incident. Captain Sheldon knew that he was standing a few feet away in the pantry door. Taking up his plate, he snapped over his shoulder:

"Steward!"

Wang was at his elbow in an instant. The captain thrust the biscuit into his trembling hand.

"Look at that! Take them all away, and bring some bread."

"Yes, sir, Cappen." The Chinaman mumbled incoherently, trying to cover his confusion. His innate sense of the etiquette of human relations, which even after fifty years of service had not accommodated itself to the brusque callousness of European manners, felt bitterly outraged; no way had been left him to save face. Yet other and stronger emotions quickly submerged the insult. The biscuit plate rattled like a castanet as he set it down on the pantry dresser. As he cut into a new loaf of bread, he shook his head slowly from side to side, like an animal in pain, stopping in the midst of the operation to bend above the offending biscuit and examine it closely. He loosened the cockroach with the point of the bread knife; it fell to the plate, a dark spot on the white china. Under his breath he gave a staccato sigh: "Ah-ah-ah-ah-ah."

Captain Sheldon found himself unable to forget this trivial incident; he kept brooding over it all the evening. At breakfast next morning it came to his mind again, and followed him intermittently throughout the day — a day of petty mishaps and annoyances, one of those days when everything aboard the vessel seemed to be going wrong, when even the best efforts of officers and men to please him resulted in misfortune, and the simplest words rubbed the wrong way. Captain Sheldon was nearing the end of a long and tedious passage, with nerves and temper badly frayed.

Coming below an hour after dinner, in hopes of finding a little peace, he met the heavy odor of opium smoke floating through the cabin. The door into the forward cabin had been left open. He strode out angrily; the steward's door was open, too. Glancing into the stateroom, he saw the old Chinaman stretched on the bed, staring with glassy eyes at the ceiling, the pipe slipping from his fingers. Thin wisps of opium smoke curled up from the bowl and drifted out into the cabin.

Captain Sheldon's patience snapped suddenly. By God, this was too much! First, bugs in the breads; and now . . . the lazy old swine, lying there in an opium dream, too indolent even to close the door! The ship's discipline was going plumb to hell. His authority was becoming a joke. A dirty steward! By God, he wouldn't stand it any longer.

"Steward! Steward! Wake up, there!"

"What, Cappen?"

By a violent effort, Wang pulled himself out of the delicious stupor and sat up on the edge of the bunk. The drug had not fully overcome him; in a long lifetime, he never had exceeded the moderate daily pipeful that would put him to sleep for only half an hour.

"Steward, I can't permit this any longer. You've left your door open, and stunk up the whole cabin with the damned stuff."

"My s'pose close him, Cappen. Maybe wind swing him open."

"You didn't close it! You don't finish anything, now-a-days. It's got to stop, I tell you. I can see what the trouble is. This devilish opium is getting the best of you. It's got to stop — and the best way to stop, is to begin now. . . . Give me all the opium you've got."

"Yes, sir, Cappen."

The import of the captain's words brought the old Chinaman to his senses with a rush. He got up unsteadily, went to his chest, and began fumbling in the lower corner. Soon he brought out a number of small square packages done up in Chinese paper.

"Cappen, what fashion you do?"

Captain Sheldon snatched the packages from the steward's hand.

"I'm going to throw it all overboard! If you've got any more of the stuff hidden away, you're not to smoke it — do you understand? I won't have such a mess in my cabin."

"Cappen, no can do!"

Wang was panting; a shrill note of anguish came in his voice. He reached out a trembling hand toward the precious drug.

"Yes, you can, and you will. It's nothing but a nasty, degenerate habit. You're too old for such things. It's making you dirty and

careless. Brace up, now — show that you're good for something.
You used to be the best steward in the fleet. I'm only trying to help
you out. If things were to go on like this much longer, I'd have
to find a new steward in Hong Kong."

Captain Sheldon, struggling to regain control of himself after
the outburst of temper, stamped off through the after cabin. Wang
heard him go up the companion. He sat down again on the edge
of the bunk, a crumpled heap, inert and silent, his eyes dulled by
a fear beyond any he had yet known. For fifty years he had smoked
daily that tiny pipeful of opium. With all that life had brought
him, could he summon strength for this new and terrible ordeal?

II

Fire, like the rain, falls on the just and the unjust alike, and eats
up a tall ship at sea as readily as it guts a splendid castle. They were
half way across from Luzon to the China coast, only a few hundred
miles from Hong Kong and the end of the passage, when the blaze
was discovered in the fore hold, already well under way. Quickly
it became unmanageable. Through a day and a night of frantic
effort the whole ship's company fought the flames, retreating aft
inch by inch while destruction followed them relentlessly under
decks. In the gleam of a dawn striking across a smooth sea and
lighting up the pale faces gathered on top of the after house, it
became apparent that the ship was doomed.

Daylight found them in the boats, standing off to watch the last
lurid scene. The ship burned fiercely throughout the forenoon. At
midday, under a blistering sun, her bows seemed suddenly to
crumple and dissolve; surrounded by a cloud of steam, she settled
forward with a loud hissing noise, and slowly vanished under the
waters of the China Sea.

Captain Sheldon, sitting upright in the stern of the long-boat,
watched the scene with set jaw and snapping eyes. It was his first
disaster, the first time he had met destiny coming the other way.
A fierce anger, like the fire he had just been fighting, ran in his
blood. He was beside himself. It seemed inconceivable that there
was no way to bring his ship back out of the deep; that the very
means of authority had vanished, that he was powerless, that the
event was sealed for all time. He wanted to strike out blindly, hit
something, crush something.

Well he knew that if any blame attached to the matter, it rested on him alone. For some occult reason, as it now seemed, the mate a few days before had broached the subject of fire, in conversation at the supper table. Not that fire was to be expected; no one ever had heard of it with such a cargo. Why had the mate chosen that day, of all others, when the captain had lost his patience with old Wang, to talk about fire throughout the supper period, to follow him on deck with the subject in the evening? The talk had aroused the perversity of his own opposition. The mate, waxing eloquent and imaginative, had at length succeeded in frightening himself; had wanted to take off the fore hatch in the dog watch, just to look into the hold. Had he done so then, the fire probably would have been discovered in season for it to be overcome. But Captain Sheldon, sarcastic and bristling with arbitrariness, had commanded him flatly to leave the fore hatch alone.

Well, no use in crying over spilt milk. The ship was gone.

"Give way!" he shouted across the water to the mate's boat. "Keep along with me. We'll strike in for the coast, and follow it down."

All afternoon they rowed silently in the broiling heat and mirror-like calm. The coast of China came in sight, a range of high blue-gray mountains far inland. Nearer at hand, a group of outlying islands appeared on the horizon. Captain Sheldon swung his course to the westward, heading directly into the blinding sun that by this time had sunk low in the western sky.

In the extreme bow of the long-boat sat the old steward, gazing straight ahead with unseeing eyes. His head was uncovered; the sun beat down on him without effect. He made no move, uttered no sound. Alone and helpless, he suffered the throes of the most desperate struggle that human consciousness affords — the struggle of the will against the call of a body habituated to opium.

In the latter part of the afternoon they sighted a big Chinese junk, close inshore against the islands. A little breeze had begun to ruffle the water. On the impulse of the moment, Captain Sheldon decided to board the junk and have himself carried to Hong Kong under sail. The idea caught and suited his fancy; he couldn't bear to think of arriving in port in open boats. Instructions were shouted to the mate's boat, the head of the long-boat was again swung around, and a course was laid to intercept the brown-sailed native craft under the lee of the land.

All this passed unnoticed by the silent figure in the bow, wandering blindly through a grim vale of endeavor. As time went on, however, Wang seemed to realize that a change had taken place in the plan of their progress. The sun no longer shown full in his face. He glanced up dully, caught a vague sight of the junk, now close aboard and standing, to his veiled eyes, like a dark blot on the clear rim of the horizon; then pulled himself hastily together and made a low inquiry of the man at the bow oar. The answer seemed to galvanize his tortured body into action. He began to scramble aft under the moving oars.

"Here, what's the trouble forward?" Captain Sheldon tried to make out the cause of the commotion.

"Wang wants to come aft, sir."

"What for? Shove him into the bottom of the boat."

"He says he must see you, sir."

"Oh, the devil. . . . Well, let him come. He needn't hold up the boat for that."

Many hands helped the old Chinaman aft. Muttering rapidly to himself, he sank into a place beside the captain.

"What's that you say?" demanded Captain Sheldon. "What are you trying to hatch up now?"

Wang made a vague beckoning gesture in the captain's face. Behind all that floated wildly through his mind, stood the fixed thought that he must not shame "Young Cappen" by openly imparting information.

"Are you sick or crazy?" demanded Captain Sheldon again, bending above the maundering old man.

"Cappen, junk he no good!" whispered Wang feverishly. "No can do, Cappen! Must go 'way, chop-chop. Night come soon. Maybe no see."

Captain Sheldon gave a loud laugh. He spoke for all to hear.

"What damned nonsense have you got into your head now?"

"No, sir, Cappen. Look-see!" Wang grasped the other's arm with frantic strength, pulling him down. "You no savvy he, Cappen. Killee quick, no good! You no wanchee he. Go Hong Kong side, chop-chop. Night come, maybe can do. Cappen, my savvy plenty what for!"

"Oh, shut up, you raving old idiot!" cried Captain Sheldon, roughly.

At this inopportune moment the mate, ranging alongside in his boat, offered a suggestion. They were closing in with the junk now; a row of yellow faces peered over the side toward them, watching with narrow bright eyes every movement of the approaching boats.

"Captain Sheldon, I don't like the looks of that crowd," said the mate nervously. "Hadn't we better sheer off, sir?"

"No, certainly not!" shouted the angry captain. "I suppose I'm still in charge here, even if the ship is gone. Do you think I haven't any judgment? By God, between a timid mate and a crazy steward. . . . Give way, boys, there's nothing to be afraid of!"

The breeze by this time had died away, the junk was scarcely moving. A moment later their oars rattled against the side. Captain Sheldon scrambled aboard. He gave a rapid glance along the low main-deck, but saw nothing to arouse his suspicion. A man, evidently the captain of the craft, was advancing toward him; the crew were crowding around to overhear the conversation. But all this was only natural. An ordinary trading junk, of course; heaven alone knew what all these native craft really did. After a moment's scrutiny, he dismissed from his mind any thought that may secretly have been aroused by Wang's warning and the mate's unfortunate remark.

"You makee lose ship — ha?" The captain of the junk accosted him in good pidgin English.

"Yes — she burned this morning. I want you to take me to Hong Kong."

Within half an hour the bargain had been struck, and they were comfortably established on the new deck. The breeze had freshened, the junk's head had been put about, the two ship's boats trailed astern in single file at the end of a long line. The *Retriever's* company had partaken of a Chinese supper; many of them were spending the last hour of daylight in examining the queer craft, passing remarks on her strange nautical points, while the native crew watched their movements with furtive gaze.

Captain Sheldon paced to and fro on the high poop deck, chewing the end of a cigar and ruminating on the unaccountable turns of fortune. The adventure of boarding the junk had for a time broken the savage current of his thoughts; but now, with the affair settled and night closing in, the mood of anger and bitterness claimed him again with redoubled intensity.

The mate ranged up beside him with a friendly air. He felt the need of a reconciliation.

"You'll be interested to hear, Captain, that old Wang has found a pipeful of opium."

"The devil you say! I wondered where the old rascal had disappeared to. How do you know?"

"He's been hanging around the Chinese crew, sir, ever since we came aboard. I went through their quarters down below forward a while ago, and there he lay in one of their bunks, dead to the world, with the pipe across his chest."

"The useless old sot!" exclaimed Captain Sheldon. "I had made up my mind to get rid of him this time, anyway. You know he has been in the family, so to speak. But I don't like the idea of his going off with this native gang. Combined with the opium business, it looks suspicious. You'd better keep an eye on him. He's got a grudge against me, you know, since I took away his stuff."

"I guess they'll all bear watching, sir."

"Oh, nonsense! There isn't the slightest cause for alarm. It's perfectly evident that this craft is a peaceful trader, and we could handle the whole crew of 'em if they commenced to make trouble. They won't, though, never fear; a Chinaman is too big a coward. This captain seems to be quite an intelligent fellow; I've just been having a yarn with him. He has given up his room to me; well, not much of a room, nothing but a bunk and a door, but such as it is, it's all he has. Funny quarters they have down below, like a labyrinth of passages, all leading nowhere."

The mate laughed. "Funny enough forward, too; a damned stinking hole, if you ask me, sir."

While they were talking on the poop, Wang appeared on deck forward, went to the weather rail, and sniffed a deep breath of the land breeze. He had had an hour's opium sleep—an hour of heaven, an hour of life again. Now he could command his faculties. Blindness was no hindrance to work in the dark; was even an advantage, since for many months he had been accustomed to feeling and sensing his way. Fate had been good to him, at the last. Now he possessed the strength to do what he would have to do.

The familiar voices of the mate and the captain came to his ears, but he did not glance in their direction. The least move on his part to give information would have been his last. He had heard enough already to know that the death of the whole ship's company that night was being actively planned, for the sake of the boats and the mysterious tin box that Captain Sheldon carried.

III

In spite of physical exhaustion, it was nearly midnight before Captain Sheldon left the deck and crawled into the narrow den under the poop-deck that had been given up to him by the Chinese captain. He could not get to sleep for a long while. He was taking his loss very hard; that inflexible, proud disposition would almost have met death sooner than admit an error. At length, however, he fell into a light and uneasy slumber.

He was awakened some time later by a faint touch on the arm — a touch that started him from sleep without alarming him into action. A voice whispered softly in his ear:

"Cappen! Cappen! This b'long Wang. No makee speak." A firm hand was laid over his mouth.

In the pitchy darkness of the close room, Captain Sheldon could see absolutely nothing. Listening intently, he heard stealthy movements outside the door. On deck there was utter silence. He became aware instinctively that the junk no longer was moving, that the wind had gone.

He lay perfectly still. The suddenness of the occasion had brought an unaccountable conflict of impulses and emotions. He felt that an alarming crisis was in the air. Along with this feeling came another, strange enough at such a time — a sense of confidence in the old steward. He immediately had recognized the voice in his ear. Why hadn't he jumped out of bed? Why wasn't he lying there in momentary expectation of a knife in the ribs — why didn't he throw himself aside to avoid it? He could not understand his own immobility; yet he remained quiet. Something in the old Chinaman's whisper held him in its command. Pride had succumbed to intrinsic authority.

The rapid whisper began again, panting and insistent.

"Cappen, you come now. Mus' come quick. My savvy how can do. Maybe got time. S'pose stay here, finishee chop-chop." The

hand was removed from his mouth, as if conscious that discretion
had sufficiently been imposed.

"What has happened, Wang?" whispered the agitated captain.

"Makee kill, all same I know."

"Where's the mate? Where's the crew?"

"All go, Cappen." Again the hand came over his mouth. "You
come quick. Bym'by, no can do."

Captain Sheldon flung the steward's arm aside and sat up
wildly. "Good God, let me go, Wang! I must go out. . . . "

"Cappen, makee no bobbery."

"Where's my revolver?" The captain was hunting distractedly
through the bed.

"He go, too." The whisper took on a despairing tone. "Cappen, s'pose you gotee match?"

"Yes."

"Makee one light."

Captain Sheldon found the box and struck a match. The tiny
illumination filled the narrow cabin. As the flame brightened,
Wang rolled over on the floor, disclosing one hand held against
his left breast, a hand holding a bloody wad of tunic against a
hidden wound. A sop of blood on the floor marked the spot
where he had been lying.

The match burned out. Again came the painful whisper.

"Maybe can do now. Bym'by, no can do."

"My God, Wang! You're wounded! How can we get out? I'll
carry you."

"No, sir, Cappen. My savvy way. You feelee here, Cappen."

The steward already was fumbling with his free hand at a
ringbolt in the floor. He guided the captain's arm to it. Captain
Sheldon grasped the ringbolt, pulled up a trap-door that seemed
to lead into the hold. Letting himself over the edge, his feet
found a deck not far below. He stood upright in the opening, and
lifted Wang bodily to the lower level. The old Chinaman struggled to be put down.

"Wang, keep still — let me carry you."

"No, sir, Cappen. Walkee-walkee, can do. You no savvy way."

Stooping and keeping an arm half around him, Captain Sheldon followed Wang through a shallow lazaret. It led forward into
the open hold. They passed beneath a hatch, where Wang drew
aside in the deeper shadow, listening. Not a sound came from

CALL MIKE SCHELL
WITH INFO ABOUT
BIKE

ASK ABOUT INS.
SOCIAL SEC. DISAB.
FEE?
~~WORK~~
CAN THEY GIVE MY
JOB AWAY?

MEDICAL RELEASE

overhead. Again they stole forward. The wounded man held on indomitably, bearing his pain in a silence that seemed almost supernatural, as if unknown to the other he had been rendered invulnerable by a magic spell. Beyond the hatch they entered a narrow passage-way, and came out suddenly into the junk's forecastle, the quarters of the Chinese crew. A ladder led to another open hatch in the deck above.

As they reached the foot of the ladder, a fearful yelling suddenly broke out toward the stern, a sound of savage anger. Naked feet pattered on the deck overhead, going aft. Wang grasped the captain's arm.

"S'pose breakee in door, no findee. One minute have got! Boat stand off, waitee! Go quick, Cappen, jump overboard!"

Captain Sheldon heard him with a shock of incredulity. "The boats are standing off? The crew haven't been killed?"

"No, sir, Cappen. All hand savee! You go now."

He felt the old man sag in his arms.

"Wang, I can't leave you here!"

"Why for, Cappen? Wang no good. Quick! Makee jump!"

The voice broke; the frail body crumpled and slipped to the floor.

Gathering all his strength, Captain Sheldon slung the old steward's unconscious form over his shoulder and swarmed up the ladder. As he gained the deck, a tall figure dashed between him and the rail; other figures were racing through the waist of the junk. An angry chatter broke out at the foot of the ladder up which he had just come.

Holding Wang to one side, he struck out heavily at the man who blocked his path, felling him to the deck. Darkness and surprise saved the day for him; their quarry had appeared like a whirlwind in their very midst. The next instant Captain Sheldon had gained the rail, and jumped clear of the junk's side. The two bodies made a loud splash that echoed through the calmness of the night. As he came to the surface, desperately striking away from the junk and trying to keep Wang's head above water, he heard a shout a little distance off in the darkness, and the rattle of oars as the boats sprang into action.

IV

The long-boat was the first to reach him. They pulled him in with his burden still in his arms. The mate, appearing beside them in the other boat, gave vent to his anxiety.

"Good God, Captain Sheldon, I thought you were done for! Why didn't you come, sir? Wang gave me your orders; we hauled up the boats very quietly as you said, and got into them, while he kept the Chinamen busy forward with talk. He said you would come, but we were discovered, and I had to sheer off. I was afraid they'd sink the boats, before we could do anything. I didn't know what weapons they had. I was just planning an attack, sir. Then I thought I saw them stab old Wang. . . . "

"I've got Wang," said Captain Sheldon solemnly. "They did stab him. Those weren't my orders — they were his. And he's the only one to pay the price!" The young captain was beginning to face a harder lesson than the mere loss of a vessel.

"I don't understand, sir. Wasn't it the right thing to do?" The mate was completely puzzled by this new development.

"Yes, yes, it was the right thing to do!" cried Captain Sheldon impatiently. "He was right, and I was wrong. Now leave me alone."

He bent above the shrunken form of the old steward. Wang's eyelids fluttered; he was slowly regaining consciousness.

"Wang, why didn't you come and tell me, in time to save all this?"

The Chinaman's eyes regarded him with a stare of mingled surprise and affection, a stare that somehow suggested a wise and quiet amusement.

"My tellee you, Cappen. You no savvy. S'pose no savvy, no can do. Mus' wait, makee savvy."

It was a terrible condemnation. Captain Sheldon ground his teeth at the bitter truth of it. His own obstinacy, his own evil! Nothing that Wang could have said, before the thing had happened, would possibly have changed his mind. He had committed himself to error. The old servant had been forced to save them single-handed, to retrieve his master's failure with his own life.

Wang was muttering, as he neared the end. He was about to join "Old Cappen," with a good report and a clean record. No one could have known the depth of the calm that had come to that aged heart. Even the awful pain of the wound had stopped, under the shock of the cool water. He seemed to be drifting off into an eternal opium dream.

"What is it, Wang? Can I do anything for you?"

"No, sir, Cappen. Bym'by, finishee."

He lay quiet for a moment, then plucked at the other's sleeve.

"Old Cappen say, boy step high. Look out! Maybe more-better stop, look-see."

Captain Sheldon buried his face in his hands. Had the words come with lesser force, they would have infuriated him; had the advice been given as advice, it would have defeated its own ends. But now it came with the authority of death, sealed with the final service. It came with the meaning of life, and could not be denied.

AH-MAN

THE STORY OF A CHINESE STEWARD

———————●————

He sat on a sea-chest in Fred's South Street store, immovable, stolid, waiting for the captain to come in. He was small, even for a Chinaman, a bony, dried-up little man in European clothes, drooping, alien, and undisturbed by the clamor of the street outside and the constant passing of sailors.

I saw him as soon as I came through the door, and it seemed like a glimpse of the strange, impassive land that I used to know—the land that has sat immovable for centuries, waiting for the word. He stared straight ahead with glazed, unwavering eyes. No one noticed him. He paid no attention to the conversation, though I instinctively knew that he understood English. An air of age and mystery hung about him; I felt that he knew infinitely more than all of us put together. Nothing escaped him, and yet he made no sign. How much he might have hidden in a lifetime beneath those unfathomable eyes!

Then Dashy Noyes came in and stopped in front of him.

"Ah-Man!" he said in a strange voice. "Where in th' devil did *you* come from?"

The Chinaman looked up without moving a muscle except his eyes. "No Ah-Man," he said. "Me Wu-Sing."

"Wu-Sing?" said Dashy, regarding him thoughtfully. "What ship you go in?"

"Me go Cap'n Tlue, ship *Ice-e-Berg.*" He spoke in that sing-song dialect impossible to show in words.

Dashy looked hard at him, and seemed to be figuring something over in his mind. They were an odd pair, facing each other in that dim room. I found myself wondering what was in the wind.

Then Dashy turned away. "All right," he said.

The Chinaman sat with oblivious indifference until Captain True came in on his way to the ship. After some talk among the captains, they went out, the steward keeping a respectful distance in the rear.

Some days later I stood in Battery Park with Dashy Noyes, and watched the *Iceberg* tow down the stream. She was loaded with case-oil and bound out for Hong-Kong.

"I reckon he'll never come t' th' States again," said Dashy, his eyes on the passing ship.

"Who?" I asked.

"Ah-Man."

"What, the Chinese steward? I thought he said his name was something else."

"He did—but it ain't," said Dashy. "He's Ah-Man all right. I couldn't forget that face. I had occasion t' remember it, one voyage."

We had taken a turn or two along the bulkhead before he spoke again. "A wonderful race!" he ripped out. "Wonderful! Very few white men know anything about 'em at all. They're superior. If we had half their brains an' a quarter o' their nerve, th' world wouldn't be big enough t' hold us. That man, now—'d you notice him that day in Fred's? You'd never think he was about as sca't as a man could be, would you? You'd never think, t' see him lookin' at me, that I was th' one man in th' world he'd been sca't t' meet f'r years?

"No, sir! He never turned a hair—just looked at me an' lied. God knows what was goin' on inside his head. You *never* c'n find out what they're thinkin' about—only just what they wan' t' tell you. They think a lot, that's all I know. That little Chinaman was doin' some o' th' tallest ol' thinkin' that ever happened, an' he took one o' th' longest chances that I ever see tackled! He was hangin' by a hair, I tell you, an' he set there an' never quivered an eyelid! Things like that show you why a Chinaman c'n beat any white man alive playin' poker. They'd look at death just as steady as they'd look at a hand o' cards."

Dashy Noyes stopped and cast another glance at the fast-re-treating ship. "Ah-Man!" he said. "I've of'en wondered where he was, an' whatever happened to 'im. He went out in such a blaze o' glory that I'll never forget th' man. He was one o' th' few mysteries you meet. An', besides, I never c'n forget what he did aboard that ship. It wa'n't his fault, exactly—but it was a horrible thing! *Horrible!* An' yet I never could find it in my heart t' blame him altogether. The Ol' Man Randall was more than half responsible, an' that hellish opium did th' rest. It finished me out East f'r a while. I struck f'r home th' first chance I got, an' th' devil an' all his angels wouldn't make me go with a Chinese steward again.

"I was on th' beach in Singapore that time, when th' little bark *Georgietta* come in. She traded up an' down th' China Sea; I'd seen her half a dozen times in different ports. Ol' Man Randall owned her himself, an' made a pile o' money out of 'er in his day. His mate was sick, an' I happened t' meet 'im th' mornin' that he put th' man ashore.

" 'Hello, Noyes,' says 'e, 'what are you doin' nowadays?'

" 'Watchin' th' ships come in, sir,' says I. 'D' you need a man?'

" 'Yes,' says 'e,—'like hell. Can you come aboard at once?'

"I wanted t' ship f'r home, but there wa'n't many chances fr'm Singapore just then.

" 'Where are you bound?' says I.

" 'Shanghai, with bark, an' iron-wood,' says 'e, puffin' like a whale. 'Lord, but it's hot!' he says, an' mops his face with a towel that he used t' always carry on his arm.

"Cap'n Randall was a big, heavy bulk of a man, full o' blood an' wisdom. He thought it was wisdom. He had ideas about everything, settled ideas that you couldn't ha' started with a yoke of oxen. I never see him ashore when he wasn't holdin' forth, moppin' his face every minute with that towel. He sweat somethin' awful, an' talked in a kind o' puffin' way, like a man comin' up t' th' top o' th' water t' breathe. Goin' along th' street he seemed t' plug up th' road; an' when you got him inside, he filled th' room. Wherever he was, he was th' most important thing in sight. A most overbearin' man. Even wi' th' cap'ns ashore, he crowded everybody out, an' that deep voice o' his would rumble on by the hour—interestin', in a way, but devilish monotonous. An' aboard th' ship in that little cubby-hole of a forrard cabin, sometimes you'd think the end of it would blow off when he got t' hollerin' an' arguin' with 'imself.

"I wonder that I come t' go with 'im, knowin' him as I did by reputation; but a young feller don't bother much about them

things. He took me right off in his sampan that mornin', an' I
turned to at noon.

"Th' first time I set eyes on Ah-Man was at th' dinner-table.
He looked as old an' shriveled up then as he did sittin' on that
chest the other afternoon. Funny about them people—they
never seem t' change. Every time I used t' go t' Hong-Kong, th'
sampan-men an' th' bumboat-men an' all them fellers would look
about th' same. Now an' then one of 'em 'uld drop out, an' each
trip there'd be two or three new babies in every boat, but that's
all. Time don't seem t' touch 'em. Nothin' touches 'em, f'r that
matter; they peg right along till one day they curl up an' die. I
never see one die, but I suppose they do.

"But there was somethin' about Ah-Man different fr'm any
steward I ever run up against. I can't explain it exactly, but I got
an idea he didn't belong in th' pantry. They're all reserved, an'
they've all got better manners than white men, but he was a little
better than th' best. I watched him that day at dinner, tryin' t'
make out what it was that sort of impressed me. Devil, I couldn't
place it—they're all a puzzle. 'He ain't no steward,' says I t'
myself; an' then, 'What in hell *is* he?' I says. That was it—what
was he? When he wa'n't movin', he'd stand like a statue, lookin'
away off somewhere. I see a China priest in Canton once look
just that way, with rows an' rows o' worshipers, thumpin' their
heads on th' ground in front of 'im. It seemed like there was two
men, one of 'em doin' steward's work like a machine, an' the
other one somethin' else. A mystery.

"Ol' Man Randall talked all through dinner. A new man was
fish f'r his net. He wanted so an' so done, an' he wanted it done
such an' such a way. He believed this an' that an' the other, an'
he'd trot out a mess o' facts a yard long t' support his theories. A
powerful man, full o' confidence. When he made a motion with
his hands, it was like rubbin' out other people's marks on a
blackboard. He wanted a clean slate an' no favor.

"By-an'-bye th' steward went forrard f'r th' dessert.

" 'Fine steward you've got there, sir,' says I. 'Rather remarkable
f'r a Chinaman, ain't he?'

" 'Yes, he's a good servant,' says th' Cap'n. 'When I break him
o' smokin' opium he can't be beat.'

" 'Well, a lot of 'em smokes it, sir,' says I. 'I can't see that it
makes much difference.'

" 'I don't like it!' he says, wavin' his hands. 'I can't stand it! I won't have it! There ain't no sense in it! The idea of a man bein' a slave t' such a drug. I'll stop it short when we get t' sea.'

"I was surprised t' hear Mrs. Randall, the Cap'n's wife, speak up at that. 'George,' she says, 'I wish you'd leave him alone. I don't like t' have you interferin' with them things.'

" 'That's all foolishness!' he says to 'er. 'That's just like a woman's way o' lookin' at things. Why, he won't do anything— you see. When I say quit, he'll quit. I tell you, it's goin' t' be stopped short off. I won't have a steward o' mine dead t' th' world f'r two hours every afternoon!'

"Mrs. Randall didn't answer. She had found out it wa'n't no use. She was a little tremblin' woman, like lots o' women you see at home. I never had much t' do with her except at table, an' then she didn't do any talkin'. The Ol' Man had knocked that out of 'er long ago. She seemed t' keep on livin' fr'm a sense o' duty. Land knows, there wa'n't much left f'r her t' live for. I never heard any o' their family history, but th' Cap'n told me once that they had lost their only child at sea. Year after year she'd been with him an' listened to 'im,—gone ashore now an' then in port, as she used to that time in Singapore,—an' called it a life, I suppose. She looked tired t' death. The only time I ever see her brighten up was once just before she sailed, when they got a bunch o' letters fr'm home. She an' th' Cap'n talked about th' home news all that noon at th' dinner-table, an I could see in a flash what sort o' woman she might ha' been. A home-body, thinkin' all th' time o' home.

"I recollect that first afternoon aboard th' *Georgietta* as if 'twas yesterday. One o' them bright, glitterin' days, with a strong sea-breeze blowin' across th' harbor an' kickin' up a muddy sea. I leaned over th' rail an' watched th' shore. Singapore! There's everything in Singapore! Th' brightest flowers, th' prettiest girls—everything! An' th' sea-breeze blowin' every afternoon. Wonder what it's like now? I ain't been there f'r fifteen years.

"A big shaggy dog that Cap'n Randall kept aboard th' ship come an' put his nose over th' rail beside me. I like a dog. This one was bully an' good-natured—never got in th' road an' never made any trouble. I thought a lot of 'im after I'd been aboard awhile. Nights he'd come nosin' around an' wan' t' be rubbed. A feller gets attached to a dumb animal like that—I wouldn't ha' seen him ill-used f'r worlds.

"About three o'clock that afternoon, as I was passin' th' galley, I caught a whiff of opium-smoke. I dodged in, an' there lay Ah-Man on th' floor o' th' cook's room, with his head on a junk o' wood. I always liked t' watch a man smoke th' stuff. He handled it like he done everything else—dignified. It seemed t' be just a part of 'is life, like eatin'. Kind o' fascinated me t' watch th' gradual motions that he went through, an' hear that little pipe sputter. Somehow, seein' him lie there in that position, th' room dim with sickish smoke, took you right into China at one jump, an' made you wonder what was behind it—the mystery.

"He smoked regular at half-past two every afternoon, I found out. Then he'd sleep till four, an' get up an' go t' work, hummin' one o' them outlandish tunes. How long he'd done it I don't know, but I c'n understand what it meant to 'im.

"Well, we sailed in about a month, pretty deep wi' the iron-wood an' overrun with scorpions fr'm th' rolls o' bark. It was another bright, windy afternoon when we got under way. Goin' out we run close by a bark at anchor, right across her stern. Mrs. Randall was on deck, wavin t' the other ship, as we went by, an' a woman aboard her waved back. They was folks fr'm th' same place at home. I c'n see 'em wavin' yet, Mrs. Randall with a little shawl around her head, an' that big dog beside her barkin' fr all he was worth. It was an old story t' her, sayin' good-by t' port— she'd done it all her life. No one'll ever know what she went through, or what a brave woman she was.

"That evenin' th' Cap'n an' I had our first row about th' steward.

" 'Mr. Noyes,' says 'e, comin' forrard t' where I was sittin' on th' booby-hatch, 'I want you t' go an' get all the opium th' steward's got, an' bring it t' me.'

" 'He probably keeps it in his room here, sir,' says I. 'I'd rather you'd speak to 'im about it yourself when he comes aft.'

" 'Why, wha' d' you mean?' says 'e.

" 'I don't like t' take it away fr'm him, Cap'n, that's all,' says I. 'If you think it ought t' be done, I wish you'd do it yourself.'

" 'Are you sca't of a Chinaman?' says 'e. 'D' you mean t' tell me that you don't dare to ask him fr that opium?'

" 'No, I'm not sca't of 'im,' says I, 'an' yet, in a way, I am. I don't think any good'll come of it. I've seen 'em smoke this way before, an' it don't do no harm. You never c'n tell what'll happen if you take it away. I understand 'em pretty well, an' I advise you not t' do it.'

" 'I guess I know as much about Chinamen as you do,' says 'e. 'I been sailin' on this coast close on to ten years now. It's just a foolish notion they've got into their heads, this opium habit. I'll show you how little foundation there is in it.'

" 'Maybe,' says I. 'But my experience is, you c'n sail th' coast o' China fifty years an' never know any more about a Chinaman. What he does he'll keep on doin'. What he wants he'll get. An' he's so much smarter than us that most o' th' time he gets what he wants an' makes us think he don't.'

" 'Shucks!' says Cap'n Randall. 'They're just like any other men. What put that idea into your head? He won't fool me, not if I know myself. I'll search his dunnage, an' then if he hides any o' th' stuff we'll catch him smokin' it. It's goin' t' be stopped, or I'll know th' reason why!'

" 'You have t' have your little nip before breakfast every mornin', sir,' says I.

" 'Well, what's that got t' do with it?' says 'e, gettin' mad. 'You don't compare a drink o' whisky to a pipe of opium, do you?'

" 'I don't see much difference,' says I.

" 'You're a fool,' says 'e.

" 'Fool I may be, sir,' says I, 'but fools is th' ones that's got somethin' yet t' learn. Thank God, I don't know it all.'

"Just then, th' steward come aft, an' the Ol' Man follered him below. I heard some loud talk in th' forrard cabin, but couldn't make out what was said. Th' row was still goin' on when Mrs. Randall come around th' corner o' the after-house. She was frightened, an' run t' me.

" 'What is it?' she says.

" 'Th' Cap'n's takin' away th' steward's opium,' says I.

"She was half cryin' then. 'I wish he wouldn't,' she says. 'I'm afraid somethin' might happen.'

" 'Oh, it's all right,' says I. 'He won't make no trouble.'

" 'You can't trust 'em,' she says, an' went away aft cryin'. She had more sense in her little finger than th' Cap'n had in his whole big lump of a body!

"About half an hour after that th' steward come up behind me without makin' a sound. I jumped around like lightnin' when he spoke, an' see his face close t' mine.

" 'Wha' for Cap'n he take opium?' he says, kind o' whisperin'.

" 'No smoke,' says I. 'Cap'n no waunchee.'

"He got off a long string o' Chinese at me, like two dogs fightin'.

" 'Go below,' says I. 'Go sleep. Mornin' come, you feel better.'

"It set me thinkin', though. What's th' use o' doin' things like that? It's men like Cap'n Randall that makes half th' trouble in th' world, an' then lays it off onto somebody else. Men that don't understand, an' can't see. It's a good thing t' be self-centered, but when you get t' be the only man alive, it's carryin' it too far. I've seen lots like him—lots o' white men handlin' foreigners as if they was so much cattle. Just because *we* don't do it, or just because *we* don't choose t' have it done, we'd change th' ways o' centuries. Better ways than our own, too, half th' time—ways that was bein' followed back along when our forefathers was eatin' raw meat an' poundin' stone, with a hunk o' sheep's hide hung around their middle.

"F'r a week things went on about th' same, an' I didn't notice much. Every day at table Ah-Man was just as soft an' easy. When th' Cap'n 'd speak to 'im, he was right on deck. I never see but few Chinamen that was sassy when they wa'n't on good terms with anyone. They was brought up different—it ain't their custom. You take a man with thousands o' years back of 'im, an' he c'n afford t' keep his mouth shut. We have t' fight f'r what *we* get, but a Chinaman don't look at life that way. He's busy savin' face, an' life don't mean anything itself. Queer combination—an' this one in particular seemed farther away than the most of 'em. It was easy t' see that he was a better-class Chinaman, with education. I've met a few of 'em in my time—honorable gentlemen, with big ideas—so big that I'm beginnin' t' think we never understood half of 'em. They only showed us what was necessary in a friendly way; th' rest of it was hidden behind them wax faces. They've got th' power t' keep their mouths shut—th' most marvelous thing!

"I suppose Ah-Man was sufferin' tortures that week, but it never dawned on me till one night in th' mornin' watch when I caught him prowlin' around decks. He tried t' get out o' sight, but I run forrard an' grabbed him.

" 'Here, wha' for you no stay below?' I says.

" 'Me no sleep seven night!' he says, an' stuck his hands up in front o' my face wi' th' fingers spread out, that way.

" 'You go below. I see Cap'n to-morrow,' I says, an' he went off with his teeth chatterin'.

"I couldn't believe it, but in an hour or so, when th' cook got up, I went along t' th' galley an' asked him about it. Th' cook was a fat Canton Chinaman, an' never smoked.

"It was th' truth: Ah-Man hadn't had a wink o' sleep that week. I couldn't get much out o' th' cook. 'Steward he no sleep,' that's about all he'd say. Just as I was leavin' th' galley door, he broke out at me. 'Some day Cap'n he catchee hell!' he says.

" 'Wha' d' you mean?' says I. 'Don't you let that steward go t' cuttin' up any funny business.'

" 'No savee,' he says; an' I do' know whether he meant me or him. Then he pointed up over his head with a big carvin'-knife that he had in his hand. 'God,' he says, an' finished up with a long mess o' Chinese gobblin'. I couldn't make out what he was drivin' at; but I see now, because I've got a notion o' what th' steward must ha' been.

"Next mornin', when th' Cap'n come on deck, I went aft.

" 'Cap'n,' says I, 'I don't like this thing at all. I found th' steward on deck last night, an' he ain't slept this week.'

" 'What of it?' says 'e. 'He'll sleep when he gets tired o' this game. It's probably a big bluff, anyway.'

" 'Too much like a white man's bluff,' says I. 'They don't bluff that way. If I was you, I'd give him a little opium.'

" 'Well, you ain't me,' he says. 'Leave him alone. Don't you go sidin' in with 'im. I wan' t' teach him a lesson he'll remember.'

" 'A man can't go on like that, losin' sleep, sir,' I says.

" 'Leave him alone—you hear me?' says 'e. 'He ain't been losin' enough sleep t' lay him up. I ain't noticed anything.'

" 'You can't,' says I; 'he won't let you. But some day he'll go an jump overboard, or put poison in th' food, or cut up some monkey-shine.'

" 'Anyone 'uld think, t' hear you talk,' says 'e, 'that you was some old woman like my wife. I tell you, things like that don't happen nowadays. We ain't a gang o' blamed savages. I do' want t' hear another word about this. I'm tired an' sick o' th' whole business.'

" 'Well, sir,' says I, 'this is th' last word, then. It's your pidgin, an' I'll keep out of it. But I think you're wrong fr'm start t' finish, sir.'

"That night was fine, with a big moon. It was just at th' change
o' th' monsoon, an' about three bells we got a puff o' wind fr'm th'
south'ard. We was makin' up towards th' coast o' Luzon then, an'
'ad a splendid run fr'm Singapore. I braced th' yards, come aft an'
had a look at th' compass, an' set down on th' weather-bitts. It
was a seven- or eight-knot breeze that struck us, an' she was
slippin' along at a great rate. I set there singing t' myself, an'
thinkin' about every namable thing under the sun. The air
smelled good, though there wa'n't no land in sight.

"Finally, I got t' thinkin' about th' steward, an' wonderin' if,
after all, I wa'n't too anxious about a little thing. I'd told th' men
t' watch out for 'im forrard if he come on deck in th' night. It
didn't hardly seem reasonable that he'd do anything. We fool
ourselves like that a lot o' times.

"I was singin' away, when th' man at th' wheel yells at me.

" 'Look out behind you!' he says.

"I jumped ahead against th' rail, an', just as I did, somethin'
went 'punk!' into th' bitts behind me. When I turned around, th'
steward was standin' there with his arms stuck up in the air, an'
in front of 'im, buried in th' bitts, was th' little hatchet that they
used in th' galley t' chop kindlin'-wood. He must 'ave aimed an
awful blow at me, fr th' thing had gone clean through th' copper
top o' th' bitts like paper, an' stuck in th' wood a couple of inches.

"Th' man at th' wheel let a yell, an' had 'im down before I
could move. Then th' watch come runnin' aft, an' we tied him up
an' put him down in th' lazare-e-t. It all happened in a few
minutes, but I did a pile o' thinkin' in them few minutes. When
I come t' loosen th' hatchet fr'm th' bitts, I found that it was all
covered with blood.

"That sent me below on th' dead run. Th' light was burnin' in
the after-cabin, an' I stopped a second. 'Cap'n! Cap'n!' I says, but
I knew without waitin' that there wouldn't be no answer. Then
I took th' lamp down fr'm th' bracket an' went into th' Cap'n's
room.

"No one but a Chinaman could ha' done what he'd done. He
must ha' found 'em both asleep, an' killed 'em quick without
makin' any noise. They was in th' bunk, dead, an' all chopped up
in little pieces. I never wan' t' see a sight like that again! All in
little pieces—legs, an' arms, an' even th' bodies, all over th' bed.
Th' Cap'n's head was right on the edge o' th' bunk, an' his long

beard hung down over. It was th' first thing I see. I come out an' closed th' door.

"I couldn't seem t' get my bearin's after that, an' instead o' goin' up aft, I went out into th' forrard cabin wi' th' lamp still in my hand. There I fell over th' dead body o' th' dog. He was killed in th' same way, all hacked out o' shape. Somehow, that took th' starch out o' me. I put th' lamp down on th' table an' fell onto th' settee. I hadn't lost my grip t' see what was in th' Cap'n's room, but th' dog knocked all th' wind out o' my sails! It wa'n't human, t' do a thing like that—chop 'em all up in little pieces! Th' dog must ha' been th' first. God, I could seem t' see that Chinaman choppin' away! I got sick, an' threw up all over th' forrard cabin table.

"That night was like a dream t' me. Think of it! We had t' clean that cabin up, though we couldn't get many o' th' men t' go down. I didn't blame 'em. All hands was on deck all night. Along towards mornin' I went up aft an' tried t' get away fr'm it fr a while—tried t' think. Th' steward was in irons down in th' lazare-e-t, ravin' crazy. I sent fr th' cook, an' he come aft, sca't blue an' chatterin' like a monkey. I knew he might be in it an' he might not, an' it didn't matter much either way. Th' second mate was fr lockin' him up or pitchin' him overboard, but I wa'n't afraid of anything more happenin'. Nothin' more *could* happen.

"O' course th' cook didn't know anything about it. All I could get out of 'im was th' same old story: 'Cap'n he take opium; Ah-Man he no can do.' I sent him off forrard an' went down t' hunt fr that opium. It was in the upper drawer o' th' medicine-chest, all rolled up in Chinese paper, just th' way th' steward had passed it over. I went out an' found his pipe, an' took th' whole business down in th' lazare-e-t. He was lyin' on his back, workin' his lips across his teeth, an' every now an' then he'd let a yell like an animal. I took out my revolver, an' unlocked the irons, an' put the opium things in his hands.

" 'Smoke!' says I. 'I guess you've earned it!'

"That mornin' I changed th' course fr Hong-Kong. I couldn't bring myself t' go any further up th' Sea. It took us another week t' get across, with light, bafflin' winds—a hundred miles or so a day. Every afternoon I went through th' same performance in th' lazare-e-t, an' after every smoke I could see him comin' back t' reason. Th' last two or three days I tried t' talk to 'im. I told him

what he had done, an' he seemed t' know all about it. But I run
up against a snag when I asked him why. 'Cap'n he take opium,'
says 'e. Th' bare fact that I couldn't understand without askin'
was enough fr *him*. He had his reasons. Sittin' there watchin'
him an' thinkin' it over, I decided that he wa'n't crazy when he
started in. It was deliberate. His honor 'd been touched in some
mysterious way. He was simply tryin' t' get his face back again. I
feel th' point of it myself; he *made* me feel it, just by th' way he
kept his dignity, lyin' there in irons. I see what a big thing
his honor was—bigger than mine was t' me, though he wa'n't
blowin' about it fr'm mornin' till night. An' so he just planned
th' thing, deliberately. It was the only way out of it. 'Cap'n
take opium, me no sleep.' Don't sound hardly enough t' slice
two people all up for, does it? But until you learn who he was an'
what he was an' all about them thousands o' years he had t' live
by, an' until you understand what face is,—unless you're a Chinaman yourself,—you'll never know how a man could do that
thing in cold blood.

"When we got up close outside Hong-Kong one night, it fell
flat calm. She slat all night in a regular ol' typhoon swell, an' in
th' mornin' things looked pretty dark an' nasty. I knew if we
could get a little wind we'd soon slip in, but it wa'n't *that* I was
worryin' about. We was right in amongst th' fishin' fleet, an' I
didn't wan' t' be becalmed there too long. I learned afterwards
that we was sighted fr'm th' peak just after dawn, but that didn't
help me at th' time.

"If you've never seen th' fishin' fleet off Hong-Kong, you can't
realize what a strange sight it is. Millions o' little junks, dodgin'
up an' down when there's any wind, an' paddlin' around in calms.
I been caught amongst 'em that way two or three times, an' it
always gives me th' creeps, somehow. Makes you feel nervous, there's so many of 'em all around you. Them was th' days,
too, when th' Chinese wa'n't so peaceable as they are now. There
was plenty o' pirates in th' China Sea then; an' t' be surrounded
by them cussed junks an' feel shut in an' helpless wa'n't no
pleasant sensation.

"That mornin' there must ha' been a dozen of 'em close aboard,
an' we could hear their everlasting chatterin' an' powwow goin'
on across th' water. I watched 'em wi' th' glass, an' imagined that
they was plannin' somethin'. I suppose they was tryin' t' get up

courage t' come alongside, but that didn't enter my head then. They sounded threatenin'. There's always somethin' terrifyin' about a big mob of 'em. The experience I'd just been through wa'n't exactly quietin' t' th' nerves, either.

"So when I see one o' them junks makin' for us I was really anxious. I'd never heard o' their attackin' a ship so close t' Hong-Kong, but I was ready f'r anything. Th' way it turned out, I guess they just wanted t' sell fish, an' it might ha' been all right but f'r Ah-Man down in th' lazare-e-t. But, anyhow, as soon as I see her rowin' towards us,—a big feller she was, too,—I armed th' men. We had a lot o' fire-arms aboard—it wa'n't safe t' go without 'em in them seas.

"When she got alongside, I leaned over th' rail.

" 'Wha' d' you want?' says I.

"They jabbered back at me, an' waved fish in their hands. Must ha' been a dozen men in her, an' none of 'em understood English. They threw a line aboard, an' I fired it back on their deck. Then they made fast t' th' lower mizzen-channels. I pointed guns at 'em, an' hollered, but they wouldn't pay no attention.

"Th' minute she was fast, two or three of 'em swarmed aboard. I tried t' stop 'em, but short o' shootin' 'em down there didn't seem t' be no way. They was bound t' sell fish. They passed a couple o' baskets aboard an' brought 'em along t' me, talkin' th' most outlandish lingo as if I understood every word.

" 'Shut up your noise!' says I, an' went below t' get some money. Says I t' myself, 'I'll give 'em half a dollar, if that's what they want, an' get 'em over th' rail an' out o' this ship.' I couldn't bear t' have 'em around—they made me sick; but I was gettin' over my scare.

"Just then I heard a rumpus on deck. 'Come up, sir, quick!' sings out th' man at th' wheel.

"I jumped up th' companionway in time t' see th' lazare-e-t hatch fly off, an' Ah-Man standin' there with 'is head just showin'. He yelled somethin' in Chinese, an' all them fishermen fell flat on their faces on th' deck. I remembered that I'd forgotten t' lash th' hatch down when I come out o' th' lazare-e-t th' last time—I knew he couldn't get out alone.

"What it was he said to 'em I can't imagine. Th' sight of 'is face above th' hatch-combin' give me a shock. It seemed t' be th' most natural thing in th' world t' him f'r them fishermen t' fall down.

He was expectin' it—was used to it. I stood like a fool with my mouth open, watchin' fr just a second. It had got beyond me—'way beyond, thousands o' years. He'd fetched 'em with a word—some religious thing, it must ha' been. But you can't imagine how dumbfoundin' it was.

"Then he yelled again, an' two of 'em jumped towards th' hatch. About that time I yelled an' jumped, an' th' first thing I did was t' tumble over one o' them fishermen just gettin' up on his feet. Th' man at th' wheel was down, too, with a couple of 'em on top of him.

" 'Shall we shoot, sir?' sings out a man fr'm th' top o' th' house.

"I was tryin' t' throw off my man, an' I couldn't see.

" 'Wait!' I yells. 'You're liable t' shoot th' wrong man. Keep 'em back fr'm th' junk!'

"Then I felt th' man above me quit an' pull himself away. I jumped onto my feet, an' see them all makin' fr th' side. But it was too late. 'Let 'em go!' I sung out t' th' men.

"It had all happened before I fairly got on my feet. Ah-Man was standin' on th' rail aft, tryin' t' jerk the irons loose. He stood there just fr a second. Then he give it up, shouted something that all th' junks close by could hear, an' jumped overboard without a look around.

"Th' rest of 'em was after him in th' same second, leavin' th' two baskets o' fish on deck. I run t' th' rail, an' found that they had cut th' junk adrift an' was pushin' off, howlin' an' jabberin' like mad. Astern of us, th' fellers in th' water was swimmin' with Ah-Man. I had a mind t' take a shot at 'em, an' then I says, 'What's th' use?' They'd got away; it might make trouble; an' land knows we'd had enough trouble fr one voyage. There was a thousand Chinamen within a mile of us.

"I watched 'em swim him alongside an' haul him aboard, with 'is arms still in irons behind his back. Then they turned around an' made them long sweeps buckle, rowin' towards th' land. As far as I could see 'em, there was a terrible commotion goin' on on deck. Each junk they'd pass, they'd wave their arms an' seem t' tell some news. But no one come near us all day, an' we got in at night.

"An' that's th' man I find sittin' on a chest in Fred's! Who he was, where he'd been since I see him goin' over th' rail o' that fishin'-junk, why he was back here in a ship's pantry—I can't

make out any of it. Th' same ol' dried-up face—an' that's all
we know. Just like th' country he comes from, that th' white
men think they're gettin' to understand. They know a little
rim around th' coast, an' they've got it laid down on th' chart,
but behind that coast-line th' heart o' th' country is a mystery:
millions o' souls, thousands o' years, secrets they'll *never* get
at, *never* could understand! Why, these Chinamen—they beat
the Dutch!"

THE GAME OF LIFE AND DEATH

There aren't any more of those evenings under the awning in Hong Kong harbor, the evenings that Nichols used to like so well. The ships and the trade have dropped away; and Nichols is gone, too, for that matter. But we who are left remember him always in connection with those friendly gatherings. We came to look for his little bark on our arrival; and more than often she would be lying under Kowloon-side, a small vessel painted in the most extraordinary colors, cream-white above and bottle-green below the water line, with a good deal of bright yellow on the woodwork about her decks.

Nichols stood apart, a singular and interesting man. His experience in the coastwise trade of China had been remarkable. A certain alien strain had crept into his blood; he held the reputation of knowing half a dozen Chinese dialects, and dealing in matters beyond the impenetrable border of the land.

As I came up the *Omega's* gangway one evening, Nichols was hanging paper lanterns beneath the awning. He expected the captains of the fleet on board to bid him good-bye. Together we sat by the rail and watched the sampans gather from the ships. A puff of off-shore breeze lifted the awning, rustling among the paper globes. The quiet harbor lay like a pool at the foot of the Peak. Men drifted in by twos and threes, dropping into comfortable deck-chairs. Glasses clinked, cigars were lighted. The talk turned to typhoons of the past; and Nichols told a tale.

I

"I wouldn't ask you to believe me," he began, "if I couldn't refer you to Lee Fu Chang. You know him; he's probably chartered all of you for home, at different times. He is the soul of honor, and would confirm my most incredible detail. The next time any of you fellows have occasion to call at his office, bear my story in mind and take another look at him. You'll see him as he chooses to have it, for purposes of business; a tall and rather stout Chinaman, smiling, dignified, graceful, offering you a chair beside a heavily carved blackwood table, and a cup of tea in an eggshell from his own hands. You may imagine that his thoughts are bounded by the walls of that little room, piled high with rolls of silk, embellished with fantastic decorations and ornaments, the symbols of his trade. He sits there so placidly, seems so utterly at rest. You would be astonished and disconcerted to know what's going on behind his eyes.

" 'Babbling fool,' he is thinking, 'I see that you are not for long. My race, enduring quietly, and waiting, has acquired much wisdom through many years. The progress of races is accomplished only in the soul of the individual; and the soul of the individual increases, not according to its knowledge of many extraneous matters, but rather according to its wisdom in a few essential matters. Nothing can be important, if through it the life of the race fails.'

"Then, maybe, Lee Fu will run over your charter-party with you; and while you're giving it a final examination, he'll lean back in his chair and fold his hands. 'What other race than mine, my friend,' he'll go on thinking, 'could throw off the evil of opium by the assembled efforts of individual wills? What other race than mine could have kept its lands in a state of undiminished fertility for forty centuries? What other race than mine could have developed an immunity to its native diseases through the fundamental process of natural selection? These matters, my friend, touch the life of the race. They are greater things than to have made many inventions, or triumphed in many wars.'

"By this time, you'll have finished reading your charter-party. Lee Fu will receive it from your hand, and fold it carefully; and as he puts it away in its proper pigeon-hole, he'll say to himself, 'My friend, I hate you, as a member of your mean and lying race. I see you coming to China for gold, with words of hypocrisy in your mouths. You have forced the opium upon us at the point of the sword. In the name of your religion, you have seized our lands. We see at last that there is no truth in you, nor any good intention; but that your civilization rests wholly upon the power of wealth and arms. From now, China shall rise against you. The best she will take, and the worst she will throw aside. You are not worthy to survive. Wait a thousand years, and I will draw up a charter-party with you again.' "

Nichols waved a thin and expressive hand. "These Chinamen!" he said. "They have a latent power. Witness their game of poker. There's an enterprise that fits the Chinese character; it's philosophical, it requires a soul. They play it, stolid and inscrutable, with joy in their hearts. The contest goes on above the cards, an elusive passage of spirits, a clash of intangible energy, that in some way thrills and electrifies the beholder, though it's never betrayed by a glance or a movement or a word. I'm sure that Lee Fu Chang took a certain fierce pleasure in the game that night. In memory I feel it, too; but that's quite different. I'm free to admit that at the time the stakes were a trifle too heavy to attract my Occidental soul.

II

"I was bound from Hong Kong to Amoy; and Lee Fu Chang had taken passage with me, to attend to interests of his in the latter port. We had been friends for many years; I was then sailing on his charter. The old *Omega*, here, was a stauncher vessel in those days; although she lasts me very well. Jove, you should have seen her when they towed us into Hong Kong after the typhoon; a total wreck aloft, leaking, and badly stove about the decks. Worst of all, there was the terrible mess forward. We'd thrown the bodies overboard, but the blood remained. It took us a couple of months to get her into shape again, lying under the sheer-legs there, on Kowloon-side. For one thing, I had the decks around the forecastle carefully planed. It was a disastrous trip for me; but, on the whole, I considered myself very lucky. To men who sympathized with me I answered that I wasn't complaining. No. Every time that I passed through the forward cabin and remembered what I'd seen there, I thanked my particular stars for being alive. God knows what might have become of us; the imagination halts at the possibilities. Torture, captivity, nameless ends—it isn't pleasant to contemplate. I can see them yet, a cabin-full of yellow masks, concealing a cabin-full of hearts that would have stopped at nothing; all watching the game, watching for a turn of the cards, for a sign to strike. No, it was good luck, the best of luck; a few masts are immaterial. Such cards are always good luck, though the heavens fall; especially when they're the only cards that will win.

"We sailed from Hong Kong in August, near the break of the southwest monsoon. A bad time to be starting north; but I've never hesitated at beating up or down the sea, as some men do. As for typhoons, there had been news of one outside the previous week; and I hoped to slip up along the coast before another put in an appearance.

"For a number of days we had light weather and a fair wind, the tailing-off of the southerly monsoon. Lee Fu and I played cards. He likes, as he expresses it, to keep his hands occupied, and does his thinking while he plays; a different attitude toward cards than the European one of playing them to pass away the time. We began at poker; but with all his preoccupation, not in the least assumed, I couldn't make the game interesting for him. I was born with a Caucasian face. We all have them—twitching faces, full of nerves, and eyes that are too closely hooked to the brain. Lee Fu's face is smooth and calm like a face of frozen butter. His eyes seem not to move of themselves; now and then he'll turn his head slowly, and point them at you. It's disquieting, at a critical point in a losing game, to find a pair of eyes like that fixed upon you. I couldn't play his game of poker for a minute; so we took up cribbage. Now, I like cribbage; the cards play the game for you, mostly, and your soul doesn't get stirred up with trying to read another man's mind, and keeping your own mouth shut. So we cribbed it, morning, noon, and night. It was dull for Lee Fu.

"After a few days, the wind became variable; but the general weather seemed so quiet that I hung to the land, for the sake of the night breeze off-shore, watching all the while for typhoon signs out in the Channel. In five days, owing to contrary currents, we had made less than three hundred miles up the coast. There's a light on Lamock Island, which we passed on the evening of the fourth day, leaving it a dozen miles to port. Lee Fu was on deck with me that evening; and soon after we had passed the light he called my attention to a heavy bank of clouds low on the southeastern horizon. The words were hardly out of his mouth, when we noticed for the first time the lift of a new swell, coming in from the eastward; the vessel rose and dipped, and my heart suddenly felt as if it were rolling over to find a different position. That lift of the waters has but one meaning.

" 'A rather bad place to get caught in,' I remarked over my shoulder to Lee Fu.

"He glanced astern, then in toward the land. 'Very bad,' he said. 'I think that we will get the first wind down the coast, from north. The center of the typhoon is out there, toward Formosa.' He always speaks as if in close communication with the spirit and authority of storms.

" 'How do you know that, Lee Fu?' I asked.

" 'There are many ways, all equally hard to explain,' he answered. 'Say, by the feeling of the swell.'

"I laughed. 'Well, there's but one thing to do,' I said. 'Put her on the starboard tack, and get her out into Formosa Channel.' The wind was still to the southward then. I took a turn across the deck, and found Lee Fu's eyes fixed on me. 'What else is there to do?' I demanded.

"He considered a while before answering. 'You know Formosa Bank?' I nodded. 'In typhoons, the waves rage on those shallow waters, and no ship lives. You cannot go far in that direction. You will get the wind from the north, shifting to east; and on your lee lies the coast of China. Such a contingency would leave us a regrettably brief time yet to live.'

" 'What shall I do? The coast heads me off to the north; and south would be going directly into the face of that black cloud. I'll be hanged if I run toward a storm—couldn't, anyway, until the wind changes.'

" 'If you wish, Captain,' said Lee Fu, 'I will take you to a safe anchorage in Chauan Bay.'

"I looked at him in amazement. Take me to an anchorage on a practically uncharted coast, in the face of a typhoon! I'd seen him beat a full-rigged ship through Lymoon Pass, the narrow door to Hong Kong harbor, less than a quarter of a mile wide; I'd seen him carry a vessel out of the middle of the fleet under sternway, with royals set. I knew that he was a consummate master of any sailing craft, that he could have handled my ship perfectly; but I had no reason to suppose, at that time, that his judgment of general conditions on the high seas was better than my own. If I had let him take charge of the *Omega* then, we would have caught only the brush of the storm on the western edge, with a weather shore most of the time. Chauan Bay, I learned later, is deep and well-protected on the north. But I put her out into it, got cornered, as he said I would, and had to anchor on a lee shore in the end.

"We took the wind from about northeast; that told us that the center of the storm was south and east of us, blocking our only way to open water, and moving directly toward us at an uncertain rate. To leeward lay the China coast, in places not over a dozen miles away; if we weren't to make a harbor—and I didn't for a moment consider the possibility—there was nothing for it but to put her head off-shore on the port tack, stand out into the face of the storm, and trust to luck. It might be traveling slowly, in which case we could get across the northern front of it before the center came along; or it might deviate from the theoretical direction, as many typhoons do in the Formosa Channel, and miss us altogether. In any case, we had to have sea-room. For a number of hours the wind held within bounds; I was able to keep considerable sail on the ship up to midnight, when we were obliged to shorten down and heave her to. In that time, however, we must have made some thirty miles of offing.

"But I won't go into the details of that typhoon. It was a terrific blow. From midnight till noon of the next day, we lay hove-to on the port tack, without a change of wind; the center of the storm was coming toward us, but must have been moving very slowly. The sea, in those rather shallow waters, made up to a tremendous size; I began to be frightened for the ship. Half of the time she seemed buried, submerged; the immense waves stood above her and inundated her decks in constant succession, like the overflow from a great waterfall. Lee Fu kept the deck with me all day, wrapped in a long oilskin coat. Side by side we clung to the rail. Talk was out of the question; we hung on grimly, fought with the wind for our breath, and waited for the hours to go.

"We were coming through it very nicely, too, when, along in the latter part of the day, the wind began to veer into the east. It meant that the center was passing inshore to south of us; and, with plenty of sea-room I couldn't have asked for a more favor-able turn. But, after drifting for a good twelve hours, we had no idea within many miles of our position; and this shift of wind was driving us directly inshore. Of that we were certain; the whole coast of China lay there on our lee to catch us, perhaps fifty miles away, perhaps fifteen. The storm was moving so slowly that the wind might hold in this quarter for hours; a question of its blow-ing itself out, so that we could get sail on the ship, before it had blown us ashore. And night was coming on.

"Lee Fu edged up to me, and put his lips close to my ears. 'Anchors . . . ready . . . chains,' I heard. 'They weren't unshack-led,' I screamed. 'We can shove them off the forecastle.' I made a prying motion with my hand. He nodded, and turned away.

"There was nothing to do but wait. The wind came in fierce squalls, with undiminished violence. It held in the east. Night fell, a solid blackness, hideous with the incessant roar and crash of the seas. Moment by moment we were driving in toward the land.

"When a couple of hours must have passed I felt Lee Fu's hand on my arm. A lull came, and I heard him distinctly: 'Shoal water!' I had noticed the fearful jerking of the vessel, that could mean only a shortened sea. In the appalling darkness I leaned forward to listen; and suddenly a new note came to my ears, breaking across the thunder of the storm. It was a sharp, insistent note, pounding through the gale like the slat of a sail adrift; a faint sound, but perfectly distinguishable, as if a mouth were whisper-ing horrible words close to my ear. Breakers! We had used up our distance, and were on the lee shore.

"How we got the masts cut away I can't remember. I've a recollection of lifting an ax to strike at the mizzen rigging, and having it snatched away by the wind before I could bring it down. I sawed the lanyards off with my pocket knife. Lee Fu attended to the main. These two masts went clean at the deck; the foremast went at the masthead. The mate and second mate must have gone overboard at this time, among the wreckage; we never saw them again.

"Then we were on the forecastle-head, prying at the anchors with capstan-bars. After a long, long time—a time that seemed ages—we got them both over the side. My crew, all Chinamen, worked well. We had lost the sound of the breakers; I couldn't understand it. All at once, as we swung around, we were in the midst of them. In the morning, when we were able to look around and get our bearing, I saw how it had been. We rode not two ship's lengths from the rocks; though we had probably dragged in the latter part of the night. When she lifted her stern on the pitch of a swell, we looked across a mile or two of bleak and ragged country; and in the offing, directly ahead of us, lay a nest of black rocks, sticking up ten or twenty feet above the breakers. These snags had given us the warning; we'd been by before we had heard them—must have passed them within a hundred yards. So it had been none too soon that our anchors had bit the night before, at the end of every inch of chain that we had in the lockers.

"Did any of you fellows ever ride out a hurricane at anchor in an open seaway? We lay like a huge log of wood, wallowing low in the water; and every sea broke clean over us from bow to stern, exactly as a comber curls over a man bathing on the beach. How my crew saved themselves, how Lee Fu and I got aft, what happened to any of us, I have no idea. Some time later, as I was clinging to the rail by the quarterbitts, I found Lee Fu at my side. There was no use in taking such punishment; if the anchors held and the ship kept afloat, we would come through; if not, we couldn't reach the shore alive by any possible chance. I nodded my head in the direction of the companionway; and when the next lull came—what passed for a lull in that hell of wind and water—we managed to get the door open and scramble below.

"In the shelter of the cabin, after many hours on deck, the scene seemed strange. The motions of the ship were inhuman, like the writhings of a tortured man. We couldn't anticipate the next jump—would be flung suddenly forward, or our feet would be knocked from under us without warning. Standing braced in the doorway of his room, Lee Fu took off his oilskin coat and wiped his face. His embroidered garments were drenched and stained; I noticed that he had broken two of his long finger-nails. Not an expression disturbed the placidity of his face; an idea crossed my mind, that he was making preparations for bed. He could have done that, too, and slept comfortably; death was nothing but death—why be disturbed? But another matter of the body interested him more; while I struggled to get out of my own wet clothes, he made his way into the forward cabin, and soon returned with a loaf of bread and a jar of marmalade. There were a few tins of sardines and a case of beer, in a locker under the starboard couch; we braced our feet against the big chair screwed to the deck, and made a hearty meal. I hadn't stopped to think how hungry and thirsty I had been.

" 'It looks like a slim chance, Lee Fu,' I said, listening to the turmoil overhead and around us. 'I'm afraid that this is the finish of all things.'

" 'Such talk is nonsense,' he answered sharply. 'The matter is now beyond us, in the hands of the gods. It should concern us no longer.'

"I smiled. 'The anchors took hold, anyway. My anchors and chains are heavy, for a vessel of the *Omega's* size.'

"Lee Fu got up, handed himself over to the chart table, took a pack of cards and a cribbage board from the drawer, and brought them to the couch. 'Captain, let us play,' he said.

"My heart turned against it. 'How can I?' I demanded. 'Listen to that! . . . Not just now.'

" 'Nevertheless, force yourself,' he said. 'Play.'

"So we played.

III

"The wind screamed overhead all night; the ship wallowed and plunged, groaning at every seam; the seas thundered upon her and roared along her decks. We sat on the starboard couch, playing cribbage; strange as it may seem, the game helped me through the night. Or perhaps it was the quiet influence of a man whose soul was sure. At dawn the typhoon broke; and we were still afloat. We lay, as I've told you, with our stern brushing the rocks; the spot couldn't have been more exposed. We had fetched up against a long point that ran southerly, like a breakwater, in front of a deep bay. Off to the southeast was the reef of rocks that we had passed as we drifted in; a row of jagged teeth, gnashing themselves at our escape. The point was barren and deserted; we saw no human being on the land. Something about the situation seemed uncanny; the sea rolled in heavily from the open Channel, bursting with a continual roar on the iron ledges astern; and there we rode, in ten fathoms of water with muddy bottom, almost touching the land, and yet cut off from it—a land of which we knew nothing and could learn nothing, but which had the appearance, as we examined it, of a mysterious new continent, as yet undiscovered and uninhabited by man. A weird coast, gray and gloomy without a tree or a sign of green: had we been blown off the good old earth altogether, to some demoniac shore? My nerves were on edge; more than once that day, as I glanced astern, I felt that unseen eyes might be watching me, that evil things might be going on in the deep and dark caverns of that broken land.

"And still there was nothing for us to do. The ship didn't leak badly; a few hours' pumping through the day kept her free. As for a jury rig, the best that I could hope to do would be to get up something at the fore, enough to run her back to Hong Kong before the northeast monsoon, when it set in. I figured, from the time we'd been hove-to, that we must have landed somewhere along the coast between Swa-tau and Hong Hai Bay; I knew that we couldn't very well be to the westward of Hong Kong. But my mate and second mate were missing, I myself was completely fagged, and my Chinese crew, good enough at handling the vessel, would have been heavy at a rigging job; the sea continued high, and there would have been little prospect of accomplishing much anyway; so I decided to rest fore and aft through that day, and be ready for real work the next morning. I longed for more room under our stern, but couldn't have moved the ship in such a sea; hesitated to heave her ahead on the chains, for fear of starting something; and meanwhile comforted myself with the knowledge that she had held in this position through the worst of the typhoon.

"Night came on, dark as a pocket; I set an anchor-watch, though nothing afloat would be liable to bother us, and went below for a much-needed nap. I slept soundly till midnight; when I got up, Lee Fu sat reading in the after cabin.

" 'Haven't you been asleep, Lee Fu?' I asked in surprise. 'Why don't you put up your book and turn in?'

" 'I am wakeful, Captain,' he said. 'I have just come down from the deck. The wind has gone and the sea is dropping fast. She rides beautifully.'

" 'What's worrying you?' I asked, as I went by him. The question was fortuitous; I made it without thought, expected no answer, got none, and went on my way. I spent five or ten minutes on deck, but couldn't see my hand before me. Off over the water, a few stars had begun to appear through rifts in the heavy clouds. I interviewed my anchor-watch, saw that everything was all right, came aft, listened a moment at the head of the companion, sniffed the land-smell in the air, and went below.

" 'It's devilish dark,' I said to Lee Fu as I came in. 'I prophesy that we have no wind for a day or two.'

" 'Yes, very dark,' he said. 'Too dark, in many ways. Captain, shall we play a game of cards?'

"I'd been about to propose the same—wanted to keep awake the rest of the night. We decided to play on the forward cabin table, where a bracket-lamp against the mast gave the best light. Minute by minute as we sat there the sea went down. I felt the ship grow quiet; it seemed very still, too, in the cabins, after the creaking and groaning that had filled our ears so long. My nerves relaxed in the deep silence; life became real, possible, on an even keel again. We had come home to ships and the world, and could settle down once more, forgetful of the inexorable destiny. I leaned back on the settee, and lost game after game of cribbage with the best of grace.

"At length Lee Fu looked over at me with a smile. 'We must change the game,' he said. 'Let us try poker. Your luck may be in that to-night.'

"I brushed the cribbage board aside. 'Deal,' I answered.

"He held up a warning hand. 'Listen . . . what was that?'

"Something had struck the ship forward, a dull thudding sound. We felt a slight shock pass along the deck under our feet. My first rapid thought was that she had gone adrift, and touched the bottom; then I knew that it couldn't be. The touch of a ship on bottom is distinctive, unmistakable; it travels up your spine, jars your teeth, speaks of the solid earth, that seems to stiffen and rise against the least impact of a floating vessel. This was a hollow sound, a bump, a shock of wood on wood. Something alongside . . . a boat, a vessel . . . a junk. I leaped to my feet. At the same instant from forward came a wild and longdrawn yell.

"Lee Fu blocked my way to the door. 'Do not go out!' he said sharply. 'This is what I feared.'

" 'What?' I cried. Feet were pattering overhead along the house. A frantic howling had risen forward—sharp screams of pain and terror—awful sounds.

" 'Sit down,' said Lee Fu calmly. 'It is useless now. Sit down!'
He forced me back onto the settee.

" 'In the name of God, what is it?' I cried.

" 'Men from shore—wreckers, thieves, pirates,' he replied. 'I
knew that they would come.'

" 'Pirates!' I exclaimed. 'Here—now—in this day?' I hadn't
been many years then in the China Sea.

" 'In lonely places, Captain,' said Lee Fu, 'this day is not
different from any other day.'

" 'Why didn't you warn me?'

" 'What would have been the use? I hoped that we were not
seen; but it makes no matter. We are helpless, at their mercy.
They can come in thousands. Hundreds of them are now on
board your ship.'

"I gripped his arm. 'What are they doing forward?' I asked.

" 'Killing the men,' said Lee Fu. 'They are already beyond
our aid.'

"I caught my breath and stood up, listening. In the acute
silence I heard loud whispers, muttering voices, and the swish of
bare feet in the alleyway. Suddenly the unearthly yelling broke
out again, nearer now, in the waist of the ship. I started for the
door, and paused, absolutely undone.

" 'Lee Fu, I must go out,' I said.

"He had seated himself again at the table, and was dealing out
two hands of cards. Tapping with his long nails on the polished
wood, he glanced up at me. 'Do you wish to die?' he asked. 'You
would never carry your head through the companion door. Sit
down.'

" 'Die?' I cried wildly. 'For God's sake, what's the use of staying
here? The cabin isn't locked; there isn't a key in a door!'

" 'I know,' he answered in an even voice. 'Sit down, and
we will play a game—the game of life and death. Be quiet, and
sit down!'

"I dropped into my seat without volition. It's impossible to
impart to you the singular horror of those few moments. I felt, I
remember, as if I had been drugged into a state of semi-conscious-
ness; a succession of events had in some way become enormously
distorted, hideously changed, like things seen at the height of a
fever. I sat inert and numb, hearing clearly the gathering of
stealthy forces on deck—scufflings, noises of many feet, sharp

words, startling and unintelligible cries. Then I picked up the five cards that Lee Fu had dealt me, and gazed at them like a man in a dream.

"Some time must have passed while we sat listening—while we sat absolutely motionless, facing each other and holding our cards. Faint sounds broke out now in the after cabin; we heard lowered voices behind the two closed doors. My eyes wandered—rested at last on Lee Fu's face. He was looking at his cards. He carefully picked out three of them and threw them on the table.

" 'How many will you have?' he asked, his voice at its ordinary pitch, clear and undisturbed. Suddenly he leaned across the table, and his eyes opened wide, showing the depths that are seldom revealed. 'Play, for the sake of your God!' he whispered fiercely. 'Much depends upon you. Play!'

"I selected a card at random and threw it down. As I drew out a second card, I became aware instinctively that we were not alone. I felt the power of eyes . . . then heard the creaking of the hinges as the doors that led into the after cabin opened quietly. Heard, too, a mutter from across the table—'Do not turn.' No fear of that—I didn't dare; but in a flash of understanding, his idea had come to me. I took a physical grip, as it were, of every nerve in my body, and threw down the second card.

" 'I will take two cards,' I said, in the best voice that I could muster.

"I believe that nothing in heaven or earth could have stopped them from rushing at us, but the very unexpectedness of what they found. They had been gathering, assembling, preparing themselves for an attack—one can well imagine. One can see them crouching aft, fearing to open the companion door—stealing at length down the companionway, astonished at the quiet, peering into my room, into the two cabin staterooms, exchanging swift glances, whispering their amazement—pausing suddenly, as they heard voices in the forward cabin—listening —finally opening the door. The picture framed there must have excited their surprise—two men, one a Chinaman, one a European, playing earnestly at cards, while all around them death stalked and blood was flowing. It was a dramatic masterpiece. But I saw, as I sat there with a thousand thoughts surging through my brain, that Lee Fu was bidding for a still higher trump, striking a deeper note than would appear. He was making an appeal to a national characteristic. These Chinamen!—their lives are games of cards. There in the forward cabin, the first hand of a tremendous struggle was played. I looked again at Lee Fu, saw him turn his head slowly; followed his glance, and beheld the after cabin doors filled with staring faces and half-naked forms, arrested, as it were, on the threshold of a great and absorbing mystery. Lee Fu regarded them coldly; then raised his hand in a gesture commanding silence, and turned his impenetrable visage back to the game.

"We played slowly, intensely; my head seemed tight, and it took me a long while to operate my cards. As we played, Chinamen by the dozen filed silently into the room, sliding behind the settees, crowding against the walls, watching us catlike with their flat, beady eyes. One glance at them had been enough. But their presence enthralled me; it took all the power of my will to hold my attention to the game. While I riveted my eyes on the cards I saw constantly a picture of the men standing opposite me. I wanted to look at them, I itched to look at them; but something told me that I mustn't. I saw them, just the same—can never forget them. They stood closely pressed together, line behind line of evil faces, breathing down upon us, a cruel and bloodthirsty guard; while we played for the minutes as they passed, like men working desperately in a nightmare over some extravagant and useless business.

"Lee Fu won steadily. I happened to have a large sum of money about me, that I'd carried to use on the ship and had no safe place to tuck away in; and this I doled out dollar by dollar. The pile on the opposite side of the table soon grew to considerable proportions. Now and then the trace of a smile crossed Lee Fu's face. They saw it; by the tone of the whispered comment that went on behind my back, I knew that they despised my weakness at the game. Cold sweat stood on my forehead; and that helped too, because I seemed to be taking my loss hard. As a matter of fact, I was grinding my teeth to keep from shouting aloud. I thought, without exaggeration, that I'd go mad. There was something sickening about the awful business; it seemed so utterly hopeless to me. The stink of those Chinamen was abominable, too.

"At length I put up my last dollar, and Lee Fu won. I leaned back, and looked across the table littered with cards; waited there, like a man with his head on the block. The belly of a

Chinaman pressed against my shoulders; I braced my feet under the table, and held back with all my strength. This was the end of the rope—and I was anxious enough to have it over with.

"Then Lee Fu, without a tremor, took up the second hand of the bigger game. Pointing with a clawlike forefinger to a man standing near the head of the table, he motioned him toward my seat.

" 'Sit down and play,' he said, in the Canton dialect that he had taught me.

"Nothing could have been more daring, more opportune. They had been watching us, whetting their appetites; seeing the white man lose, too, and the Chinaman win. Their gambling spirit had been thoroughly aroused. And now, at the height of the interest, the game was suddenly cut off; and as suddenly, an opportunity was offered for its renewal. An opportunity, moreover, with the interest enormously multiplied, with the possibilities of excitement increased beyond bounds. I stood up; and without a word the other man, as if drawn by a magnet, took my place opposite Lee Fu.

"I noticed him for the first time then. He was undoubtedly the leader of the crew. His face was intelligent, his whole appearance far above that of the other men, who were of the lowest coolie caste. He was dressed like a clerk: white trousers, a short black coat, and a close-fitting black cap. Lee Fu's eyes, it seems, had been busy while he played.

"I moved toward the head of the table, surrounded by wet, slimy bodies; and the two Chinamen began to play. The rows of faces on either side of the cabin crowded closer, emitting grunts and exclamations of approval. Standing there at the heart of this extraordinary scene, I seemed to drift off into a region of total unsubstantiality. For a long while my thoughts were wandering and inattentive; I tried to retrace the last few hours, to piece the crazy circumstances together; and as I worked my way up to the present situation, I gradually became aware that I was witnessing a rare and powerful exhibition—a battle in the air. Men have paid heavily to see the wonders of art, to hear music played, to be touched to the core by a perfection of illusion. Well, here was the reality . . . and free, too, or maybe bought at the final and complete price which opens still more mysterious doors. And I was touched, believe me! I was thrilled in every nerve, by waves, by surges of emotion; I was dazzled, staggered, appalled, at the fearfulness of the stroke, and at its diabolical cleverness. For I saw at last the full value of the stake for which my friend Lee Fu Chang played.

"They sat with the cards between them, absolutely quiescent save for the movements of their hands. Their faces were inscrutable. As I watched them, I felt like a man trying to read deep and pregnant words on a blank page. With all their immobility, they didn't give an impression of indifference. Far from it. Behind those placid countenances revealing no trace of thought, the imagination was stirred to discern a veritable ocean of sensations and ideas: in one, watchfulness that mustn't show in the eyes, anxiety that mustn't influence a decision, hope and impatience that mustn't outreach themselves, despair that mustn't creep into the voice; plans and plans, being advanced, analyzed, weighed, approved or thrown aside; the consummate game itself being carried on without hesitation or mistake; and all concealed behind the veil: in the other, surprise, distrust, excitement, keen curiosity, and supreme carelessness, for of course there was no danger to himself in any possible outcome. . . . Think of it, you fellows! These two men, both of the incomprehensible race whose real life goes on beyond our horizon—these two playing a game for pleasure, as it seemed, playing to pass the time; and yet throwing into the scene by the very incongruity of their nerveless attitudes, the glamour of a hidden and deathly struggle, a combat of the secret, elemental forces of the mind. It was stunning, marvelous . . . and terrible. Not a covert glance, not a twitch of a muscle, not a quickened breath. They were the sum and expression of complete impersonality. And, to add the crowning touch, I saw that each perfectly understood the other—understood that the mask before him screened all that moves in the human heart and soul."

Nichols paused in his tale; someone touched my elbow, and I found a Chinaman bending above me. I started from my chair. It was the steward offering drinks on a tray.

"Nichols, you've woven a spell," I said.

He sipped his liquor in silence, then gave a smile. "The European nerves," he said. "Imagination . . . without control. Don't deny the Chinaman the imagination, or the nerves, either; but acknowledge how overwrought you are. You are the slave, instead of the master. You should take a lesson from my friend Lee Fu Chang.

"While the game went on, more and more men kept filing into the forward cabin. I was shoved against the edge of the table; I could feel them pressing behind me, coming down the forward companionway. There must have been fifty cutthroats about us; the after cabin was full, too, and you could hear them passing word of the game back to the rear. Their faces were savage, brutish, ferocious; they grunted and snarled, baring white teeth; they leered at me malevolently, thrusting their yellow visages forward to catch my attention. I returned their scrutiny with a blank gaze glanced to my left, and saw extended a smooth yellow arm, dripping with blood; shuddered and turned my eyes back to the game.

"The leader of the crew had pulled from some inside pocket a bag of coin, a considerable sum of money. He was no stranger to the game. My head had cleared now, with the removal of the dreadful necessity for action; I was able to follow and grasp the details of what was going on. Considered apart, the delicacy of the game was amazing; you who have never seen Chinamen play poker can hardly appreciate it. It seemed to make no difference what they held—they didn't depend on the cards. Bluff was the game. Time and again they bet on hands that any one of us would have thrown down; and both having the same style of attack, as you might say, the same daring, the same abandon, it was surprising how often they matched with nothing, and clashed over empty hands.

"Knowing what was in his mind, I saw after a little while that the honors went to Lee Fu Chang. At the opening of the game he had won a few hands; and immediately afterward had lost heavily, to an accompaniment of guttural cries from the infernal crew. Then he had begun to win again, slowly—so slowly that with each gain he held the gambling spirit of his countrymen, with each loss he drew them farther on. Like a man manipulating the fine wires of some instrument, he played surely, cunningly this masterful double game. His adversary, it soon developed, was a poker-player to be reckoned with. How to clean him out, and yet keep the flame alive among his men; more than this, how to lash them, madden them, intoxicate them, so that at the last the flame would burn brightest:—here was a problem for all acuteness and power. The strain upon me, though I had nothing but a passive part, was terrific.

"But after suspense that seemed to be stretched out through long hours, standing there and watching Lee Fu's winnings ebb and flow, the tide coming in each time with an amount slightly increased, I felt approaching the culmination that he desired. It was in the air—he had them! I knew it from sudden movements of the crowd, from the rapid shuffling of feet, from the swaying of shoulders and the jerking of heads, from smothered but violent words. Slight things, but evidences of an excitement, barely controlled. It was in the air. They had forgotten life, gain, and the business of the night; they were mad with the game.

"Lee Fu picked up his hand, and glanced across at his opponent's resources. They were growing very small.

" 'I want no cards,' he said. 'I will bet five dollars.'

"The other drew two cards, examined them, and slipped his hand together into a neat pack.

" 'Five dollars more,' he said.

"The betting continued; we leaned forward above the table. Ten, twenty, fifty dollars—at length Lee Fu's opponent threw down his last dollar, and called. He spread out his cards before him one by one, a flush in hearts.

" 'I have a full house,' said Lee Fu, showing his cards, and raking the pile toward his side of the table.

"The other man got up. Lee Fu sat motionless, silently regarding him. He seemed lost in thought; his hands played with the heap of silver and gold on the table. I held my breath. A moment passed, a finespun interval. Suddenly Lee Fu spoke in a voice of fire.

" 'Sit down!' he said. 'I will give you a stake worth playing for. I will bet all that is here, many dollars, all that I have; together with two lives and a fine ship of European build. If you win, they are yours, to do with as you will. But if I win you and your men are to leave us as you found us, and go. Now we will play . . . one hand. Sit down!'

"The Chinaman seemed to break and falter—turned to his men, speaking in a rapid patter of dialect. I caught a few words. An argument was going on; they didn't fully understand the offer and the terms. But when he had spoken for a time, I saw their eagerness shining in their eyes. An explosion of cries burst out;

wiry arms shot forth, pointing toward the table and the game. The man sat down. His face for a moment lost its immobility; he stretched out his hands like a man inspired.

" 'Play!' he cried.

"Swifter than thought, Lee Fu had dealt the cards. He picked up his hand, held it before him an instant, selected deliberately one card, and threw it away; the other four he made into a pack, and placed face downward on the table. I thought rapidly. He might be holding two pair; he might be hoping to complete a flush, with a number of chances; or he might be bidding for a straight, in which case his hand would be worthless if one particular card didn't come his way. I tried to read his face. Anything to end the awful suspense—hope or despair, it didn't much matter. But only the blank page confronted me.

"The other had thrown away two cards. My instant thought was that he held three of a kind. They would beat Lee Fu's two pair—would beat anything that Lee Fu held now, for who could hope to complete a scattered hand at such a pass? We were beaten already. And yet . . .

"Without a word, Lee Fu dealt his adversary two cards; then took the next card on the pack, his card, and calmly looked at it. A glance was enough—he placed it face downward on the top of the other four. A pause fell, and the eyes of the two men met across the table.

"Until that instant I hadn't realized the added grimness of this hand. There was to be no betting, no issue of personalities, no escape from the decree—nothing but luck, the cold and unchangeable cards. We lost or we won. Life hung by a hair. . . . I watched it straining. And yet some of the madness of the game must have taken hold even of me; for I remember that, as I waited for their eyes to finish the battle, my nerves quieted and my heart grew still. Beyond the bounds of terror lies a realm of delirious and ghastly joy.

"The outlaw laid down his cards. He held a straight flush in spades, headed by the queen.

"Wonderful luck!—he had completed this hand with two cards out; he had not held three of a kind. Irresistible luck—fatal luck. I gasped, and my eyes wandered to Lee Fu. Perhaps I felt that in the stress of our predicament, the emotions that gripped me might at last find an answer there. His face was placid, smooth, serene, like the face of a Buddha carved out of soft stone. Meditatively, he picked up the little pack of his hand and turned the upper card, the card that he had drawn. It was the ace of hearts. He turned the others slowly, placing the cards in a methodical row, his eyes on each card as it fell, as if confirming the miracle for his own satisfaction—king, queen, knave, and ten-spot, all of hearts. He had completed a royal flush, the highest combination that the cards afford.

IV

"I leaned against the table, faint and exhausted. The two men stood up, facing each other. Lee Fu waved a hand, a slight gesture toward the cards. The tiers of faces pressed forward, gazing wildly, incredulously. A murmur ran through the room, increasing to a spluttering outburst of jargon. The leader cried out sharply: the uproar ceased. For some seconds a tense silence held, while they looked their fill.

"Then Lee Fu's opponent raised his hand, and uttered a command. The yellow forms began to stream past me, making for the forward companionway; I felt them brush my elbows, I smelled their breath as they muttered imprecations in my face; some of them spat at me. They melted from the room like ghosts, furtive and noiseless; before I had taken my eyes from the cards that had spelled out deliverance we were alone with the leader of the crew.

"He rested his hands on the table, devouring the cards with his gaze. He was loath to leave. A shout came down the companion. He started, dragged himself to the door, and turned. There, as if overcome by the inadequacy of all speech and expression, he made a hopeless movement with his shoulders, and suddenly was gone. We stood like wooden images, hearing his thick-soled shoes clatter up the stairs.

"They were gone. I sank to the settee, bolt upright, and waited in an appalling silence—waited and listened, fearing that what had come to pass was only another trick of fate, expecting minute by minute that they would be back, armed with death . . . that they were already turning, gathering outside the door. Lee Fu stood above his marvelous cards, without motion or sound. Ten minutes must have gone by. But after those departing steps on the stairs we heard no more. They had vanished whence they came. They had slunk off like men in fear, like men rebuked by fate; they had withdrawn quietly, hoping to be unobserved of the gods, ere they had overstepped too far the forbidden line. They had incurred dire penalties; they had opposed one obviously under divine protection. Me, the white devil, they had hated; they had spat upon me. But they had left me alive, and gone. I bowed my head on the table, and let my nerves have their run.

"When I looked up, Lee Fu was fingering the pile of coin that was the least of his winnings. He spread both hands flat upon it, and pressed down, thinking his own thoughts. With a rush, the realization, the awakening, came to me. He had won all—*all!* The ship, our lives . . . and this, too, the last straw. Reckoned by the coin of the earth, he had made a good night of it. He had won perhaps a thousand dollars; he had cleaned them out. These men had stood beside us, filling the cabin, ready to strike us down; they had left with us, as it were, a few slight tokens—their ready money and their odor; and they were *gone.* They had returned to the barren, unnatural country of their habitation; a shore of death, defended by outlying reefs—a land where no man was seen to move by day. Before God, if it hadn't been for what we found, I could have discredited my best senses, could have doubted their reality altogether.

"After an hour of waiting we went on deck, and picked our way cautiously forward among the wreckage. The ship seemed deserted. I lit a lantern in the galley; the first ray of light along the deck disclosed the reason of the deep silence. We were alone on the vessel, Lee Fu and I. My Chinamen had been killed to the last man. They lay in hideous postures, as if thrown down violently from a great height. A pile of bodies choked each forecastle door. The knife had done it all.

"I staggered aft, and walked blindly down the port alleyway, trying to get as far off as I could. The lantern had gone out; I remember that I flung it overboard. A puff of cool land-breeze, thick with the odor of flowers, came across the water. Life seemed very sweet. Land was near—I smelled it. The world waited for me; it was still the same. When we touch death with our finger-tips, and feel how cold it is, we discover that we're all selfish beasts at heart. I drank in deep draughts of living air, and gloried in the postponement of my dissolution, in the opportunity to follow for a while longer the trivial round of my habits and affairs.

" 'Lee Fu, I have to thank you for my life,' I said. He had ranged up beside me at the rail.

" 'No, no, Captain," he remonstrated. 'You do not understand. The gods have favored us.'

" 'No one but you,' I said, 'could have played and won that game.'

" 'My friend,' answered Lee Fu, 'the Gods were trying me. I felt it, and had faith. Your European way is very bad. You would have taken upon yourself the work of the gods, and solved your own destiny. You would have flourished your revolver, and shot a few; and finally many would have killed you in horrible ways, as you have seen. An uninteresting method, you admit. It seemed better to play; and we were amply repaid by the game. As for the matter of winning or losing, that concerned us not at all. I left it entirely with the gods. They sent the cards.' "

THE LEAK

Clangity-clang! Clangity-clang! Clangity-clang! The incessant sound of the pumps drummed through the gale; forward, aft, below in the cabin, it penetrated like the stroke of doom. Captain Blair hung to the weather rail, listening to the metallic beat; it had been in his ears for days, sleeping or waking, so that now he heard nothing else. Clangity-clang! Clangity-clang! Clangity-clang! How long would she last at this rate? Another week? Another day?

Overhead the wind howled in the rigging; the old bark staggered with a stiff, unwieldy motion, wallowing like a log in the wicked cross-sea of the Gulf Stream. He felt her distress under his feet. She was fighting a good fight; but she was old. The spirit of battle had gone from her, the youth, the energy, the power. This terrible cargo—nitrate from Pisagua, heavy as lead! It bore down massively within her; from her bottom and 'tween decks the bags of nitrate rose in two huge elongated pyramids, running the length of the ship, free of the sides, so that a man could walk around them. By this time the bags had consolidated; they would have to be dug apart with pickaxes; they formed two enormous rigid and rock-like lumps in the bowels of the vessel, threatening to tear her bodily open as she wrenched from crest to trough of the sea. Nitrate puts a frightful strain upon any ship. She was old.

Captain Blair had rounded the Horn with her; he was bringing her "on the coast" in the winter time. All the passage he had dreaded this last and worst encounter with the elements, but he had hardly anticipated so much ill-luck. He had hoped against hope, even, that he might slip in from Hatteras between storms. Lucky men sometimes did. There were more reasons than one, this time, behind his prayer for a favorable slant. He *had* to get in quickly; his wife lay sick in bed down below.

Clangity-clang! Clangity-clang! Clangity-clang! He left the rail, pacing the deck fiercely, buffeted by rain and spray as he faced forward, blown aft at a jog-trot as he turned his back to the wind. The gale had grown colder; it showed signs of snow. As he struggled to and fro an endless stream of thoughts passed like fire through his head.

A week now of unremitting northeast gale; a week of constant trouble, of deepening anxiety. Day after day he had paced his little corner of the quarter-deck, cold, wet, with raw face and chafed wrists, until he had forgotten that he owned such a thing as a body. He had scarcely slept for forty-eight hours. All this didn't matter, was nothing, if they could only have got somewhere. But the bark had been hove-to on the port tack, drifting back across the Gulf Stream, steadily away from port. It was the only course. To wear her around and head inshore would have been madness, would have accomplished no end. Hatteras, a treacherous low cape with outlying sand banks, lay in wait for those who defied the lee shore in a northeaster; that terrible lee shore stretching south from New York for hundreds of miles, a straight line of merciless sand, the grave-yard of ships and men.

On the second day of this last gale the bark had sprung a leak without warning. Her strength, holding out till the final test, had suddenly given way. Since then they had stood at the pumps night and day. They had pumped with the whole watch, six men, three on a side; they had done nothing but pump. They had barely been able to keep her free.

Clangity-clang! Clangity-clang! Clangity-clang! Captain Blair could never accustom himself to the sound; he listened to it acutely, as if it had just begun; it vibrated behind every thought, ceaseless, urgent, diabolical. It didn't belong to a ship, that sound; it was driving him mad. Why were they so hard on him? Why? Why? He stopped short, shaking his clenched hands in the face of the gale. Why wouldn't they let up a little? What had he done? He *must* get in—couldn't they see? His wife was dying!

The mate came aft, drew up beside him, shouted in his ear. "Gaining a little, sir!"

Captain Blair nodded. Words choked him; he drove his nails into the palms of his hands. "Keep on pumping!"

A squall burst upon them, bowing their heads, driving them to the rail for a hold. The mate's answer was snatched away, like water blown from the mouth of a pipe. "Men . . . pump . . . much longer!"

"For God's sake, shut up and go forward!"

The mate gazed at Captain Blair in perplexity for a moment, then turned and battled down the alleyway. A terrific sea shook the old bark from stem to stern; the crest of it leaped aboard between the main and mizzen rigging, and swirled aft in a river of foam. The captain received it grimly, standing with feet braced apart, letting the water spurt to the tops of his rubber boots. He wondered if any men had been washed away from the pumps. When the lull came he listened. Clangity-clang! Clangity-clang! Clangity-clang!

What was she thinking about, down below—the wife who had gone with him bravely on so many voyages, who had made life all that it was to him by her love and sacrifice? That heavy sea must have startled her. Perhaps she had heard them shouting when the mate had come aft. Sounds had a way of carrying to the cabin. He must go down and reassure her.

He threw back the sliding door of the companion, stepped inside, and shut the cover carefully as he descended. Darkness was coming on; the steward had lighted the lamp in the after cabin. Captain Blair glanced at the chart pegged out on the table, and swore below his breath. For three days he had not seen the sun. What was the use of a chart, if they were never to know their position, if they were never to get anywhere?

A weak voice spoke from the room abaft the cabin. "Is that you, Bert? What is it? Oh, what is it?"

He went in without taking off his oilskin coat. The room looked cheerless; the air was close, damp, chilly, full of the depression of sickness and the odors that came up from the hold of the leaking vessel. In the shadow of the bunk lay his wife, chocked off with pillows, so that the ship's rolling and pitching would disturb her as little as possible. She turned her face as he entered, and attempted a smile.

"Has anything happened?" she asked again, fearfully.

"No," he answered. "Nothing." He took the hand that she stretched out over the edge of the bunk. "I just came down to see how you were."

"How cold your hands are! Give me the other."

"They only seem cold to you."

"I was frightened. I heard someone shout—and then that awful sea!"

"Down here it sounds worse than it is. That wasn't bad."

"I always think of you—of what might happen."

"Nonsense! You ought to know me well enough—nothing can happen to *me.*"

"You don't stop to think. You're so impulsive."

He laughed—he had heard it often. "As if there wasn't enough to worry about!" he said. "But I think the gale is nearly over."

"Oh, I hope so! Is she still leaking?"

"Not so badly now."

"Then everything is better?"

"Yes—everything. How are you feeling to-night, girlie?"

She pressed his cold hands. "Better, I think. It pains a little—when she pitches. Isn't it very rough?"

He choked, and suddenly bowed his head on the edge of the bunk.

"My poor boy!" She stroked his cheek, half-crying. "It's been so hard on you! You mustn't worry about me, dear. I'll be all right. You have the ship on your shoulders."

He sank beside the bunk, trying to hide the tears. The ship on his shoulders? More than that! More than that! She was helping, doing what she could. She knew.

Another sea breached the vessel, and his wife clung to him in terror until it had passed over. She had never been able to overcome her fear of these waves that made the ship tremble as if she had struck a rock; with an experience covering many years and countless gales, they always sent her heart into her mouth. She had not been cut out for the sea.

Captain Blair could feel what was going on above his head; his sailor-instinct told him that the old bark was hard pressed. He listened; and in the brief lull that came after the shock of the sea, the pumps drummed on like a heart palpitating somewhere deep in the vitals of the ship. Clangity-clang! Clangity-clang! Clangity-clang!

II

Should he put back to Bermuda? The question pursued him about the decks; it faced him in the darkness at every turn. He had left his wife sleeping; she might sleep for a few minutes, for half an hour—it never lasted long. Should he keep up the fight? Should he give in? What should he do?

He knew what it meant to put back to Bermuda. They would rob him of the bark; they lived on disabled vessels there, like vultures in the wake of an army. The cargo would be unloaded, probably reshipped; the bark would have to be repaired. All this would cost more than she was worth. He owned a quarter of her himself; it represented twenty hard years of following the sea. How could he afford to lose it? He was young no longer; where would he begin anew? And then, there was his duty to the owners; his duty as a master mariner to get the ship, his trust, to her destination.

These things would weigh nothing if his wife died. *Died!* The thought lashed him like a whip. Hidden by the night, his voice drowned by the roar of the storm, he cried out in torment and beat the rail with his fists. What to do? Were there capable doctors at Bermuda? Would it avail anything, in the end, if he put back? Might it not be a disastrous mistake? He knew vaguely that some serious operation would be necessary to save his wife.

The week passed before him, day after day of drifting, while he had hoped for a change—all wasted time now, gone forever. He was a sailor, a man of duty; his training had been to put duty first and sentiment last. He began to think that this was all wrong. Experience, convention, the very creed of an onerous and sometimes bitter life, were going by the board. What could it possibly matter—success, reputation, savings, life itself? His wife might die!

Yet he had kept on; he wanted still to keep on. It *must* be right—he felt it strongly. It was a test, they were trying him again; it was the same old fight of truth, the fight that he had always been in, coming now in a new guise—but harder this time, with a keener stroke, with a deeper thrust. His wife! They had touched him vitally. They were unfair.

"No!" he cried aloud, out of a desperate heart. "I mustn't put back—not yet. I'll fight—like the old bark—a while longer, as long as I can!"

A little later he went below and found his wife still asleep. For a while he stood beside the bunk, watching her pallid face— thinking. Was he being fair to her? Yes!—the highest fairness— right. He loved her. If he could be sure of help for her at Bermuda there would be no question. But they might be longer, now, in getting to Bermuda, than if they kept on to New York. And she understood.

Once more he took up the watch on deck; he felt that sleep would never touch him again. Clinging to the weather rail he peered to windward as if trying to discern the secrets of the storm. The wind screamed in his ears; a huge wave lifted its white shoulder above him, showing a weird light against the solid blackness of sky and sea. The miles upon miles of waste and angry waters surrounding him, became a vivid entity to his distracted mind. Off there, the land, a long line, not very high, just rising above the sea—a continent, teeming with life, solid ground for the feet of men. Then water, nothing but water, rising and falling, lashed to fury and destruction, black with the shadow of overhanging clouds. Here a ship, a tiny object, lost in the night, struggling alone against the power of the sea. Off there to leeward a small island—a long way off, and very small. Wind, and rain, and despair. God in Heaven! What to do? What to do?

III

In the early morning the storm broke unexpectedly. The wind jumped into the northwest, the vessel headed up, and within an hour the sea had begun to fall. As it grew calmer the seams of the old bark tightened, and they were able to ease up a little on the pumps. They made sail at once; voices rang out, a cheerful activity awoke on the storm-swept deck. The sun broke through the clouds soon after dawn; at eight o'clock Captain Blair got a clear altitude for the first time in seven days.

He ran below often during the forenoon to speak with his wife. The change of weather was like a breath of new life to her. She lay propped up in the bunk, feasting her eyes on the sunlight that streamed through the open window. With something to look forward to, something to take up her mind, the pain was easier to bear; she allowed herself to hope again. If only the ship would stay quiet! It seemed to her that she could not have lived through another day of the storm.

At noon she heard her husband come below to work his sight. Ordinarily she had helped him at this duty, looking up logarithms, bending with him above the table while he pricked off the latitude and longitude. Then they would hold a discussion over the day's run; or, perhaps, she would measure with the dividers the remaining distance to port, and speculate as to how much longer they would be.

"Bring in the chart, and show me where we are," she called from the bunk.

He held it upright for her, and pointed out the little circle that marked their position. "Not as bad as I feared," he said. "The Gulf Stream has set us north. I thought we must be in it."

"Then we'll have to beat up, if this wind holds?"

He nodded, proud of her knowledge. It had always been a secret trouble to him that, with all their sailing together, she had not entered more fully into the spirit of the sea-life, or learned to enjoy the side of it that meant such a deep satisfaction to him.

"It *must* hold!" she cried suddenly. "Of course it will hold. A clearing-off wind, after this storm! It ought to blow for weeks."

"Yes, dear," he said. "We're going to get in now." She could not see the old expression in his eyes, the look of a hunted animal.

He bent down to kiss her. She was trying to speak again.

"What is it, dear?"

"Hurry! Oh, hurry!"

A broken cry escaped him. "I'll take the masts out of her! I'll get in some way! My poor girl—"

"I know you will," she said. "And you'll be careful, too."

As the sun went down that afternoon, Captain Blair stopped his pacing and stood by the weather rail for some time, scanning the heavens. The west glowed with a pale yellow light, the sea had grown quite smooth, the bark heeled sharply to a stiff breeze. He gazed at the placid yellow sunset in bitterness of heart. It seemed so perfect, so beautiful; and yet, according to every sign that he knew, it was false and ominous. He hated a Nature that could be guilty of such treachery.

The mate came up beside him, full of excitement at their good
luck. "This is something like it, sir!" he exclaimed. "I can almost
see the old Statue up the bay."

Captain Blair shook his head. "It won't last!" he said sharply.

"Why, cap'n, there isn't a cloud in the sky!"

"Never mind—I've seen this before. The wind didn't go
around the right way; it backed into the nor'west. It has too much
northerly in it now. I'll give us one day of clear weather; to-morrow we have a change."

The mate walked away, disappointed; Captain Blair waited
alone to see the last of the sun. This was better than the storm,
at any rate, and he gave thanks for it; but he had come "on the
coast" too many times to build castles in the air. He had an even
chance of getting in—that was all.

"I'm glad I didn't put back," he said to himself. "I'm glad I
decided before the gale broke. I may get my reward."

That night a wide, brassy ring encircled the moon. Three
bright stars twinkled within its circumference. On the following
day the northwest wind died out gradually, and a gray film of
clouds spread over the sky. A faint breeze sprang up from the
eastward, a raw, cold wind, carrying a hint of snow. Still the sea
remained smooth. For two days and two nights this strange state
of the weather continued. They kept on, heading diagonally in
for New York, making a fair course and sailing by dead-reckon-
ing. On the morning of the third day they picked up the edge of
soundings with the deep-sea lead, and knew that they were
within a hundred miles of port.

IV

The weather that morning looked very threatening. Overhead
the haze had grown thicker; the wind moaned in the rigging with
an insistent note; the swell running in from the open Atlantic
had in it a new lift, a menace of latent power. A storm was close
at hand.

Captain Blair paced the quarter-deck in agony, as he felt
the forces of the elements gathering against him. He weighed
his chances over item by item; there were many contingencies
that had to be taken into account, each offering problems and

difficulties. Caught by a northeast snowstorm in the angle made by Long Island and the Jersey coast, he could hope for no mercy. A strong ship might possibly be driven to sea again out of that pocket, under a press of canvas; but he would not dare to carry sail too hard on the old bark. Dismasted! The thought made him physically weak. Helpless, drifting, cast ashore! No—if the storm came on he would be obliged, in common caution, to heave her to under shortened sail. Then, suppose she wasn't able to scratch by that snare to leeward, the dread corner of Hatteras? If she didn't weather it, the alternative was to fetch up on a leeshore—to die. He must guard against being drawn too far into the trap. No ship ever made the approaches to New York harbor in a snowstorm.

His only hope of arrival lay in picking up a tug. Often he had met them here, a hundred miles at sea. They were always cruising about, on the lookout for ships. He remembered a time when, with a fair wind and pleasant weather, he had refused a tow until he was abreast the Scotland Lightship. He had saved a few dollars then; now he would sell his soul for the same chance.

Noon passed, and still he headed inshore under shortened sail. How long could he tempt Providence? How long? Another hour would turn the scales; by that time he would *have* to get in, somehow—or lose the ship on the Jersey Shore. The storm was making up minute by minute. He searched the horizon for a trail of smoke, for the sails of a cutter. Where were all the towboats? That harbor just beyond the horizon was full of them. Where were the pilot-boats? *Was he to be kept outside, after all?*

In his mind's eye he saw the coasts to leeward and across his bow; they seemed to press in upon him, narrowing their angle, closing on his tracks. Again he went over the courses, figuring the least possible margin of safety. If the gale held in the northeast, and he wore around on the port tack, he ought to slide off between southeast and south-southeast by driving the bark a little. That would open up the leak once more. It would probably open up anyway. But the wind might come on too heavy to allow him to carry even a little sail; worse than this, it might draw in from east-northeast, or from *due east,* around the end of Long Island. They were lost already if it came from due east!

He stopped short, facing the truth. Luck was against him. He need hope for no tugboat; he felt in his bones that they would not be permitted to get in. The air thickened to leeward; a section of horizon disappeared behind a white veil. Snow was coming up the wind. Inch by inch the horizon vanished, swallowed up by the approaching terror. In ten minutes the face of the sea would be completely hidden. And still no tug in sight.

"Land ahead!" sang out a voice forward.

Captain Blair whirled, uttering a savage oath. "Fire Island! God! No use!" He would not look; going to the stern, he shut his eyes and stood silent for some time.

He had made up his mind. Night and a snowstorm were upon him; and he had put the old bark into the very jaws of death. Time to finish playing and get to work—time to tear out hope from the heart—time to do what had to be done—time to forget what might have been.

"Wear ship!" His voice rang out sharply above the rising gale. "Mr. Forsyth, lower the spanker down on deck. Get your men on the weather braces. Let her run off a little, there."

Almost in. Captain Blair rested his hands on the stern-rail, and gazed dully at the low sandy coast of Fire Island, a fading line on the northern horizon. Almost in! A few flakes of snow drove past the stern; an opaque cloud crept stealthily toward them on the water. The captain's eyes fell to the wake, watching the old bark gather headway on the port tack. When he looked up the land had been obliterated. He was not to see it again for many days.

Back into the storm, into the open Atlantic, across the Gulf Stream—back to the old fight—back to the endless exile—back to the reproach of failure, to the anguish and despair in eyes that he loved. "Hurry! Oh, hurry!" she had begged him. Hurry away! Hurry offshore! Drive—drive—drive. Pound—pound—pound. Claw to windward. Race through the gale. Strain—surge. Howl, wind. Laugh, death. Open, seams. Back to the pumps. Back to sea—and almost in.

He entered his wife's room quietly, and took her hand without speaking. For a moment they gazed at each other, a world of pain and love in their eyes.

"I heard," she said.

Something gave way suddenly in his brain; he sank to his knees beside the bunk, sobbing like a child. "I had to do it! I had to do it! I promised to get you in to-day!"

"Never mind. We'll get in to-morrow."

"No! No! No! Never! Never! We'll never get in!"

"You mustn't say such things."

"I can't stand it! It's too much."

"You must, dear. Be brave—for my sake."

He looked at her, speechless. A great cry tore from the depths of his soul—"Oh-h-h!" Didn't he know? "I'm a weak wretch, dear, to break down like this. It's *you* who are suffering, it's *you* who are being brave! You make me ashamed. You are the bravest woman that ever lived. But I love you so much. Sometimes I feel absolutely lost. It's in my mind."

"Poor boy—I know. Don't think of me. I'm feeling better to-day. Think only of the ship."

He turned away, looking at the blank wall of the room. "I promised to get you in."

"You're doing the best you can. That is enough for me."

Hour after hour he sat in the gloomy cabin, gripping the arms of the chair with both hands, staring straight ahead. The night passed slowly. What was the use of going on deck? They were only driving through the storm—driving away. If anything happened the mate would call him. He could feel the condition of the ship by her plunges; when it got too bad he would go up and take in the reefed upper-top sails.

The mate came to the forward-cabin door, knocked, and stuck in his head. He was covered with ice and snow; two pendants of frozen tobacco juice hung from the ends of his mustache.

"She's leaking again, sir," he said. "Pretty badly. Eighteen inches—"

"Pump, then!"

The door closed; the mate stamped away through the forward-cabin. A squall struck the vessel; she careened wildly, the voices of her hull shrieking aloud under the strain. Captain Blair sat on, motionless, with unwinking eyes. He saw into the future plainly. God was indeed hard on him. Why? Why? Why? What had *he* done?

The wind lulled; and a familiar sound struck his ears, throbbing through the ship like the vibrations of distant machinery. Clangity-clang! Clangity-clang! Clangity-clang!

V

It was on a night two weeks later that the old bark crept past the lights of Atlantic City. The long northeaster had blown her far to sea; but it had cleared off properly at last, coming around to the southward with a short gale that had brought them back a good two hundred miles. The offshore wind that had followed, clear, squally, piercing cold, had yet allowed them to hold their own and keep up under the lee of the land. Now it had blown itself out to a gentle breeze; the sea was as level as a floor. A high peace brooded above the world; out of a guileless sky the serene stars looked down in surprise and curiosity. The old bark crept on, deep, ice-covered, in sore distress. Her ropes were frozen in the runners; her decks were piled with snow. In the great stillness her pumps clanged fiercely, flinging their challenge to an encroaching sea.

Captain Blair watched the line of brilliant lights along the western horizon. They were happy in there; they were laughing, dancing, carousing! They had been at it when he wore ship off Fire Island, two weeks ago. Perhaps they'd enjoyed the snowstorm, glad of any diversion. What did they care? What did they feel? What did they know? When they looked seaward from the boardwalk, admiring the handsome ships, did they suppose that God was marshalling them back and forth on the water for their amusement? The pretty ships! Hell!—what of the men? Did those parasites ever look beyond their own selfish, thoughtless lives? He cursed them—he hated them.

A rare smell of the land filled his nostrils; even in winter the earth sends out a message to her sons on the sea. He breathed it deeply, letting it sink into his soul. His wife still lived—lingered somewhere between life and death. Would she live through what was yet to come?

He knew that he would get in this time. Nothing could stop him now. The elements had done their worst—he had won. There would be another day or two of calm, pleasant weather; the token of it ran in that crisp, sweet air. As he paced the deck, memories crowded upon him—visions of a certain seaport village, of the faces of men and women long since dead, of simple boyhood scenes; sights of the street there, running up a hill, of the familiar houses, of his house, where his mother now lived alone. Home! God, were they to go home again? Then, in a flash, his thoughts leaped forward into the recent gale. He saw the menace of the angry Atlantic, he felt the struggle of the old bark, he heard the pumps pounding above the noise of the storm. The men had sobbed with the cold as they bent to the handles. They were still at it. Clangity-clang! Clangity-clang! Clangity-clang! That sound would haunt him to the grave. But they had weathered the gale at last, they had won—

Would his wife live—even now, even now?

The mate came stumbling aft. "Cap'n! Steamer dead ahead! I see her red and green."

Captain Blair's heart leaped in his breast. Could it be a towboat, so far outside, in the middle of the night? He waited five minutes; the lights were almost upon them, still showing both red and green. A whistle shrieked—the sweetest sound that had ever greeted his ears. It was a towboat, making directly for the bark.

"Stop those pumps!" cried the captain. "It'll never do to let him know that we're leaking."

The tug rounded-to on the bark's weather quarter, with a loud hissing of steam. A far-away hail came across the water.

"Ship ahoy? What ship is that?"

"Bark *Adelaide,* from Pisagua to New York."

"Do you want a tow?"

"How much will you take me in for?"

"One hundred and fifty dollars!"

"Hook onto us!" Captain Blair ground his teeth. "Fifty dollars too much," he said to himself. "It's worth it—I'll pay it myself."

The tug veered closer to the quarter.

"What kind of a passage have you had, Cap'n Blair?"

"Why, hello, Dan Reilly, is that you? Where were all you fellows two weeks ago?"

"Were you off here then?"

A lump of bitterness and misery rose in Captain Blair's throat. *"Was I off here then?"* he shouted furiously. "I've been twenty-five days from Hatteras to New York! My wife is sick. So get us in as quick as God will let you!"

Under the high, clear stars, across the glassy water, the old bark trailed in from sea. Amidships her pumps clanged ceaselessly; ropes lay about the deck in confusion, where they had managed to start the frozen gear and get in the canvas. Aloft a few men worked slowly and painfully, trying to furl the upper sails. In past the twin lightships, in past the winking eye of Navesink—boarded by the pilot—into the mouth of the old ship-channel, in past the Romer bug-light, in past the range-lights on Sandy Hook, in past the blaze of Coney Island—in from sea. The glow of the great city filled the northern sky; the land loomed closer in the darkness; lights multiplied, shifted, approached—the lights of port. Life touched them once more; their ears caught the faint, ghostly murmur of the awakening land. Over the waste astern, the open Atlantic, dawn broke in a cloudless sky.

They saw the city, the towering buildings, the wide sweep of Brooklyn Bridge. They saw the Statue, calm, aloof, indifferent to storms, unmoved at life or death. They saw the land to port and starboard, the hills of Staten Island, the gleaming fields of snow, the houses rising roof on roof, the spires, the forts, the broad harbor, the swift ferries, the bustling tugs. Only the sailor knows the full beauty of the land, the hidden truth. Only the sailor, in from sea.

He sat in the after-cabin, waiting to hear their fate. In the deep silence of the ship resting at anchor, the pumps clanged with a loud, monotonous sound. He gripped the arms of the chair with both hands; his soul shrank before the greatest fear that he had ever known. The door behind him opened and closed. The doctor stepped out into the cabin.

"What chance, doctor? For God's sake, say something!"

"I can't tell—I can't be sure. She must be taken to a hospital at once."

"I've kept the towboat alongside. Will you see to the business, doctor? I'll go with you; but you must take entire charge. I don't know much about hospitals. I've been through a hard time, sir."

VI

Late that night Captain Blair came off aboard in a shore boat, and climbed the side ladder. The mate met him at the rail.

"What news, cap'n?" he asked hesitatingly.

"She pulled through, Mr. Forsyth."

"Thank God, sir!"

Captain Blair turned away with tears in his eyes. He could not trust himself to speak.

Down below a dim light burned above the chart-table. He stopped in the center of the cabin, and looked around like a man in a dream. The hour in the hospital stood before him, was burned into his memory for all time. She had been off some-where, in some horrible place—unconscious, perhaps dying—and nothing for him to do. But he had seen her since, she had known him.

What was it that seemed so strange about the vessel? He found himself listening. Silence. The pumps were quiet! She had stopped leaking.

He went into his wife's room. The bed had been made up freshly; the air of sickness was gone. He wouldn't sleep there—until she came back. Unutterable thoughts besieged him, flashes of pain beyond words. Storm and disappointment and torture and fear. What a life to give a woman! What a life for a man to live! They had won this time—but the cost, the frightful cost.

He saw her face as she lay on the cot in the hospital. He recalled her whisper: "This is your reward!" Black hatred of the world surged in his heart. *Reward!* Yes—but why had it been necessary for them to do such awful penance? What had *they* done?

He looked up at her picture, hanging on the wall of the room. The brave eyes seemed to chide him. If she were here now, what would she say? "You mustn't think such things!" He knelt beside the bunk, stretching his arms full length across the empty bed. "God forgive me!" he cried from a torn heart. "She'll live! She'll live!"

DE LONG

A STORY OF SUNDA STRAITS

"De Long was an interesting man," said Nichols. "In days gone by
he kept a ship-chandlery at Old Anjer, that busy port of call on
the Java shore of the Straits of Sunda, where every vessel that
came to the China Sea passed either up or down at some time
during the year. De Long met them all, in his Whitehall boat
with four natives rowing. Once seen and heard, he was never
forgotten. There are men despisable enough to be vastly interesting. One loathes them, abhors them—and is fascinated by them;
one finds oneself repeating their words with a certain flavor of
contemptuous enjoyment, and not at all displeased at the
prospect of meeting them again. A real liking for them is almost
sure to grow; one begins to, in a way, condone their meanness,
is a trifle sorry for them, perhaps sees how it might have come
about. Of this anomalous company was De Long. An interesting
man, a personality; and his death was in keeping with his life. Let
me tell you about him—it won't take long."

A few of us had gathered that evening on board the bark
Omega, to welcome Nichols once more to the harbor-society of
Singapore. He had arrived at noon from Batavia, standing across
with the early seabreeze from the mouth of Rhio Strait. For some
time his trips had kept him off among the islands; of the fleet that
he had left in Singapore three months before, my ship alone
remained. I'd introduced the later arrivals; and talk had drifted
down through Banka and across the Java Sea, along the route
that Nichols had just sailed.

I

"I remember well the first time that I saw De Long," he said.
"It was on my maiden voyage at sea; I had come out East, a boy
of seventeen, with Captain H— in the old ship *Rainbow*. We
anchored at Anjer for mail and fresh provisions, and I was bow-
man in the boat that took the captain ashore. The scene, our first
landfall after the long, hard voyage, and my first glimpse of the
fabled East, land of desire and charm for boys, was impressed upon
my mind for all time. This Anjer where we had called, Old Anjer,
the original town of that name, lay some miles away from Fourth
Point, the place that you know as Anjer to-day. On the charts of
Sunda, you've perhaps noticed across the face of the Java coast
this legend: "All these villages totally destroyed by the volcanic
eruption of August, 1883." Krakatoa did it—a tall conical peak
rising in mid-straits, that one day split apart and fell outboard
before their eyes, loosing the fires of hell. It's as if the names only,
registered on charts and sailing directions at the Hydrographic
Offices of distant nations, were intangible enough to float free of
the devastating tidal wave; and many of them, perhaps, were
swept away never to return. This one, it seems, was uprooted
along with its village, and stranded some distance along the shore,
where men who stood in by a recollection of Anjer roadstead would
never find the place. The wave passed, and Old Anjer was gone.

We rowed up a little river that morning, an Eastern river, very
picturesque to young eyes, very quiet and peaceful to eyes accustomed for months to a wide horizon, to the expanses of turbulent
oceans; and landed on a strip of white beach under an immense
banyan tree. I remember the captain pointing with a sort of
personal pride to this great tree, and informing us that it was
known among seamen as the biggest banyan in all the East. I'm
sure, I have never since seen a bigger. It was a marvel to me then;
a real banyan tree, in every respect like the picture in the geography that I'd studied at school. A regiment of soldiers might
have camped beneath it; hundreds of dark trunks rose from the
ground on every hand, supporting a stratum of luxuriant veg-
etable life, an elevated island, an upper world; the thick tentacle-
like branches and heavy foliage fairly darkened the sky. In the
rear of this banyan the two rival ship-chandlers, De Long and
Shute, had their respective stores; odd little buildings, low and

ramshackle, each set in its half-cleared enclosure littered with
refuse, and facing the gloom of the immense tree. De Long and
Shute were expert pilots for the China and Java Seas, and rivals
in that business as well. Behind their ship-chandleries lay the
village, a settlement of considerable size. The aisles of banyan led
in every direction toward clusters of native dwellings; men,
women, and children passed constantly beneath its shade, going
to and from the boats at the landing; it must in a certain sense
have dominated their lives. I remember Old Anjer chiefly as a
village of a tree.

"We hauled the boat out on the landing, a strip of perfect
beach. The captain had been wondering as we came in, at the
lack of formality in our reception; a few natives gathered about,
lending us a hand with the boat, but none of them seemed to
have an official capacity. 'The beggar must be sick,' remarked
Captain H—. 'I've never known him to turn this trick before. If
he doesn't look out, I'll take my trade to Shute. And where in the
devil is Shute, if you please? What's happened to this place,
anyway?' As if conjured by his words, two natives suddenly appeared in hot haste, flying through the dusk of the banyan and
shrieked with a sound half of laughter and half of dismay. Behind
them rolled and puffed an enormous man of short stature, bran-
dishing a stick, cursing, snarling, and very much out of breath,
whom I instantly knew from previous descriptions to be De Long.
Behind him, still, an emaciated individual lurched from the
gloom—a man apparently in the last stages of some terrible
fever. This, I learned later, was Shute, the rival ship-chandler; a
Yankee of the shrewdest sort, and one of those singular physical
specimens which, while in perfect and tenacious health, give the
impression of decay, disease, and scarcely restrained mortality.

" 'Captain! Captain!' gasped the leader of this strange pair.
'You know me, old De Long? I am your man! Forgive and pardon!
I slept. I am but just returned from piloting—a hard trip, Captain. I slept; and these sons of the devil, these—!' He exploded
with vile imprecations. 'They kept no watch! They awoke me
not! Hell and corruption!—that I might lost you! Go back, you
Shute—go back to starve. Even at running have I won. This is
my man; dealings many and good we have before.'

" 'That's all very well, De Long,' said Captain H— severely.
'But what kind of a way is this, I ask you, for a man to call at

Anjer? Here I run in with a fair wind, in a great hurry to be off
again. I expect to be met before I reach the anchorage. Minute
after minute I look for boats. No De Long. No Shute. I thought
I remembered that men here were eager for trade. I get my *own
boat* overboard. I come ashore——'

" 'Captain, no more!' wailed De Long, beating the air in
agony. 'Have I not told?—a blunder most terrible! A man must
sleep. Never trust another. These——s a lesson to remember
shall have. Never shall such blunder happen again. Never,
never! Hear me, now! Never, Captain, if you but pardon and
forgive.'

" 'Where were you, Shute?' the Captain demanded.

" 'Inland buyin' chickens.' The man's voice was astonishing, a
sepulchral, echoing, indefinite sound. 'You slipped in close along
shore, Cap'n, and wasn't seen.' He jerked his head backward.
'Native festival in the village yesterday,' he explained.

"Captain H— faced the pair, looking from one to the other.
'Well, what shall I do after such treatment? Take my boat and go
to some other village, where they keep awake? I intended to
make large purchases, but don't see any inducements to do business here. Or shall I split up my trade between the two of you? Or
shall I give you your just deserts, De Long, quit you altogether,
and see what Shute can do for me? I can't be bothered with a man
who sleeps all the time.'

"De Long covered his face with fat yellow hands, in the attitude of a man receiving his deathblow. 'Captain, no!' he
screamed. 'Not so, not so! You do me greatest wrong! Remember
our past dealings, honorable to both. Ten, fifteen years have you
trade with old De Long, always to utmost satisfaction. And
now—ah, God! Could I know you come, even at Java Head I
meet you, though life pay so to do!'

" 'Talk is cheap,' observed the Captain, 'What do you say,
Shute? What's your price on those chickens that you've been
buying, and on a few bananas and yams?'

" 'No, no!' De Long broke in, his hands fluttering like leaves.
'No, I say—it must not be! Never shall this robber Shute supply
you, Captain, my friend. Rotten are his yams, green his bananas.
Nothing of good he has. Your crew from him will catch a belly-
ache. Worse, worse! Beware of him!'

" 'What do you say, Shute?' persisted the Captain.

"Shute gave him a fleeting and luminous glance. 'I say you mean to trade with De Long,' he boomed. 'Don't let him fleece you too close, Cap'n.' The next instant he had vanished into the banyan-shade.

"A shrill cackle of laughter went up from De Long. 'Ha, ha, ha! This Shute!—good fellow, knows his place. Captain, why you frighten old De Long? Ah, God—I am water inside! But come.' He took the Captain by the arm. 'I show you yams like white meal, and from the bunch bananas dropping—all cheap, very cheap, nothing at all. They are sweet to the taste after beef and bread—make rich the blood of men. Prepare your crew for Hong Kong—eh? Ha! ha!'

"This was De Long. Myself and another boy brought the provisions to the boat, each trip passing under the width of the mighty banyan tree. And each trip at the store I watched and listened to De Long. His face was peculiar; I thought then, before I'd seen one, that he must be a Chinaman. A broad, flat oval of yellowish skin, a mouth like a round hole, a stub of a nose, eyes brown, wide, and sometimes handsome, rather exceptional eyes: these made up his features, and gave him that Mongolian cast. His whole aspect spoke of cunning, greed, deception, perfidy, and general shabbiness of the spiritual fiber. I watched him with delight, with something suspiciously like a secret and boyish admiration. And I remembered him.

II

"It was some years afterward that I met De Long on an equal footing, as you might say, and made the acquaintance of the man. I'd been on a number of Eastern voyages, and had worked up to a ship of my own; but for some reason or other had missed him each time that I passed through Sunda Straits. Either he would be off piloting some ship when I called at Anjer, or a fair wind would take me by with such a rush that I merely hove-to for the mailboat. Shute had boarded me once or twice, however, and I had given him a little trade; but the man never ceased to be obnoxious to me. There were Yankees enough on the home-end of the route to be cheated by, without running against them everywhere; in Eastern waters I wanted to be cheated by an alien of some sort, to at least have a new turn and piquancy lent to the

sordid old game. At length I arrived one time in the Straits of
Sunda on the break of the northeast monsoon; it broke unusually
early that year, and spoiled my hopes of running up the Sea
without a hitch. The wind was variable and squally; I'd had a long
passage, and greatly needed fresh food and vegetables for my men.
Struggling with a head-current down the Straits for a number of
days, we finally fetched in toward Anjer early one forenoon.

"As the shore drew nearer and nearer, and I got a sight of palm
trees and white beaches, I decided all in an instant to lay up there
at anchor for a day or two, take things easy, and go ashore. There
were two or three vessels in the roadstead, with sails loosed; but
I didn't care about them. I wanted to investigate. The Java shore
of Sunda, in those years before the eruption, rose in virgin beauty
and magnificence from the water's edge to the hills and mountains
a short distance inland. Perhaps it was because we used to come
upon it fresh from the sea that it seemed so very wonderful; but
the pure intrinsic charm of Java stands apart from that of all other
islands I have seen. A voice calls from the jungle as you sail by;
and when the wind drops at evening and a land breeze wafts down
from the hills, you long to anchor and go ashore—and never
return. I had been waiting for this chance; the boat couldn't swing
over the side soon enough for me.

"But Shute came to disturb my fancy before I could get away.
Like my old captain, I'd been on the lookout for boats, and
wondering why they didn't come. There were plenty of native
dugouts, paddling from every direction along the shore; and at last
I caught sight of what I expected, a Whitehall boat skipping
through the water toward the vessel, spray spouting from her oars,
her men rowing a quick stroke in time to the grunts and yells of
a bareheaded European sitting in the stern. A look with the glasses
disclosed the flying arms of an animated skeleton—Shute instead
of De Long. He boarded us as we let go the anchor. I was a trifle
disappointed, and made short work of him.

" 'It's no use this time, Shute,' I told him. 'I suppose De Long
is still in business ashore?'

" 'Oh, yes. But what's the matter, Cap'n?' he asked. 'Wasn't
everything all right last time?'

" 'Perfectly,' I answered. 'I have no complaint to make. But I
have a definite reason for making a change.'

" 'I don't see—' he objected.

" 'I want to investigate a memory,' I said.

" 'A what?'

" 'A memory,' I repeated. 'Never mind. It's absolutely no use for you to make me any prices. It's absolutely no use for you to stay aboard. I am determined to trade with De Long.'

"He backed away as if from a violent and unaccountable contagion, and gazed at me from the rail with open mouth. 'Investigate . . . well, I'll be damned!' he said; and disappeared over the side without further words.

"After I'd seen the ship properly anchored, given orders to furl everything aloft, and read my letters (for the mailboat had crossed Shute going in), I jumped into my own dinghy and made for the shore. The wind had died away to a flat calm; the sun boiled down without a shadow on the roadstead and the shimmering green land. When we reached the mouth of the little river I looked ahead for the great banyan tree. There it stood, a tremendous solid mass in the landscape, an astonishing thing to have actually grown from the ground; and there in the lee of it lay the strip of white beach, a landing arranged by nature for those who in the course of time could not have failed to attach themselves to the tree. It all seemed very natural; and so I wasn't surprised, as I stepped from the bow of the boat, to see emerging from the shade and rolling toward me along the sand a grotesque figure which I recognized as that of De Long. He wasn't so massive a man in general as I remembered; but his paunch retained every inch of its fabulous girth. It seemed inflated—a growth, an appendage, like the stomach of the fish that boys blow up and then throw overboard, to watch it float around. He came on puffing loudly, waving his arms with distracted gestures about his head.

" 'Captain, Captain!' he called. 'Patience!—I hurry—old De Long. Away was I with all my men upon the river, executing the order of Captain P—.' He reached me exhausted and dripping with sweat. 'Come this way,' he purred, grabbing my hand in both of his. 'Listen, Captain. I tell you, that dam Shute he is no good. You trade with him—I know. I know your ship. Every ship I know, coming to Anjer—thousands, American, English, Dutch, French, of all the world! Yes, very good. You trade with Shute. But this time you will try De Long—eh, no? The captains tell you, old De Long is best. They say, next time try him to see. Come, now, and I will show.'

" 'Shute met me in the roads,' I said. 'Didn't you see his boat?'

" 'Ah!—devils of hell!' wailed De Long. 'I saw! For shame would I eat the sand beneath your feet! But Captain, a little order?—a slight order for old De Long?—a beginning only? Come and see finest yams. Perhaps my wife is there.'

" 'You were asleep,' I said. 'This is the second time I've caught you napping.'

" 'Never! Never before! Far, and dangerously upon the Strait, sails old De Long, always awake, always seeking the ships, always first on board. "Ha, Captain, you are back again?" "Ha, old De Long, dare-devil, why not at the Cape of Good Hope take up your station, to board us there?" Yes, yes. But this time, Captain, I have great business on hand. It happen so. Never before, and never again!'

" 'What about Captain H— in the ship *Rainbow*, eight or nine years ago?'

"He paused in the midst of mopping his face to give me a cunning look. 'Captain H— I remember well. Fine man, trade always with De Long. He tell you some story—eh?'

" 'He told me nothing,' I said. 'I was one of the boys in his boat that day.'

"Suddenly De Long crumpled with noiseless laughter; his body shook and heaved; slight sounds went on within him, little clicks and puffs, like the noise of escaping steam. 'Then why you make me lie?' he at length got out. 'Captain H—, he was the same. Always his joke with poor De Long! You mean it not—ha, ha! It is to trade with old De Long that you come on shore. But I, how shall I know? I suffer here. I cannot joke with trade. With your jokes some day you kill De Long. That will be funny—eh? Come, listen—a great joke, boys: old fat De Long is dead. Oh yes; his heart failed when he thought to lose a little trade. Ha, ha! A great joke is life, Captain. Wait some years.'

"So I let him capture me, with enough resistance to keep him voluble; and away we went among the roots and stems of the banyan, his arm linked in mine and his voice whispering hoarsely at my side. Heaven knows how many strains of blood ran in De Long. Sitting in the coolness of his veranda I examined him leisurely over my cigar. I knew his reputation; many stories had reached me during the years since I'd first seen him—stories that spoke of personality and that had never completely satisfied me.

He was said to be a rich man, and a miser. Captains locked up their valuables when he came aboard for any length of time. A crime was supposed to have driven him to Anjer; but such a conjecture was only to be expected from the natural curiosity and aspersion of man. Nothing definite, you see. He did have Chinese features, I made out; a Chinaman must have had a hand in his family not far back. More than the features, there was a certain secretive attitude of mind, a reticence not concealed by the flood of talk, a baffling and inscrutable look in the eyes—a trait of character, in short, that's fiber and tissue of a Chinaman. He denied it absolutely; called himself a half-Dutchman and half-Portuguese, but admitted a Javanese grandmother. One found oneself, almost unconsciously, asking him intimate and personal questions, outrageous questions; his lack of sensitiveness, of pride, of decency, was so very evident that it amounted to a native innocence—or would have amounted to something of the sort if he could have controlled his shifty eyes.

" 'What makes you lie so, like the devil?' I asked, after a while. He'd been telling me of an impossible order for provisions that some captain had given him the week before.

" 'Lie?' he repeated incredulously.

" 'Yes, *lie*, ' I said. 'I won't go any farther than that just now.'

"He pursed up his round mouth, gazed among the rafters of the veranda, and suddenly blew his breath out with a cynical laugh. 'All men lie,' he observed. 'Whenever lips are opened a lie is on the tongue.' Bending forward, he tapped me on the knee. 'If I lie, I also believe nothing,' he pointed out. 'You believe something, and you do not lie so like the devil all the time. Similar process. We reach similar result, eh?—pleasure, pain. I, myself; and you, yourself. In long runs, Captain, perhaps I am so happy as you.'

" 'What's that?' I demanded. 'What do you mean?' I wasn't prepared for a sophist in the jungle; though maybe that's where they thrive. I looked him over with new interest. 'Such talk spoils the world, De Long,' I said.

" 'No,' he contradicted. 'It but makes possible to live. For all purposes have I found it best. Kill the world with lies, or the world kills you with lies.'

" 'Then there's nothing that you can trust?'

"He folded his hands across his paunch. 'Nothing. All lies, and I no longer care. I grow old.'

"While we'd been talking, two people had come out of the shadow of the banyan and approached the house. I saw that they were a white man and a Eurasian woman. The woman was young and beautiful, dressed in a quaint costume more native than civilized. They walked on without speaking or looking at each other, coming toward the steps of the veranda. Beside me, De Long got up heavily. His hands wandered at his sides, as if feeling for pockets that weren't there.

" 'Captain, my wife is come,' he said abruptly, when they had reached the steps. 'My wife was walking with Captain P—.' The woman started and smiled, holding me with her eyes. She hadn't looked up before, probably hadn't anticipated finding anyone at all on the veranda. I was completely taken aback.

" 'Your wife?' I queried.

"De Long bobbed his head. 'Why not? You think she is my daughter?' The shadow of an emotion crossed his face. 'Ask Captain P—,' he said.

"The tone, hasty, incautious, vindictive, was one that I would hardly have expected from De Long; though the meanness of it was all his own. She whirled on him fiercely. 'You are an evil old fool!' she cried.

" 'Enough!' he commanded, stamping his foot. 'Go in!'

"She held his eye, laughing scornfully. 'Go in!' she mocked. 'I go where I wish, De Long. You cannot make me go out or in.'

"The captain, standing on the steps, played with his watch chain, turned and surveyed the harbor. De Long rolled down to him, his enormous bulk trembling all over like jelly. 'Captain P—, come sit on my veranda, smoke, drink what you like. Some whiskey, eh?—or little gin?'

" 'No, I must be off,' said Captain P—.

" 'But here is Captain Nichols, good comrade, just in from sea. He stops to make visit, and trade with old De Long.'

" 'Sorry—but I see there's a breeze coming down the Straits, Captain Nichols. You know what that means.'

" 'You're bound out, then?' I inquired. 'Which is your vessel?'

" 'The black bark, lying just outside your ship. Yes, Singapore to Melbourne, and back from Newcastle with coals to Singapore.'

" 'A nice trip,' I observed. 'Nice country—I haven't been down there for years.'

" 'It's a sort of regular run with me. Well, De Long, I believe we're all square?'

" 'Yes,' said De Long. 'All square.'

" 'Glad to have met you, Captain Nichols. Goodbye.' He turned to the woman. 'Good-bye,' he said.

"She gave him a level, steady look. 'Go!' she said in a low voice. 'Never return!' The words were simple—and desperately unconventional. They tore to shreds our flimsy fabric of talk, brought us up all-standing, as it were, and thoroughly frightened De Long.

" 'Captain, take no notice!' he begged, wringing his hands. 'No hard feelings are. Call to see us when from Newcastle you come, and we have ready the chickens of which you spoke.'

" 'Yes, call upon De Long!' cried the woman. 'He must have trade!' With a quick turn she fled up the steps; then hesitated and sank into a chair. The captain shrugged his shoulders, laughed, and started down the path. Cringing and whining, De Long followed him into the gloom of the banyan, leaving his wife with me on the veranda.

"She was laughing to herself like a child. 'Fool! Fool!' she cried softly. Looking off above the great tree, 'De Long is an old fool,' she announced. When I made no answer, she turned to me. 'So I heard you say,' I remarked. Her eyes traveled over me, rested finally in my own; and for some minutes we gazed at each other without speaking. At length she moved, drew herself together, and leaned toward me over the arm of the chair. 'You will stay for dinner?' she asked. I nodded. She was an alluring figure to look upon, slender and swaying and delicate, like a flower that's grown in the shadow; her skin was dusky, her face was round and smooth; big, wide-open eyes trembled in a maze of lashes, and her arms hung in a helpless fashion at her sides.

" 'De Long is great for trade,' she said suddenly. 'So you will find. I have not seen you before?'

"It seemed to be a question. 'No,' I said, 'I've always traded with Shute. I haven't been ashore here for many years. This time I decided to trade with De Long.'

" 'Trade,' she whispered. With a quick motion she sprang to her feet and stood before me. 'Trade!' she cried breathlessly. 'Life for trade! Honor for trade! Love for trade! So much I learn.' She brought her hands together with a sharp sound. 'Tell me, is death also for trade? I think not. One bargain De Long shall lose!' As if confounded by words that had come without volition, she covered her face and ran toward the door, vanishing before my astonished gaze.

"What in the devil was up, I asked myself, in this land of sunshine and splendor, in this land that looked from the water as if it had never known sorrow, strife, or disillusionment? This girl, a decoy for trade? Detestable, inconceivable! Then what? Why that outburst from De Long, so inimical to the interests of trade, which had immediately to be swallowed? The woman's scorn of him I could comprehend; but why her repulse of the captain? If she didn't like the situation, why was she in it? Could her resentment have been induced, or at least heightened, by the fact that a young stranger sat watching on the veranda? Then how far was she the innocent victim? Did De Long himself know exactly? Did he care?

"And yet, she had a manner of pride and circumspection; that flash of anger at his insinuation had appeared genuine enough.

"These thoughts, and many more, passed through my head as I saw De Long returning under the banyan. From where I sat I could follow the path nearly to the landing. He came on ponderously, sweating through the strip of hot sunlight, turning his head from side to side like a wild beast in the open. 'Where is she?' he gasped, mopping his face. I nodded toward the house. He mounted the steps; the rattan chair creaked and snapped as he collapsed beside me. 'These dam women need the lash!' he snarled.

" 'They get it,' I remarked. 'A word is a lash to a good woman.'

" 'No good women are!' he cried. 'Bad women, and worse women. Unfortunate am I, Captain, to have married the worst.'

" 'You old scoundrel!' I exclaimed. 'Is it possible that you believe your own lies?' By Jove, I'd entered with a man into a discussion of his own wife—but all decorum vanished in the presence of De Long.

" 'Yet this is truth,' he answered. 'Watch when she looks at me, and then at you—'

" 'Hold on,' I interrupted. 'You can leave me out of this.'

"He gave me a cunning look. 'Captain, men to me are plain. Already now, it is as if I know you many years. I say, De Long,

here is strange man. A different. Safe. How you like, Captain—
eh? True, I think. Else why I speak these things?'

" 'Thanks,' I said. 'But that is something you can trust.'

"He shrugged his shoulders. 'Oh, I think you have best intention for a little while. But my wife, she would not understand.'

"I was amused, disgusted—and interested, as I told you. 'De
Long, this is a bad business,' I said harshly. 'Do you find that it
pays?'

"He sighed profoundly. 'Seldom life pay,' he answered. 'Thus
you see me, old De Long.' He waved a hand. 'You tell me,
Captain—what to do?'

"I wasn't prepared for such a question. For the moment it
touched me, it seemed to be a note of sincerity in the midst of
utter guile. I had to smile at myself when I remembered that the
rascal was pretty deliberately doing what he chose to do. And
yet, he did appear troubled; in his devious way he meant it, he
wanted my advice. 'That depends upon how much you care,' I
said.

" 'How much I care,' he repeated. 'But tell me what.'

" 'You could easily close up your business here, and take your
wife away. You're probably a rich man now. Take her to Batavia,
to Singapore, to Hong Kong; give her dresses and jewels, excitement, something to think about—'

" 'What, leave my trade?' he cried. 'My friends, my customers
of long establishment? For this, no man is called upon! It cannot
be!'

" 'Your affections seem to be badly divided, De Long,' I said.
'Then perhaps, in time, you'll become reconciled to the present
arrangement.'

"He opened his mouth wide, as if to roar out his mind—then
controlled himself. 'You think, Captain,' he asked, 'that in
Batavia, in Singapore, in Hong Kong, with dresses and jewels,
my wife would for long remain true?' His eyes narrowed, peering
at me shrewdly. 'Much I give her,' he said. 'A house, dresses,
jewels, finer than before. The Queen of Anjer may she be! Here
is a little world. How useless, more to do!'

"I wondered if he realized how preposterously useless anything
would be. 'Why did you marry her?' I asked.

" 'Ah!—why? That question, many ask themselves. Why? Yet

always the same. Because she is beautiful—because a man am I, and all men fools. No proper reason, eh? Because into the world woman was sent, a curse for man!'

" 'And in the meanwhile,' I observed, 'your wife's charms attract a little trade.'

"He raised his eyebrows. 'So? Yes, perhaps. Why not? Both trade and happiness must I lose? No! It is the way of the world.'

"She came to the door just then to call us in; stood there a moment watching us, framed in the square of deeper shadow. Whatever this pass meant to De Long, I knew that it was very hard on her. A woman spirited, wilful, and true enough, I judged; the outright feminine, venturing recklessly in quest of its love. But truth of that sort couldn't endure for any length of time in such an atmosphere.

"She disappeared within the house; as we got up to follow her, De Long touched my arm. 'Expect always evil,' he said. 'Then nothing is good, and evil not so bad.'

" 'Shut up!' I snapped. 'I'm tired of you and your world.'

"He chuckled at my shoulder. 'I would make good an evil world by hauling down the flag of goodness. But at the masthead you keep it, and perhaps only one thing of many in all life reaches so high.'

" 'For God's sake,' I cried, 'try at least to make them all a little higher!'

" 'And fail.' He snapped his fingers. 'Too late!' he said. 'I have seen—what I have seen.'

III

"I spent the afternoon ashore, walking with De Long through the village, while he picked up a supply of chickens for me at different houses; spending an hour on Shute's veranda, in conversation with an English captain; and later, wandering alone under the great banyan, examining; the countless trunks that dripped like streams of black pitch out of the foliage above, trying to estimate them, enjoying the immensity, the sense of wonder and awe. There De Long found me, toward the close of the afternoon, and pressed me to stay ashore for another meal. The day was closing without the usual squall; the breeze off the Straits had died away, preparing to come down in the evening from the hills. My boat was at the landing; I told the men to go aboard for their supper, and return for me at eight o'clock.

"After our own supper at De Long's we sat on the little veranda and watched the moon rise over the hills—three of us, De Long, his wife, and I. The fragrance, the calm, the infinite peace of the scene, seemed incompatible with hearts of hatred and wrong. She hadn't appeared at the midday meal—had probably been sulking somewhere in the depths of the house; but during the afternoon they had evidently patched up their difficulty. I could imagine the conference: De Long threatening, storming, begging, abject and insincere, hitting upon the unwisest things to say, following the wrong line altogether; the woman aloof and disdainful, loathing the words and the man who uttered them, desperate, in revolt at life and fate—but concealing her heart now, reserving for her own knowledge the completeness of their estrangement; at last submitting to the situation, unbending suddenly, lying as if by nature, and cleverly acting the lie; resolved to play with him a while longer, for inscrutable purposes of her own. She sat on the floor of the veranda beside his chair, rolling cigarettes for us, and listening without comment to the conversation. As he talked, his fat hand smoothed her shoulder; he was happy and garrulous. Now and then I caught the gleam of her eyes under the darkness of her hair.

"It was distressing, tragic—and very interesting. The moon shed a new light on the whole matter; it rose swiftly and swung clear into the ocean of the sky, suffusing the land with that soft radiance responsible for so many sensations, acts, impulses, for so much that has been decisive and vital in the history of man. Wrong?—I asked myself. Could love ever be wrong in such a place? The moon above the hills, the air sweet and warm, full of the breath of earth and the odor of flowers; breezes whispering, the leaves of the palm trees clashing faintly, a subdued murmur of waves coming up from the shore—what was there for it but to love? Wasn't this woman more honest than either De Long or I? In fact, hadn't she the essential right of the matter? I wondered— wondered, too, if De Long persuaded himself that anything had actually been gained. An old husband, a young wife—suspicions, accusations—anger and defiance. And then intrigues. One couldn't blame her; I felt like telling her so. What would have been the answer? What was she thinking about so silently, off there in the shadow? Life and love?—or the death that was to cheat life out of its final and paramount trade?

"I tried to avoid the topic of business; but De Long came back to it persistently, at unexpected openings. It was his life, the topic to which all other topics stood in a tributary relation. A mention of early days in the Straits of Sunda set him off at once. Trade wasn't what it used to be, he complained. 'Old times, Captain, they are best. Ah, yes! Then came many ships to Anjer, and money like water flowed. Big crews they carry, fifty and sixty men. And food—ah, God, for saltness!—and for drink, I swear you, they take rum and mix with the brine of the sea! So always scurvy; and from the rail they shout for fresh provisions. Ha!—then I sell yams, fruit, chickens, big of everything. Big price, big profit. Good times for trade. But now—pah!' He swore shamelessly; no doubt the woman was used to it. 'Now, Captain, few ships, few men, no scurvy, provision in the tin—what chance, I ask you, to make money? Soon is the world remade for little men.'

" 'Or maybe men themselves aren't as big as they thought,' I said. 'A captain told me in Singapore last year that De Long was barely holding his own at Anjer, while Shute grew rich under his nose. Is that the way of it?' Something about the man invited banter; he liked it, would have been disappointed at a different tone.

" 'Eh?—what!' he cried, sitting up with a jerk. 'Shute under my nose is rich, you say? Ho, ho, ho!' He shook the veranda with his mirth. 'This Shute! Ho, ho! I think, your little joke. That captain, he live in the air, not Singapore. Holding his own, he tell you, is old De Long? Ho, ho! Yes—holding his own.' He paused abruptly, glancing in my direction. 'Captain, I have a fortune,' he said. 'You like to see?'

"I didn't understand: could he be referring to the woman? 'What is it?' I asked.

" 'You tell it not?—to captains in Singapore, or in the air.'

"His wife spoke for the first time since we'd come out. 'Yes, show to the Captain,' she laughed. 'He will not tell.'

"De Long hoisted himself up and came toward me. He was fumbling with the buttons of his coat. When he had reached me, 'Feel here,' he said. He unbuttoned his waistcoat and guided my hand over the lining. I felt lumps—some heavy substance. 'What is it?' I asked again.

" 'Gold!' he said. 'Feel here.'

"I touched a leather pocket sewed into the lining of the vest. 'Diamonds!' he whispered.

" '*Diamonds!*' I exclaimed.

" 'Yes, yes,' he said. 'My diamonds. Another lie, you think? Then see! He tugged at the fastenings, drew out a long case or pouch of leather, and before my eyes poured a heap of diamonds into the palm of his hand. The moonlight struck them; they shone like a handful of lambent flame. I gasped in consternation. Bending above the jewels De Long heaved a fluttering sigh. The next second he had them back in the leather case, as if fearful of the very forces of the air.

"By Jove!—this extraordinary creature really had a fortune, carried it around with him, close to his heart, close to his mercenary soul. I lifted the flap of the vest; it was heavy with gold pieces, and felt like some curious garment made for a diver, weighted to keep him under water. The material was a stout canvas-like drill; hanging loosely, and padded with its fantastic layer of gems and bullion, it accounted for some of the man's inordinate girth.

" 'Heavens, De Long!' I cried. 'I should think you'd die in this hot weather. Why don't you invest it in something that wouldn't break your back?'

" 'Captain,' he answered shrewdly, 'of investments I have experience. Consider diamonds. Always their value rises; always are they near, to be counted, to be looked upon with eyes. No insurance, no fees of law. No little paper, for which money across the sea rests in other hands. I buy a diamond, I pay my gold; the diamond is receipt and bond. I like it best. This gold shall into diamonds change—the profits of my trade. Yes, yes—it shall be diamonds, when next to Singapore I go.'

" 'But why not deposit in a bank until you need it?'

"He gave me one of his cunning sidelong glances. 'Ah-h!— too many banks have I seen break. No, no. I will my own bank be. Your friend the captain tell you true—De Long, he hold his own.'

"The woman laughed again, a laugh of childish amusement. 'He sleeps with it!' she said, tossing me a cigarette. 'In depths of night he sweats and groans.'

"Her words brought a picture, and I marveled—marveled to think of the possibilities, and of De Long's incredible fatuity. Or was it his miserliness, irresistibly requiring the touch of every dollar that he owned? He was too sharp a man to have overlooked the danger; but a force stronger than reason held him in its power. These are the forces that differentiate us, that balk our best attempts to reduce life to a formula; they are dominant, inexorable, like deep and mighty currents sweeping us toward the brink of an abyss. So De Long drifted. Well enough now, perhaps; it was evident that the woman had no knowledge of the value of money. One might have expected her to covet the diamonds; but they were a part of De Long, loathsome and detestable, the product of trade; and besides, remember, her unsophisticated heart was busy just then upon a problem of different values, of values whose knowledge runs in the blood, whose lore is drawn in with the breath of desires and days. But when that problem was solved it occurred to me that her heart would be free to follow other matters.

"Soon afterwards we heard the rattle of my boat's oars at the landing. I'd had my fill of Anjer and De Long; his provisions were coming off in the morning, and if the breeze favored I planned to get away at noon. The two of them accompanied me with a lantern to the landing; for under the great banyan lay a darkness like the night of an eclipse. De Long overflowed with thanks and professions of friendliness; he would see me on board in the morning.

"To the woman I held out my hand. With a movement imperceptible in the deep shadow that fell across the landing she clasped my fingers for a moment—crushed them wildly, passionately, with a touch that burned like fire. She did not speak. I drew my hand away. As we backed out with the boat she stood apart from De Long, watching our departure. Diamonds and gold she had laughed at, and put aside. I saw her turn suddenly and disappear into the deeper shadow. Grunting and swearing, De Long hurried after. I was glad on the whole, to get into open water again, out from under the stifling lee of the land.

IV

"I thought of them often in the next few years," Nichols went on. "At a distance, and after an appropriate interval, the woman became only a super-numerary; De Long was the force, the central figure in that uncomfortable drama. There he sat, like a great toad squatting in the midst of a garden of flowers; there he went about his business, a miserable, unmanly, immoral creature, chained by his destiny to a passionate island and married to a daughter of the land; divided between greed and doting love, treading the mill of anger and malice, of hatred and revenge; and surrounding himself daily, no doubt, with those enemies which fear and jealousy conjure out of the very air. He probably suffered excruciatingly. And then I'd think of his fortune, a waistcoat lined with gold and diamonds, and worn day and night like a supplementary skin that had formed over him by action of the worldliness that he was so fond of preaching. Yes, there was much about him to tell of, and to remember. I looked forward to a second meeting with the man.

"Quite a number of years passed before this opportunity came my way; but when I did finally reach Old Anjer for another visit it was as if the world hadn't moved while I'd been gone. De Long met me in the Roads; I went ashore in his boat, stepped out on the strip of white beach that gleamed and glistened as if it had received a scrubbing every morning, and was ushered through the aisles of the banyan to his house, that stood facing its enclosure still half-cleared, still dirty, still littered with broken boxes, strips of torn paper, straw, old clothes, and fruit and vegetables in various stages of decay. De Long himself didn't seem a day older; the banyan had been so tremendous before that if it had grown in the interval the change was impossible to mark; and when we reached the house the Eurasian woman stood on the veranda, as young and pretty as I remembered her. She greeted me with a disinterested air; her coolness and indifference struck me unexpectedly—the only thing I'd met, so far, that seemed to indicate a change of time.

"De Long seemed genuinely glad to see me. He disclosed a more human side; chattered on with a certain freedom and relief, told me all the news of ships that had come his way, and made me feel in some unaccountable manner that I'd arrived at a welcome moment. I fancied that the old beggar was lonesome.

"The woman, as I said, was impassive, unconcerned. Not that I would have had it otherwise; but it's hard to define accurately what I'd anticipated or how I felt. I may have been disappointed; I may have been a little piqued, taking it as a personal matter.

The male animal of the human species is ridiculously sensitive to notions of this sort; and much of our virtue is streaked with broad dashes of regret. A man doesn't relish being utterly overlooked by a woman who once held his hand a trifle too long. For a while I was in quite a state of mind over the situation.

"After supper De Long and I sat on his little veranda, and blew smoke into the silent night. The woman didn't come out to roll cigarettes for us, as she had done the time before; and finally I asked De Long in a casual way where she was. He swore violently, striking the veranda-rail with clenched fist. 'How shall I know?' he cried. 'How shall I know?' The words tore from him, jarred the night, brought back the past in all its distress and misery. It seemed inconceivable that the same suffering of hearts had been going on here all this time. It occurred to me that no other ship lay in the Roads. I made no answer; but De Long wished to continue the confidence. 'An unhappy man am I!' he said, after a pause. 'Always worse and worse. Captain, what is the end?'

"I made an effort to swing him onto another track. 'Is Shute still in business over there?' I asked, nodding my head in the direction of the rival ship-chandlery.

"It was the very thing I shouldn't have said. De Long heaved himself up like a mad elephant, stamping and ranging till the whole house trembled, launching a string of filthy names toward the store in the opposite enclosure. 'Ha!—young devil!' he screamed. Young whelp of hell!' He shook his fists aloft, blaspheming the sky. Suddenly the paroxysm subsided; he sank breathless into a chair. For some moments he sat without speech or motion, an inert mountain of flesh, a lump of foulness and despair. 'A year ago,' he said at last, 'since now Shute sold the business. A good man was Shute; with him I have trouble most honorable. He fights for business, not for wives. Now comes this dog of the dung-hill, this young—' He choked, and covered his face with his hands.

"I saw too clearly what had come about: the woman had learned her values, had found her dream. She was free in the world of love. 'Why don't you let him take her?' I asked.

" 'No! Never!' cried De Long.

" 'But why not?' I insisted. 'Think of the facts.'

" 'Because he does not want her,' said De Long, dropping the pose swiftly, like a mask, and disclosing a face tortured by hope-

less anxiety. 'Because he does not love her. Because to her he
would be bad.' I felt his fingers drumming on my knee with a
machine-like beat. 'See, Captain,' he said. 'She loves him. For
months have I seen it. That, and more. But am I a fool, Captain,
that I know not men? Love?—pah! Oh, yes, he is young, fiery—
perhaps he loves a little, since to another she belongs. Not
much. Not as she loves. Ah!—I know men. I read the eye, when
at me he looks. It is me he loves!'

" 'You!' I exclaimed, for the moment not catching the point.

" 'Me,' said De Long, tapping his waistcoat significantly. 'My
fortune!' Suddenly he clutched his bosom with both hands
crossed at the wrist, as if covering as much as he could of his
precious fortune. 'They think it is, that I soon die,' he snarled,
like an animal at bay. 'In the eyes I read it. "When will this old
De Long die?" He loves my fortune; and now also, her mind upon
it runs.' With a great effort he heaved himself up and stood before
me. 'They shall not have it!' he cried hoarsely. 'Many years will
I live!'

" 'Is your secret generally known?' I asked in surprise.

"He shook his head. 'I think, not so. From her he has it. But
of what he tells, how can a man be sure?'

" 'Probably he has told no one,' I said. 'De Long, for a man of
years and business, you've been a desperate fool. Now then, why
don't you give this fellow some of your money—pay him to take
your wife away? That might satisfy the both of them.'

" 'Never!' he cried resolutely, as if a point of honor were
involved. 'Not a dollar! No, no! Many years will I live!'

" 'I doubt it,' I observed. 'They'll kill you the first chance they
get.'

" 'Doubtless,' he said phlegmatically. 'For that, am I prepared.
I sleep little, and always armed. In the village I take my meals. I
am much away.'

" 'There's still another solution,' I pointed out, curious for the
last word of such a consistent philosophy. "You can shoot the
fellow, you know, and get him out of the way altogether.'

" 'Only young men shoot,' said De Long.

" 'Are you afraid?'

"De Long had resumed his seat; holding the tips of his fat
fingers together he examined them intently in the bright moonlight. 'Perhaps,' he said at length. 'You like the truth. Consider,

Captain, truth which is never spoken. When have you shoot a man? Ha!—much you know. Tell me, to deal with death who is not afraid?'

"The following morning it remained a flat calm, with no indication of a breeze. De Long had been on board early, left some provisions, and said good-bye; but in the middle of the forenoon, having written a letter that I wanted to get into the mail, and seeing only native canoes about the ship, I sent the dinghy overboard and had myself rowed ashore. 'De Long is on the river,' they told me at the landing. 'He will return at noon.' Noon was rather an indefinite quantity at Anjer; the sun already stood high, no breeze touched the Straits, and I decided to waste a little time on shore. 'I'll wait for him on the veranda,' I said, and started off through the aisles of the banyan.

"I had no intention of stealth or silence. Walking with my eyes on the ground, alone in the oppressive midday heat of the land, and very much occupied with my own thoughts, I mounted the steps and was about to take a chair. There I looked up for the first time, and beheld a strange spectacle. Directly in front of me within the house, and a little to one side of a curtained window, stood De Long's wife clasped in the arms of a big upstanding half-breed Malay, both of them oblivious to the world. He was a fine figure of a man, tall, lithe, handsome, as are most of that blood; just the fellow, I saw instantly, that she had been seeking so long. He held her closely while they spoke in low tones; her eyes devoured him, her love emanated from her as if she had shouted it aloud. They hadn't noticed me. I waited a few moments, rooted to the floor, annoyed with myself for having blundered into such a silly position, and hoping minute by minute they would go away. Suddenly my embarrassment became mortifying; I backed noiselessly off the veranda and made my escape unobserved to the landing. It was the last time that I saw the woman in Old Anjer.

"A short while later I saw De Long, too, for the last time. As I made off from the landing in my dinghy, his whaleboat appeared at the mouth of the river; he'd been along the shore to a neighboring village, it seemed, instead of inland, as they had told me. He hauled up and waited for me; then turned at my invitation and followed me aboard to dinner. During the meal a breeze sprang up from the westward and I was for getting away at once.

We talked for half an hour on the quarter deck, while they were heaving up the anchor forward. Poor old De Long, his manner seemed more artificial than ever; in an effort to impress me, he cringed, fawned, and had an outrageous fit of servility. I estimated it as his best attempt at an expression of friendliness, and took it for what it was worth. One could hardly refrain from feeling a bit sorry for the unhappy reprobate; and particularly now, when the woman needed nobody's sympathy. He hung over the rail, gazing into the water with vacant eyes, and seemed reluctant to leave.

"'No use is life!' he whimpered. 'Ah!—this world. A good place to forget. See, Captain, even the heavens fall.' He pointed prophetically to the westward, into the wind, where the volcano of Krakatoa stood, a lone peak far out in the center of the Straits, surrounded by a pall of smoke and cloud. It had always threatened more or less, but never before had I seen it so active. The ship's deck was gritty from fine ashes sifting through the air. A few flakes lodged on De Long's outstretched hand, and he held them over for me to see. I shook my head; together we glanced aloft. The sky since noon had grown the color of copper; a lurid glow like a fire by night had taken the place of the sun. I was anxious to get away.

"I watched De Long as he was being rowed toward the shore— toward days of apprehension and nights of terror, toward hatred, treachery, and the accumulated evil of his own unworthy existence, recoiling upon him at the end of life. We'd parted at the rail. He sat huddled in the stern sheets of the boat like a man bowed under a weight of years and sorrow. But what really was bowing him over, I remember with unvarnished precision, was the weight of a fortune in gold and diamonds. He was sinking beneath a load of worldly collateral; I fancied the stern of the boat was going down.

"He passed out of sight behind the point; I raised my eyes and saw the coast of Java, blooming, luxuriant, wild with the impulse of creative life. The breeze flurried unevenly, and a breath of the earth was wafted through the air—a breath heavy with moisture, a vigorous smell of the jungle and the hills. The atmosphere had become stifling, superheated; under the lurid light the green of the land took on a dark and somber tone. Even then, that coast was doomed. The waves from Krakatoa wiped across the face of it like mighty hands, and left it desolate. Life, love, and the petty affairs of men were swallowed and swept away by a sea such as the world had never known.

V

"I was far up the China Sea when it happened, some weeks later. The wave itself didn't reach us, around so many islands and over so much shallow water; although we had tremendous and irregular tides that day. Across the open Pacific that wave had passed in a solid mound, bearing down upon unsuspecting ships and lifting them for one tremendous instant high above the floor of the sea; it had washed fiercely on the opposite coast of South America, hours later and thousands of miles away. But we, comparatively near in a land-locked harbor on the China coast, knew by the condition of the atmosphere that something fearful and momentous had taken place. A red curtain fell above us, shutting out the sun; objects half a mile away were obscured by a murky crimson mist, as if the heavens were raining fine streams of blood. Men left their work to look and listen, chattering, praying, gathering in companies, waiting frantically in the ghastly dusk for a nameless fate to be revealed. And then the reports came drifting in; reports of flood and fire, reports of a cataclysm of nature, reports of towns inundated, of islands totally destroyed, of sea turning to land and land to sea; reports of great ships flung like driftwood against the Java hills.

"Day after day in the terrible red twilight, we heard of disaster and devastation and death, until our nerves were shattered and our hearts grew afraid. That horror might break out again, it might portend the destruction of the world; many a night I turned in with the thought that I stood a chance of never seeing another morning. For days the sun didn't appear, and no rain fell; the air had turned to reddish dust, the light was more appalling than the darkness; one had the feeling that off beyond the horizon a monstrous fire burned savagely, consuming continents and islands, eating its way along the shores. I knew by rote the lay of the land in Sunda, and the accounts were very real to me. Krakatoa had literally blown up, according to the best information. The Straits were reported as closed, impassable; a huge island had risen between Java and Sumatra. The floating pumice caused this tale. Soon ships began to straggle in, with yarns that took our breath away. The heavens had rained fiery rocks on their decks, and steam from the boiling sea had risen above the royal yard. Ships buried in ashes, gray from truck to water-line, ashes in the cabins, a fine sifting of ashes in the farthest part of the lower hold; ships with charred decks and blistered paint, burned to a crisp, as it were. These were the vessels that had been in the neighborhood, but at a safe distance, about the Java Sea or coming up outside in the Indian Ocean. But in their most extrav-agant accounts they couldn't have equalled the reality, couldn't have approximated the awful upheaval, the concussion, the surge of waters, the eruption of smoke and flame, that must suddenly have been loosed in the narrow and sharply confined area of the Straits of Sunda. It was a good year afterward that I saw the place; and the ruin fairly staggered the mind.

"I had thought often of De Long, concluding that he was dead. Everyone in the coast villages, according to report, had been killed. An exaggeration, of course; many had escaped to the hills. But how could De Long, a mountain of sluggishness, have got away? I inquired diligently, but could hear no word of him. There was a bare chance that he had been absent from Anjer at the time, though he'd given up his piloting business of late years. I thought of him constantly that morning, as I came down the Straits and approached the spot where I'd seen him go out of sight behind a point fringed with palm trees, where I'd looked up and said good-bye to Old Anjer and the Java shore. The ship pushed her way through wide fields of pumice floating like flat, gray reefs on the muddy surface of the water. The land was gray and deso-late; it had a barren appearance, as if a gigantic rake had passed over the hillsides, uprooting trees like grass. Bleak spurs that I couldn't place in memory, stuck out like fangs from the coast; I sailed by them sadly, lost in uncharted waters, on the shore of an evil dream.

"Off toward Sumatra, the island which had been Krakatoa now seemed to be a number of islands. I'd known it as a perfect cone, a clean landmark rising from the water's edge to a height of over two thousand feet. The peak of it had evidently split, and the smaller section had fallen bodily outboard. You fellows recall the mark, an enormous chip riven from the side of the cone; but you've seen its outline softened by years of wind and weather.

That day it stood out roughly, and I beheld the sky through what had once been solid land.

"And you've seen the Straits of Sunda, too, since God reclaimed them, since the heart of the land burst forth again, and the palms sprang up, and the breeze forgot the message of death and the songs of mourners on the hills. They say that it's more luxuriant than before, that the fall of ashes marvelously enriched the soil. Perhaps. Time passes, and life takes up its work; the seeds of flowers come down with the evening breezes, the men return, and words of love are whispered under the moon. Nothing kills us but unbelief. And I have seen Java, green and living again; it welcomes me as of old with a breath of the land-smell, with hope and faith and joy. But it was a melancholy prospect that day of my return. Why, I had difficulty in locating the very mouth of the river where Old Anjer had been.

"A few woe-begone natives came off in a lopsided dugout, as I drifted into the roadstead of Old Anjer; but not a face among them could I recognize. I asked about the eruption; they held up their hands and answered by exclamations only. It was a matter beyond speech. The world had ended amid mountains of water and sheets of flame; they had seen it, and still lived. They knew no more. They had escaped into the hills.

"After glancing them over I took the most intelligent looking man aside. I wanted to find out two things—De Long's fate, and what had happened to the banyan tree. I had a deep curiosity to hear about the banyan tree. The man told me that it was gone. It seemed impossible. Thousands of trunks and branches as strong as iron, covering acres of shore, filling the sky with magnificence—gone!

" 'Where?' I asked.

" 'No one knows,' he answered. 'The wave came, and it was gone.'

"I closed my eyes trying to picture the scene. 'Where were you?' I inquired.

" 'On the hills,' he said. 'High!' Held his arms aloft to signify a great altitude. 'The wave reached me, but it was spent,' he said with awe.

" 'Did De Long escape?' I asked.

"The man shook his head. 'I passed him on the road. They

fought, and De Long was already dying. Many have searched, but without avail.'

" 'What do you mean?' I demanded. 'Who fought?'

" 'De Long and the other. I had newly come to the village, and did not know his name.'

" 'The Malay who kept the store?'

" 'Yes.' My informant hesitated, regarding me narrowly. 'De Long your friend?' he asked.

"I nodded. 'What were they fighting about?'

" 'I heard strange words.' Again the man hesitated, shifting his feet excitedly. 'De Long had gold and diamonds!' he exclaimed. 'Tell me if this be true?'

"It seemed like a message from beyond the grave. The precious secret had escaped, had survived death and the flood. I might have known. 'Yes,' I answered. 'De Long carried a fortune. His coat was lined with diamonds and gold. You have searched, you say?'

" 'Ah!—night and day we search,' cried the man. 'On every shore. With hooks we drag in deep water; and in shallow water we dive from boats.' He pointed inshore. 'See, they search now, where the river makes a bar.'

"I lifted my glasses, and beheld the naked forms of men leaping from a canoe. Their dark heads bobbed in the water, the sunlight flashed on their shoulders . . . they were diving for the fortune of De Long! That wave had swept him off the Straits; the bones of his fat body lay somewhere on the bottom, anchored by his gold. And these men swam about, or prowled the beaches, looking for the treasure to be cast up by the sea. It was romantic. They should have been clearing away the ruin, building homes, cultivating the land; heaven and earth and the waters under the earth had given them warning, such warning as is seldom vouchsafed to creatures inhabiting a quiet and well-ordered world. But they searched instead for a dead man's gold.

"And then I thought of the woman. She hadn't cared for the fortune, she wouldn't be searching for it now. What of her and her lover?—they probably had got away. I turned to ask the native; but he was already over the side, in violent conversation with his crew. I'd given them news indeed, revived their failing hopes; they were off in a flurry, splashing and straining, lest those

fellows inshore should steal a march on them. I felt no regret for
my words; they had reared a fitting monument to the memory of
De Long.

"Soon afterward I filled away. There was nothing to stay for,
nobody to see. I wanted to leave the place as soon as the breeze
would let me, to get it out of sight and out of mind. I was bound
to Batavia that voyage, and had to fight my way around San
Nicholas through vast fields of pumice stone. The Thousand
Islands were full of the stuff; the harbor of Batavia was full of it
when I arrived. Reminders of the eruption cropped up on every
hand; it entered into all conversation, it hung over the life of
Batavia like a pall of its own ashy cloud. And I hadn't been there
many weeks when the scene was again brought home to me—
brought home in the flesh, by the only soul I knew in Old Anjer
who had survived.

VI

"I sat alone one evening in a certain café in the heart of the
town, where I often took my dinner. Dusk was coming on; a
calm, still evening, full of the cool essence of night that you find
so often in ports where the sea breeze has been drawing in all the
afternoon. I took out a cigar, leaned back to enjoy my smoke; and
a woman came toward me, walking alone among the tables. She
was slight and graceful, dressed in a gown of dark color and
becoming lines. When she had almost reached me she looked
up—and we recognized each other. She stopped dead; then
dropped into the chair opposite, and gazed at me for some time
without speaking.

" 'You!' she said at last. 'You here?'

"I nodded, a whirl of thoughts revolving in my mind. She
hadn't been lost at Anjer, then. Where was her lover? What had
happened: I hesitated to ask. 'How did you escape?' was my first
question.

"She caught her breath, struggling with a deep emotion. 'I
went into the hills.' The inevitable answer! All who escaped
had gone into the hills.

" 'They told me at Anjer that De Long was dead,' I ventured;
it was the only fact I knew.

" 'Ah, De Long!' she cried in a low voice. 'Yes!—all were lost.

All!' She looked straight ahead with motionless eyes. 'I alone escaped,' she said bitterly. 'I should have died also, but the fear of death was upon me, and I ran. He told me to save myself, and left me for De Long. I was mad with pain. I ran, and God has cursed me with life yet to live!'

" 'They—they both died?' I asked.

" 'Both,' she answered. 'Both are gone.' She struck the table with clenched hands. 'Gone! Gone! Gone! What do I care? I love him no longer!'

" 'Why couldn't they get away with you into the hills?'

" 'The fortune delayed them,' she said in a hard, scornful voice. 'De Long could not run. The fortune was too heavy, and he was too fat. One wave had come already, a big wave, but small before those which came after. I ran to Saka, urging him to fly with me. I thought that he loved me. Ah, I was blind!' Holding her head erect, she closed her eyes, as if waiting for a blow to fall. 'He cared more to save De Long!' she cried suddenly. 'The fortune—the gold which De Long kept here, the diamonds—God! I went to him, thinking still that he loved me. I touched his hand. He was angry, and struck me on the breast. He bade me save myself. He and De Long fought together, rolling upon the ground. I heard them. Then I saw!'

"She gripped the table, swaying slightly in her chair. 'A great sound shook the air. The heavens were full of thunder, and fire streamed from the clouds. I feared death, and ran.' She paused. 'I stood on the hills, looking back,' she said. 'I cannot remember; I knew that he did not love me. All below vanished, and the wave came to my feet. It had covered him. Ah!' She bowed her head.

"How clear she made it. I saw the day, the darkness pierced by flame; I heard the roar of the wave. It had given scant warning. Imagine them starting to escape, an odd trio; the woman light and strong with the courage of love, leading the way, calling on the man to fly with her; the man stripped to the truth at last, striking her off in anger, turning to help De Long; De Long, crazed with fear, fat, breathless, undone, but clinging to his fortune in the face of death! When the man had seen that De Long could go no farther, the fight had begun—struggling, tearing, snarling, cursing, shouting aloud the incredible secret for men who paused wonderingly in their flight—the one hugging

his hoard desperately, the other beating down resistance, searching for buttons, trying to shake the great body loose from the
thing—all sanity, all reality, long since fled; while above them
the heavens split and thundered, and below them the waters
rushed to their destruction.

"She had stood on the hillside and looked back. I seem to see
her, a lonely figure poised above an abandoned world, con-
fronting with dazed and vacant eyes the might of the naked
elements, the awful wrath of God. She couldn't remember—she
had been thinking of lost love.

" 'And now you live in Batavia?' I observed aimlessly.

" 'I live in Batavia,' she said. 'I have no friends.'

" 'Once I was your friend,' I told her. It seemed the least that
I could say.

" 'Yes—I remember. You would not look, or speak to me. Ah,
I was young!'

" 'Can you do nothing—' I floundered.

" 'Nothing!' she said defiantly. 'I shall never love again. Oh, I
am not unhappy. Perhaps some day I dare to kill myself, and then
all will be well. I should have died at Anjer. I was a coward.'

"I reached in my pocket and took out all the money that I had.
This I pushed across the table. I was afraid that she wouldn't take
it, but could see no other way. 'It is yours,' I said. 'I sail to-morrow. I may not see you again.'

"She glanced at the money, then looked up at me. Two tears
came in her eyes; she brushed them sharply away. 'You are kind,'
she said. 'I need it.' Was it kindness or money that she needed?
I have never known.

"I left her sitting at the table. 'Good-bye,' she said bravely.
'When will you come to Batavia again?'

" 'I can't be sure. I'm in Singapore more often.'

" 'Perhaps some day I will go to Singapore.'

" 'Then good-bye, for a time,' I said. It was useless to stay
longer. A whiff of land breeze swept through the court, a breeze
like the night air coming down from the Anjer hills; and I went
out into the moonlight to forget her—if I could."

CARRYING SAIL

"Now, indecision is bad," said Dashy Noyes. "It's bad enough on land; it's worse aboard a ship. Cap'n Tripp had indecision—had it in his vitals, so to speak. A good master, a thorough seaman, a perfect gentleman; but bewildered by nature, sort o' boneless. Not in the body, he warn't—'twas all bones there. A tall, lank, gawky man, and homelier than mud. His face was mostly nose; a tuft o' whiskers took the place of his chin. His eyes was a whitish color; ten foot away you couldn't make 'em out. And he was slow, and soft-spoken, and uncertain; and when he give an order it was either too soon, or too late, or the thing never needed to be done. His special anxiety was carryin' sail.

"We was bound on the regulation China passage, case-oil to Hong Kong and general cargo home. I'd never seen the *Vigilant* or Cap'n Tripp before; but she happened to need a mate, and about that time I happened to need a job, so we decided to call it square.

"We sailed in mid-winter, on the tail of a nor'wester. The wind was dead aft and howlin', and the weather fine; but what did Cap'n Tripp do, when we dropped the towboat, but keep her down to lower topsails. There we was joggin' off at six or seven knots, when we might ha' been makin' twelve. The second day out I couldn't stand it any longer.

" 'Don't you want to set them upper topsails, Cap'n?' I asks, comin' aft to where he was standin' on the poop.

"He looks aloft and all around the horizon. 'No-o-o, I guess we'll let her run along easy,' he says in his deliberate way. 'You don't gain much, in the end, by carryin' sail.'

" 'Well, sir, if you call this carryin' sail—'

" 'I don't know,' he says, lookin' aloft again. 'I suppose she might stand the main upper topsail.'

" 'Stand!' I cries. 'She'd stand three royals!' 'Twas disrespect-
ful, but this joggin' along had strained my nerve.

" 'Three royals, Mr. Noyes?' asks Cap'n Tripp. 'Now, you
don't mean three royals, I guess. You young fellers are so extrav-
agant. We'll try her with the main upper topsail, and see how she
behaves.'

"I'd called the men and sent a couple of 'em aloft to loose the
sail, when I see the Old Man wave his hand. Thinkin' he probably wanted the men to loose the mainsail while they was on the
mast, I run aft to get the order.

" 'I guess we won't set it, after all, Mr. Noyes,' says he.

" 'Not set the upper topsail, sir?' I asks.

" 'No, not just now. I'll feel safer to let her run as she is.'

"I wondered what was in the wind. Cap'n Tripp seemed too
young a man to be in his dotage. I knew he wasn't drunk. So soft
and gentlemanly, and so dam nonsensical! I laughed and laughed,
as I went forrard to call down the men from the topsail yard.

"Most o' the day the Old Man shambled back and forth on the
quarter deck; and, knowin' him as I do now, I can understand
that this weighty problem was worryin' him distracted. Had he
ought to set that topsail? . . . Would she stand it? . . . O' course
she would! . . . Still, it was blowin' pretty stiff. . . . Better keep it
furled. . . . And yet, maybe, 'twould be well to set it. A very complicated, interestin' man was Cap'n Tripp. I enjoyed him thoroughly on the passage out; I didn't care what sort o' time we made.

"That gale soon backed into the nor'ard; and with each shift o'
wind the Old Man kept her off before it till finally we was runnin'
a due south course, still under them cussed lower topsails.

" 'Looks like a northeaster blowin' up, Cap'n,' I remarks a few
days later, as we was takin' the sun at noon.

" 'Yes, yes,' he answers, nervous. By the look in his eye you'd
think he was caught on a desperate lee-shore. 'But I hate to heave
her to, Mr. Noyes,' he says.

" 'One thing sure, sir,' I points out. 'You'll have your troubles
crossin' the Line, unless you get farther to windward in the
northeast trades.' Why, there we was runnin' south in fifty-five
west longitude!

" 'I know it!' says he. 'I know it. But the wind is liable to
change. I hate to heave her to. I guess we'll let her run a while
longer and see how the weather pans out.'

" 'You can go a-cruisin' in the West Injes, for all I care,' says I to myself, and goes off laughin.'

"The weather panned out rich. Next mornin' come a livin' gale out o' the northeast; the sea picked up surprisin'. And still we run before it, pointin' for Cuba and the Banks o' the Bahamas. Began to look as if we'd chase around the Atlantic till a favorin' breeze happened to shoot us across the Line.

"The sea was pretty bad that day, with a sharp, snappin' lift that kept her rollin' heavy. Along in the middle of the mornin' the Old Man come forrard a-wringin' his hands.

" 'I don't like this rollin', Mr. Noyes,' he says. 'It's bad for the masts.'

" 'Yes, sir,' I remarks.

" 'I don't hardly like to heave her to,' he says.

" 'Fly, sir,' I suggests.

" 'Mr. Noyes,' he says, reproachful, 'this is a serious matter. It's blowin' on harder every minute. We must decide what's best to do.'

" 'Heave her to, sir, and get it over with,' I says. 'She'll lay easy in the wind.'

" 'Yes,' he says, 'I guess I will. D'you suppose she'll come around without much fuss?'

" 'Cap'n,' I says, 'to tell you the honest truth, I think that with man's ingenuity and help o' Providence, we may be able to bring her into the wind.'

" 'Well, get ready forrard,' he says at last. Till he put the wheel over I was in a cold sweat for fear he'd change his mind.

"Indecision, you understand—he warn't a timid man. Once on a given tack, he hated to go about. 'Twas like pullin' teeth for him to say yes or no. Neither was he incompetent; he knew too cussed well what ought to be done. That was what worried him. But he couldn't quite make up his mind to do it, least-wise not till afterward; and when he'd said the word he'd wish he hadn't, and go and try to take it back. I figured that life must ha' been distressin' hard for the Old Man Tripp. A man who'd rather go hungry than pick out a breakfast from the bill o' fare, ain't what you might call well-fitted for a world o' pull-and-haul.

"And o' course luck went against him right along. Why, Cap'n Tripp lost more sails that voyage, for all his caution, than some cap'ns I've sailed with would blow away in a natural lifetime. The sails seemed bewitched. In calm weather they'd slat themselves to pieces against the mast; and whenever a puff o' wind struck it always carried off a sail or two. Sails would split and open up before our eyes; jibs would go clean from the bolt-ropes in the night, and we wouldn't discover the loss till mornin'. 'Twas a standin' joke with the second mate and me; we'd place a little bet on what would be the next to go.

"But the worst mess was in the doldrums. Yes, we did get down to the Line, by hook or crook, I don't exactly remember how. One evening at eight bells, we sighted a heavy squall to windward. Just then, the Old Man poked his head out o' the companionway.

" 'Squall to windward, sir,' I says. 'I'll take in the royals before I leave the deck.'

" 'Well,' says he, 'I guess you'd better let 'em stand. We'll wait and see what's in it.'

" 'Wind, sir,' I says. I knew the look o' that squall.

" 'Well, maybe it ain't much,' says he. 'I don't want to take in the royals just yet.'

"I lit my pipe and went below, leavin' the watch to the second mate. Pretty soon the old hooker bends a little to the breeze. No sound o' takin' in sail. Then down she heels with a sickenin' lurch, the gear snappin' aloft and the wind roaring overhead. I braces my feet in the corner o' the bunk, and keeps my pipe goin'. She righted little by little; somethin' strange was happenin' to her. At last it come to me—the Old Man was droppin' off before the wind rather than take in them royals.

"Then the main squall struck, and things began to happen one after the other. Pretty soon I heard the spanker boom go over— bang! Pretty soon it come back again—bang! Pretty soon broke out a terrible slattin' aloft. 'Ah-ha!' says I. 'Royals comin' in without assistance.' Bang! went the spanker boom, and all the dishes in the pantry jumped. 'Surge old spunyarn!' I says. 'He'll take the anointed masts out of her!' Any minute I expected to get a yardarm in the stomach, or the heel o' the mizzen topmast in the jaw.

"Soon I hears the Old Man hollerin' through the cabin. I has just time to tuck away my pipe and compose my features in slumber when he busts open the door. Bang! crash! goes the boom overhead. He jumps a clean two feet from the deck, and his jaw drops as he looks at me.

" '*Asleep!*' he screams. 'How can you *sleep*, Mr. Noyes, at a time like this?'

"I sits up and rubs my eyes. 'What's the trouble, Cap'n?' I asks.

" 'Trouble?' he yells. 'Listen! Can't you *hear?*'

" 'That squall must ha' struck, sir,' I observes.

"He gives me one witherin' look, and slams the door.

"When I reached the deck the fur was flyin'. She'd come into the wind again; the lee rail was level with the water. 'Twas a devil of a squall. Some able seaman had mistook the main topsail halyards for the fore topgallant brace, and let it go by the run; the yard had fetched up solid, broken into pieces, and both ends of it was rippin' up the belly o' the mainsail. Nobody knew what sails was left, and what was gone. Cap'n Tripp stood aft with folded arms, sayin' not a word. Things was makin' up their own minds about it too swift to follow.

"But the masts stayed by her, and the squall soon passed over. We cleaned her up as best we could. And then the Old Man commenced to fume and fret.

" 'What fool let go them topsail halyards?' he cries.

" 'That's somethin', Cap'n, that we'll never know,' I says.

" 'You can't splice a yard that's broke in the middle!'

" 'No, sir. There's a spare yard on deck. We'll send that up in the mornin'.'

" 'But it's the only spare spar aboard.'

" 'Yes, sir.'

" 'Now, what'll we do for sails, I'd like to know? I don't hardly want to bend the heavy-weather sails, here in the doldrums.'

" 'Better anchor, sir, and think it over.' I suggests.

" 'I wish to God I could!' he says; and the heartfelt way he brought it out tickled me down to my boots. After a while I persuaded him to go below. I reckon he'd have ended by leavin' her as she stood, there was so many different ways that everything could ha' been done.

"Well, in a few days we had her in runnin' order again. The rest o' the passage turned out fairly quiet. We pegged along and got to Anjer, hitched along up the China Sea, and managed to arrive at Hong Kong in a hundred and forty days. And more and more, as I sailed with him, I come to like the Old Man Tripp. I can't say why. He tickled me; but that warn't all. I liked him. He meant right in his heart. 'Twas the fault o' the world that he didn't make more showin'. Figure it down to rock bottom, it come to this: the man warn't selfish enough. He'd always given in to someone else; and the habit had knocked the tar completely out of him.

"The first evenin' in Hong Kong I took an hour o' comfort at the rail. Sails was unbent and stowed away. All along the slope o' the hill the lights was twinklin', and the air smelled o' land. Ships lay around us, a whole fleet o' square-rigged vessels. As I leaned there, smokin' my pipe, the Old Man Tripp come up to me.

" 'Seems good to be at anchor, sir, don't it?' I says. 'I ain't been to Hong Kong for several years.'

" 'Mr. Noyes,' says he, 'I thank God every time I arrive in port. I'm gettin' almost too old to go to sea.'

" 'You don't like it very well, sir?' I asks.

" 'It worries me more and more,' he says. 'No, I was never cut out for the sea.'

" 'Some men are born for it,' I says, 'and others don't jibe with it from the first.'

" 'Just so,' he says. 'That's it, exactly. They force themselves to go. All the boys is goin', and there don't seem nothin' else to do. They force themselves to learn, to rise; and when they get a ship, what do they find? No heart in it. The years stretch off ahead like a hopeless job. Then, maybe, they meet hard luck.' He passed his hand across his face, and heaved a sigh.

" 'It's a thankless life at best, sir.' I chimes in.

" 'It is,' he says. 'I suppose you think you know all about it. I suppose you laugh at me behind my back. I've gone by the corner. A queer old customer. Well, Mr. Noyes, I guess I know too much. There is such a thing.'

"The ship *Paul Revere* lay in Hong Kong that time. Dan Sands was mate of her, a chum o' mine from home. We figured that we'd be sailin' for New York together; and evenin's when we was callin' on each other, we'd joke over the race. I told Dan all about the Old Man Tripp and his ways o' carryin' sail.

" 'Some day when you sight a ship on the Line hove-to under a goose-winged topsail, that's us,' I'd say. 'Or maybe you might see us on the Coast in a howlin' northeaster, with royals set. If ever they do get *set*, they're liable to stay so till they blow away. If you happen to notice three royals without bolt-ropes passin' on the breeze, you'll know that we're somewhere to wind-ward bendin' sail.'

" 'The *Paul Revere* is a clipper, my boy,' he'd answer. 'You won't stand a ghost of a show with us. We'll beat you by about thirty or forty days.'

"I'd joke with Dan; but just the same it made me mad. If the *Vigilant* had been a slow old tub I might ha' stood it with a better grace; but I'd seen enough of her to know that with proper handlin' she would *sail*. 'Twas indecision that held her back. When Dan Sands waved his hand to me from the *Paul Revere*, as we was goin' out by Green Island side by side, I vowed that I'd find some way to make a decent passage home.

"Luck favored us for a good long while. We parted company with the *Paul Revere* on the second day out, and had an easy run down the China Sea. The Old Man Tripp was familiar with Eastern waters; and, as I'd said, we got the royals set and so they stayed. When we passed Anjer our rival hadn't put in an appearance. I began to have a sneakin' hope that we might beat them after all.

"The weather seemed made to order for Cap'n Tripp, a fair wind most o' the time, not too light and not too strong. It did him a world o' good. The vessel sailed herself; as days went by without the necessity o' comin' to a decision, he brightened up and took on flesh. And as for me, I prayed. I'd dodge the Old Man around the deck; I'd hardly dare to speak to him at table. For I knew that when the spell did break 'twould be without rhyme or reason.

"We rounded the Cape o' Good Hope with royals set, and took the trades across the South Atlantic. Says I to myself, 'Watch out, and stand from under!' But the southeast trades carried us without a break to the Line; and after a few day's o' doldrums, we picked up the northeasters on the other side, and started on the last leg o' the passage. Never was such a slant. Seventy days we'd been from Hong Kong to the Line in the Atlantic, no slouch of a run in old tea-clipper times. I begun to paint and polish up the *Vigilant* for port, plannin' what I'd say to Dan when he come stragglin' in.

"But a voyage ain't over till the anchor's down. The third day of the northeast trades it breezed on heavy; if they wants to, you know, the trades can blow up a swingein' buck of a wind. The

Old Man paced the quarter deck, skittish but undecided. In one way, I see, the long rest had been bad for him; he'd forgotten how annoyin' a breeze might be. He'd stop and cast his eye aloft, then look to windward, then walk off aft with his hands behind his back, and examine the wake in a brown study. I knew the symptoms; my heart dropped into my boots. And all the while the wind kept breezin' on.

"At eight bells that night I took the watch, and the Cap'n went below. He'd managed to hold out that long, or else he hadn't managed to make up his mind. A splendid evenin', I remember, with a broad track o' moonlight on the water and great clouds flyin' through the sky. Quite a sea had picked up; now and then she slapped a little spray on deck. She was just layin' down and walkin' home. I never see stiffer trades. Enough to make a feller's heart dance, with gear snappin' and crackin' aloft, and the sails full o' moonlight and good round wind.

"There I was, hangin' to the weather rail and singin' like a bluejay, when she struck a little sea. She must ha' given a heavier lurch than usual, though I scarcely noticed it. In the middle o' the second verse I was aware o' the Old Man standin' at my elbow, without coat or hat, his teeth chatterin' in his head.

" 'Mr. Noyes,' he cries, 'what are you tryin' to do?'

" 'I'm tryin' to sing, sir,' I answers. 'But my musical education was neglected.'

" 'Nonsense!' he cries. 'What is this ship doin', I want to know?'

" 'She's doin' thirteen knots, sir,' says I, 'and more to come.'

" 'I guess we'll call a halt,' he says. 'Twas the only time I ever see him riled. 'You can take in the royals and topgallant-sails, Mr. Noyes, as quick as you're able. Call all hands,' he says.

" 'Cap'n,' I begs, 'you're not goin' to shorten sail in the trade winds? This breeze is steady as a clock. The trade winds is the only thing that you can depend on, sir, in all the world.'

" 'She jumped me over in bed, Mr. Noyes,' he says. 'I won't carry sail in this reckless way. And he kept the deck till we was down to upper topsails, with the mainsail hauled up. The mainsail, mind you. I could ha' laughed at the rest, but he hauled the mainsail up. Then he went below to sleep in peace.

"There we lay dancin' up and down, hove-to in the moonlight, by the gods o' war, in the heart o' the northeast trades! And what d'you think, but about that time a great ship come swingin' along our wake under three skysails and passed us close aboard. I clapped the glasses on her and made out without a doubt that she was the *Paul Revere*.

"That settled it. My heart was broke in two. Hardly stoppin' to think, I locked the after companionway on the outside and took the key. Runnin' around the house I closed and hasped the shutters to the cabin windows. Next I slipped down into the forrard cabin, locked the two doors there and took them keys. Then I pounded till I raised the Old Man Tripp.

" 'Come to the door a minute, sir,' I cried.

" 'What is it, Mr. Noyes?' he says, rattlin' the knob.

" 'You're a prisoner, Cap'n,' says I. 'No use to make a row. You'll be comfortable, and your meals'll be sent in regular.'

" 'What do you mean?' he cries.

" 'The *Paul Revere* just passed us under skysails, sir,' I says. 'It ain't in human nature, Cap'n to stand such a thing. Now, you turn in and get your sleep. I'm goin' on deck, sir, and make sail.'

" 'Well, I wouldn't set everything, Mr. Noyes,' he says deliberate, on the other side o' the door.

" 'I'll watch her close,' I answer, chokin' a laugh. 'You ease your mind, sir, and leave the ship to me.'

"And then I drove her. Next mornin', there was the *Paul Revere* hull-down ahead. We held our own that day; the followin' night we had a lift, and picked up five miles on her. The trades fell light again; by close watchin' and trimmin' the yards I managed to close up the gap between us inch by inch. The *Vigilant* was at her best in light weather. I found a set o' stun'sails below that hadn't seen the light for years; these I rigged out on bamboo poles lashed to the yardarms. On another pole I contrived a balloon jib under the bowsprit, like a Spanish galleon. Staysails?—I covered her with staysails. She looked like a back yard with the washin' out. But all together they did the trick; on the fifth day o' my command we'd crawled up on the *Paul Revere* and was sailin' with her side by side.

"Pretty soon they sets a string o' signals—'Is Captain sick?' I suppose they'd been watchin' our quarter deck with the glasses.

"I took the signal book and hunted through it for somethin' appropriate to say. Soon I found—'Captain desires me to inform you'—and put it up. That gave me time. There was a whole page o' 'healths.' They all looked nice, but finally I picked out—'In bad health.' 'Twas noncommittal, and I hoped they'd let the matter drop.

" 'What is sickness?' they fired back at me.

"I was up a stump. Beriberi, dengy fever—what in the devil would I say? 'Toothache' caught my eye, and tempted me considerable. Then I struck 'disease,' and found what I wanted—'Infectious disease.' I put that up, and it kept 'em a proper distance. I didn't care to talk just then.

"You know how it is when two ships get together in a quiet spell. Side by side we sailed, day after day; it seemed as though we couldn't draw apart. And every day they'd set them cussed flags, askin' delicate questions about the Cap'n. It might be 'Is any improvement?' or 'Did Cap'n rest?' and I'd answer with 'Better' or 'Tolerably well.' Signals is the best language for lyin' that I ever used.

"The Old Man Tripp himself seemed happy as a clam at high water. The steward took in his meals, and each day I give him the observation at noon. Now and then I'd peek at him through the skylight; usually I'd find him readin' in the big armchair, without a care in the world.

"After we'd crossed the Gulf Stream and run into cold weather, we struck a northerly spell, and parted company with the *Paul Revere*. Then a southeaster lugged us up abreast the Delaware, and cleared off in the sou'west, a pretty chance to run us in. We passed Barnegat one day about noon; when lo and behold, off on the starboard beam a full-rigged ship hove in sight. O' course she turned out to be the *Paul Revere*.

"It was nip and tuck to the lightship then. I spread the fancy wings once more, and hung the balloon jib over the bow. From Barnegat to the Highlands we logged a clean twelve knots, passin' the lightship at three o'clock. The *Paul Revere* dropped into our wake about a mile astern.

"A pilot boarded us just beyond the lightship. I met him at the rail, tellin' him that the Cap'n was laid up below.

" 'Racin' that ship astern?' he asks.

" 'The same,' says I.

" 'I thought as much,' he remarks, glancin' aloft and bustin' into a laugh. 'By George, you deserve to win!'

"About that time, along come a little tugboat and hauled up on our weather quarter. Lookin' inshore, I see a bigger boat a-hustlin' toward us.

" 'D'you want a tow?' sings out the Cap'n o' the little tug.

" 'No, thank you, sir,' says I. 'Go back and pick up that other ship. Tell 'em, with my compliments, that they need a lift.'

"Then we got the big towboat, and beat 'em to quarantine by over an hour.

"The moment that the anchor fetched bottom, my courage ebbed. The day o' reckonin' was at hand.

" 'Doctor's comin' aboard,' says the pilot.

" 'Talk to him a minute, till I see the Cap'n,' I says.

"I waited awhile in the forrard cabin, thinkin' it over. Says I to myself, 'The jig is up. You've got to swaller your medicine.' Then I unlocked the after cabin door.

"The Old Man Tripp sat in the armchair, readin' a book. He finished his page before he looked at me.

" 'We're anchored off quarantine, sir,' I says, 'and we beat the *Paul Revere.*'

" 'Did we? Did we?' says he. 'Well, now, I'm glad to hear it.'

"I hitched from one foot to the other. 'Cap'n,' I says at last, 'I want to apologize for what I've done. I couldn't help it, sir.'

" 'Well, I guess you don't quite mean that you couldn't help it,' says he.

" 'I couldn't stand it, sir,' says I, 'to be passed hove-to in the trades.'

" 'Now, Mr. Noyes, you don't mean hove-to exactly,' he says.

" 'Cap'n,' says I, 'the doctor is comin' aboard this minute, and I told the pilot you was sick abed; and now I don't know what to do.'

"He got up kind o' slow, and smiled. It takes a homely man to smile.

" 'Well,' says he, 'I guess I'd better get to bed.' "

HOME

It was a sultry night toward the close of the southwest monsoon. Singapore sweltered under a thick, motionless heat that seemed to descend vertically out of the sky. A party on the quarter-deck of the bark *Omega* sat restless and uncomfortable, cursing the climate and the land. Kimball was there, an enormously stout man, mopping his face with the towel that he always carried thrown over his shoulder in hot weather; Gilmore was there, and Carver, and Blake, and half a dozen others—all men of New England, and of the sea. Conversation flagged; the tropics had conquered these sons of the colder zone.

"Nichols, how long have you been out East?" someone asked apathetically.

"Let's see," answered the captain of the *Omega*. "Twenty-five from sixty. . . . By Jove, it's going on thirty-five years!"

"Why in the devil don't you go home?"

"To die?"

"No, to live. To get out of this infernal hole. To see the old town, and renew your youth. Lord, I should think you'd be crazy to go!"

Nichols let his eyes roam from face to face with a keen, quizzical glance. "Yes, the old town," he said. "On a clear winter morning, for instance . . . hm-m, what? Perhaps there's been a fall of snow over night; the trees are loaded with it, the roads and paths haven't yet been broken out, the whiteness spread undisturbed. Can't you see it?" He waved a hand. "The houses along the street, the familiar houses of your boyhood, with snow banked in around 'em, with smoke rising straight up into the still air from every chimney? The boys issuing from those houses, muffled to the ears, armed with wooden shovels; attacking the great drifts, the clean, hard-packed piles that cut like cheese; singing, pounding their hands around their shoulders, shouting to each other from yard to yard? Stop a moment, and lean on your shovel. See the white fields rising behind the town, with the ragged line of evergreen trees above them, etched against a wonderful blue sky. Smell the air, that pure, clear atmosphere like nothing else in the world. Feel the cold, the stinging, invigorating cold, the potent cold that stirs a fellow's blood, that upraises him in his might, ready to conquer life and destiny. . . ."

"Hell, don't!" remonstrated a peevish voice.

Nichols laughed cynically. "Nonsense!" he said. "I touched you? you call it a longing for home? Why, you poor fools, that's simply man's perverse and devilish discontent with his surroundings. He's never quite happy, this strange creature. He'd be where he isn't, he'd have what he's never been willing to pay the price for—the cursed hypocrite. As a matter of fact, you fellows wouldn't like that cold weather if you could have it. You wouldn't enjoy digging into those snowbanks. Your feet would be numb, and your back would ache; you'd hire some poor cuss to shovel the paths for you; and you'd go indoors yourself and croon over the fire, and pile on wood, and growl, and never so much as look out on the beautiful world. You'd sigh for the tropics, for palm trees and mangoes and a sea breeze in the afternoon; for a deck-chair to stretch your lazy bodies in, and a good Chinese steward to fetch your drinks, and the sweat to trickle down your backbone. Damn you all! here you have it. Now why aren't you satisfied?"

He sat up with a jerk. "You ask me why I don't go home?" he inquired. "I'll tell you: because I affirm that I like to stay right here. I like the East. I like the hot weather, the rainy season, and all the rest of it. This country has become my home. . . . As for the other, the home of my boyhood, I have every reason for wanting not to go there. You yourselves have told me of the change. A railroad has come to town, bringing in its wake the pitiful scramble that has ruined so many fine old communities. The sea-farers have died away; the new men are strangers, Vandals in Rome. The dear old place is caught in the pitiless jaws of economic revolution. Inevitable, of course; eventually right, we hope: just as we speak of death. We have faith in the future; something truer must be in the wind—must reach us, ultimately, some time. But in the meanwhile, why in the devil should I go there, why should I want to watch my home-town die? The spot that I remember best of all—that quiet point of land to the eastward of the town, where a grove of spruce trees used to run down to the margin of the bay, where I've spent many a serious afternoon with the breeze murmuring in the branches over-head—has been stripped, you tell me, and levelled for the freight-yard of the railroad. It bristles with wharves, it stinks of smoke, it's grimy with coal dust—the dust of coal that's bound inland to run the engines of industrialism. What is it all about? What is gained? What is lost? There are other points of land, you'll tell me; points just as quiet, still untouched. But that was the point I loved. The ducks and herons go there no longer: why should I go?

"So I couldn't find the old town if I sought it," Nichols went on. "How silly, this business of transporting our bodies about the world for a change of scene. I have the town with me, I needn't seek it at all. I live at home. I spend my best hours there, visiting the shipyards, listening to the old men, our first and most untrustworthy oracles. 'Go to sea,' they advised us. 'Nothing can supersede our ships.' We went to sea; and the bottom dropped out of our world. But because I *haven't* been home, haven't actually beheld the change, the memory seems quite real to me, and I feel that the old times are living on. And now you're asking me why I don't return—destroy one of my few remaining dreams. Hm-m? . . . Oh, of course the lay of the land there hasn't been materially modified. But from what I hear, a veritable glacier has swept over the men, the ideals, the life, and left them unrecognizable."

Nichols fell silent; no one had the spirit to take up his chal-lenge. "My friends, there has been but one home-coming in our wandering life," he resumed suddenly. "One only, worthy of the name: the first home-coming, at the end of our maiden voyage. The others were merely repetitions, incidents in a settled life; we knew by that time what to expect, we anticipated the sensa-tions, the glamour of wonder and surprise had vanished, never to return. But the first home-coming was new, fresh, and abso-lutely beyond experience. It compassed all human sentiment—much that we'd never before felt, much that we'd realized but dimly, much that we'd known and suppressed, but that had suddenly become unsuppressible. Our hearts flamed, our souls reached out to embrace the world. That glory! why couldn't we have held it? why couldn't we have gone on, living in the light of that flame of love? All that we saw was beautiful, all that we touched was good, all that we conceived was born of the noble part of us, of the dream and the divinity. Why did we let it go? Listen. . . .

"I started out when I was sixteen years of age. My father had died; I had become the head of the family; and we were poor. I chose the sea; in those days there seemed to be no other choice for us boys who had grown up in the ship-yards and played with boats from the time we'd learned to walk. I shipped before the mast with my Uncle Ross in the old bark *Hudson.* She was then lying at the wharf below our house, refitting for a long foreign voyage. One morning I said good-bye to my mother, dropped over the bank by a back way so that no one should see my unmanly tears, and went aboard. My chest, made by another uncle who was a joiner, painted brown with blue trimmings, and packed by my mother, a woman experienced in fitting out sea-chests for young sailors, had been wheeled down to the ship by my brother the evening before. An off-shore breeze was springing up as I reached the vessel; we sailed within the hour. Mother stood in the kitchen door as we hauled out. She waved something white; I wondered what it was. I couldn't see very clearly. There was no time for watching—too much to be done about decks. I stole a glance now and then. I didn't wave her in return. No, I wasn't ashamed—I can't explain. The town dwindled in our wake, the hills rose up behind it, the bay widened; the land itself sank, shifted, and was gone. A new world, the world of the ocean, spread about me on every hand; I saw for the first time in my life the etched line of the whole horizon, an unbroken circle between the sea and the sky. But I couldn't bear to look at it. I felt that I never would be happy again.

"You know it, you fellows—you remember. The sinking of the heart, the weight like lead dragging upon some indefinite region within, the quick pain that grips and lets go, grips and lets go. Homesickness—the misery of the soul. There's nothing for it; in fact, one doesn't wish it to be cured. It would be disloyal. No, one bears it, looks it in the face, wrestles with it alone; and no other experience of life brings one nearer the truth, or contributes more to one's poor store of nobility. In my case, I was too familiar with the water to be seasick, and too familiar with a ship to be at all bewildered on the old *Hudson's* deck. Sea-faring had been bred into my bones; my boyhood had been a preparation for it, an apprenticeship at home. Well, I found that this didn't help me now. Because I knew so much, I think that it made my first week harder. For, in my preparation, I'd learned the pain of sea-faring as well; I'd heard sad stories along with the romantic ones; the fatalism of sailors, their superstition, their moodiness, had come down to me as an integral part of my inheritance. And here I was, already embarked upon my voyage, surrounded by a barren and desolate sea. Death seemed very near to me, I remember; much nearer than it does to-day. This, I reflected, was the beginning; before I knew it life would pass; then *finis*, the great change, whatever it might be. Really, it didn't appeal to me as being quite worth while.

"But, of course, I got over that—soon, too, surprisingly soon. So soon that I half-accused myself of the disloyalty I spoke of. Life must triumph, since we're to make out a career in the shadow of an inexorable fate. Within a week I was myself again. I liked the work; seamanship, the sailing, the handling, the care of vessels, had always held a rare fascination for me. But the training was severe. My uncle was a captain of the old school, a martinet, a stern, hard man. I had never seen this side of him ashore; we had always been good chums. From men who had sailed with him, however, I'd heard what to expect. And this preparation, too, did me no service. Perhaps I hadn't believed it. To be passed on deck without a look or a word, seemed needlessly cruel. In my uncle's eyes the worth of a training depended directly upon its severity. I had put myself into his hands to be trained; and he trained me as best he knew. I was supposed to have better stuff in me than the ordinary boy before the mast; the way to bring it out was to grind me uncommonly hard. Above all, with our known blood relationship, the least trace of favoritism must be guarded against; and in order to be sure of this he felt obliged to be particularly nasty to me. Sounds odd, doesn't it, in our soft and humanitarian day? Let me tell you a secret: the more I see of life and results, the firmer is my belief in the old-fashioned discipline.

"So I learned—learned to live. No more preparation; the real thing now. I worked like a dog; I growled, cursed, hated the officers, hated my uncle, the Old Man, worst of all. Hard-hearted old devil! all very well for him to claim the virtue of wisdom, but I was the one who had to do the sweating. I shovelled coal in the lower hold for twelve hours a day, with a shovel that seemed half as big as my body. I went aloft with my watch off the Horn, and laid out on the upper-topsail yard when rain turned to ice on the sail we were trying to reef, when every pitch of the old hooker came near tossing us overboard. Once, in the early stages of a typhoon, I volunteered to furl the main royal, which had slat itself adrift from the gaskets; accomplished the job, too, after a wild hour among the clouds. I wonder that I ever reached the deck alive; but my uncle had stood by when I'd offered to go, and had nodded his head. Out on the West Coast, at Iquiqui and Junin, I rowed stroke oar in the captain's boat; rowed him for miles up and down those exposed and windy roadsteads; rowed until I thought my arms would come out of the sockets at every stroke, until I could cheerfully have killed the Old Man, lolling back in the stern-sheets and playing with the tiller ropes. At the Chincha Islands, I had charge of one of the lighters, and took her in under the guano-shoot every morning that we were able to work cargo; a job that called for a man's strength and resolution, with the open Pacific rolling in on one hand and an iron-bound coast on the other. I ate the coarse, unpalatable food of the forecastle, and grew like a weed. I had several fights with sailors, and licked my men. I sauced the mate, and received my first licking, a substantial one. My uncle had stood by while this had happened, too. I know now that I worked, played, thought, and suffered harder than any two men aboard the ship. But at the time I had an idea that I was a miserable failure. The Old Man never opened his mouth in a word of praise; silence was his verdict for good work, and a sound rating for bad. Such training isn't conducive to egoism.

"Through all this I found little time to think of home. The town of my boyhood seemed a place far away in some indefinite region, a place detached from my present existence, a part of a discarded dream. I heard from mother regularly; cried over her letters more than once when I was tired and disheartened. My uncle seldom spoke to me of home, and then in such a way that all the pleasure of it was spoiled, and I wished that he had kept still.

" 'Come here a minute. I had a letter from your mother to-day.'

" 'Yes, sir.'

" 'She writes that she is well.'

" 'Yes, sir. I had a long letter. She said—'

" 'You mustn't fail to write her before we get away. Sunday is the time to write.'

" 'Yes, sir.'

" 'I am sending all your wages to her from here. You don't need any money, do you?'

" 'No, sir. That is—I'd like a few dollars, sir.'

" 'What for?'

" 'To buy things with.' I may have said it in a tone of faint sarcasm.

" 'To buy things with, hm? Do you think that's the way to get it?'

" 'I don't know what you mean, sir.'

" 'Well, you'd better learn. Now, go back to your work. There is nothing in this place that you want to buy.'

"These were our relations—Jove, didn't I hate him! How did he know what I wanted to buy? what business was it of his, anyway? Hadn't I earned the money? 'Go back to your work!'—well, who the devil had called me away from my work? I hadn't wanted to talk with him, wouldn't care if I never heard or saw him again. The old stinker—I was glad that I'd sauced him. . . . But I did write to my mother that very evening; I'd been neglecting the duty. I'm afraid that my letter may have been a trifle stilted; after subtracting the things that I didn't want to tell her, the narrative lacked the essence of truth. Sometimes, as I wrote, I felt like opening my heart to her; would have done so always if my newly acquired manhood hadn't revolted at the disclosure. For I was unhappy —I won't attempt to deny it. I was a desperately unhappy boy. No doubt she read it between the lines. She must have felt my reticence; must have cried over it, prayed, and bowed her head before the sad but inevitable change. She had lived quietly, but knew much of life . . . my mother.

"We were gone on that voyage three years. We went to San Francisco, from there to Australia, from there to the West Coast with coal, from there to Holland with guano, from there to the East, to Batavia, to Shanghai, and finally to Yokohama, where we loaded for New York. In Yokohama the second mate left the ship. That night my uncle called me aft.

" 'You are to go second mate on the homeward run,' he said. 'Put your things into his room, and take up your duties to-morrow morning.'

"That was all; no explanation of the duties, no word of encouragement or approval. But I was encouraged just the same; I knew that I couldn't be a total failure. The Old Man didn't think much of me; but he had given me my chance. I'd show him; I'd change his opinion of me, or break my neck in trying. With the advancement itself, I was considerably elated. My first command was for two men to bring my chest from the forecastle—put it into the second mate's room—be careful of that mahogany hand-rail—over in *that* corner—here, look out for the paint on that door! Indeed, things were vastly different now; I'd taken my first step upward. I redoubled my efforts; my responsibility weighed upon me, so that often I couldn't sleep in my watch below. Jove, I'd like to get hold of such a second mate to-day!

"During the homeward passage I was too busy to indulge myself in sentimental reflections. When, at odd moments, my fancy did reach ahead, I couldn't make the approaching event of our return seem real, probable, or even possible. I'd outgrown my boyhood, I'd completely changed my state of mind. And I thought, I remember, that by virtue of this superior indifference with which I carried myself I had been weaned from home.

"We came in through an autumn storm, the tail end of a hurricane. Wind and sea, rain, hail, and lightning, the blowing away of sails, the smashing of boats, the flooding of the cabin, the handling of canvas, the bracing of yards: these matters occupied my mind from Hatteras to Barnegat. There the pilot boarded us, a towboat picked us up; and almost before I knew it we were in. The first touch of Indian summer lay on the land. I gave the scene a glance or two, and thought it very beautiful, as all land is to sailors; but perhaps not quite so beautiful as Java or Japan.

"We hauled in to a pier on South Street, and began discharging the cargo. The crew left, the mate left; the work of the ship was done. I felt a bit dazed; a bit jealous, too, of the boss stevedore, who seemed to be of more importance than I was—I, who had stood my watch and helped to bring the ship and cargo in. I had no money; I would have cut off my hand sooner than ask the

Old Man for any, and give him the opportunity to refuse my request. He would pay me off when he got ready; then I would be finished with him for good and all. So I stayed aboard, busied myself at odd jobs about decks, and grew very restless as the days went by. Mother wrote begging me to hurry home; but I didn't answer her letters. A strange spirit had come over me. Had the chance offered, I would have run away from the *Hudson* and shipped at once for another long voyage.

"One morning the Old Man took me up to the commissioner's and paid me off. We came out of the office together and walked back along South Street toward the ship.

" 'Well, my boy,' said my uncle suddenly, 'the voyage is over. What are you going to do?'

"I stopped short, gazed at him in astonishment. His manner, the very tone of his voice, had softened. He stood before me as I remembered him, the friend of my boyhood. His eyes were no longer cold.

" 'I don't know, sir,' I answered. 'I was thinking of looking around.'

" 'You're going home, of course?'

" 'I don't know,' I repeated. 'I haven't made up my mind—'

" 'Of course you are!' he cried, in his old bluff, hearty way.

" 'Of course, sir,' I echoed.

" 'Then you'd better go along with me to-morrow morning. Here's a good restaurant; let's have a square meal now, and talk it over. Wake up, my boy. *You're going home!*'

"The words came to me like a bugle-call on the field of battle. My heart gave a great leap; the world and everything in it changed in the twinkling of an eye. The dammed-up emotion of three years swept over me like a flood. We entered the restaurant and sat down. Suddenly I lost control of myself. I leaned forward on the table and buried my face in my arms. When I at length found courage to look up I saw that my uncle had chosen a quiet corner, and that I hadn't been observed. His eyes were fixed on his plate with a wide and sober gaze.

" 'I'm a fool, sir,' I said. 'I want my mother. I want to go home.'

" 'Poor boy!' he whispered, as if speaking to himself. After a pause he addressed me directly. 'Next voyage you are to go out mate with me. You have done well.'

" 'I wish to God you'd told me so a year ago!' I cried.

"He looked me over thoughtfully. 'I might have spoiled it,' he said. 'Some day you'll understand.'

"So it came about that we were chums again, and went home together like two boys. All the journey I flattened my face against the car window, watching the land slip past, noting and exclaiming over the sweet things of the land. Beside me my uncle talked, telling tales of the town, of ships and men; drawing me back unconsciously to my boyhood, to the spirit and presence of home.

"In those days the railroad didn't reach within six miles of our town. At Portland we wired to Newall Rich, who kept the village livery stable, to meet us at the train. Now, I had never been aware of a particular fondness for Newall Rich. I'd known him, I'd laughed at his quaint sayings, I'd thrown snowballs at him and stolen rides on his teams. Once, for frightening a horse that he was driving he'd given me a cut of the whip; with a boy's philosophy I had laid it up against him. But looking over my uncle's shoulder as he wrote the telegram, the familiar name gave me an unaccountable thrill. 'Newall Rich!' I cried. 'Hm—just imagine!' Thereafter, my mind kept recurring to Newall Rich. Would he receive the message in time? would anything prevent his meeting us? would he bring the old hack? would he be as fat as ever? He would tell them over town that we were coming. I could see it plainly: had been so often an actor myself in the scene, inquiring of the boys who Newall was going after with the hack, who was coming home from sea.

"At last the train drew in to its last station; and Newall met us. As I came down the steps I caught sight of his short round figure. 'Here they are!' he chanted, dancing along the platform. 'Ha! The Honorable Commodore of the fleet!'—Newall held a humorist's license. 'And here's Bertie, little Bertie, that went away one summer day!' He immediately broke out with one of his ridiculous verses:

> 'Little Bertie
> Sailor-man,
> Tucks his shirtie
> With one hand.'

"I was vastly amused. Funny duck, Newall—good fellow as ever lived. I forgave him that cut of the whip, forgave him freely. For this was a real welcome, a welcome into the bosom of the town; when I'd gone away I hadn't been of enough importance to merit a verse from Newall. We piled into the hack—yes, he'd brought that venerable relic—our trunks were strapped on behind, and off we rattled. The windows were open, soft autumn smells came to us; the sun set as we jogged along, and twilight descended upon the land. We followed a road high above the sea, with the woods on our left and cleared land between us and the shore. Along our route lay old farmhouses, flashing their lights at us through the dusk. Gardens were waiting for the harvest; we saw ripe pumpkins among the withering corn. Peace and contentment filled the air. From the box above our heads Newall addressed his horses in a vigorous mixture of prose and verse. We were in home-country now.

" 'Uncle Ross, there's the haddock-hole off Moose Point!'

" 'Isn't it a little farther to the eastward?'

" 'No, sir. I could put you right on top of it.'

" 'We'll try it some day, my boy.'

" 'Who lives here, Uncle Ross? The white house with three elms.'

" 'I don't remember. Ask Newall.'

" 'Where are we now? I'd forgotten that there was a hill along here.'

" 'Yes, a fellow forgets those things at sea.'

"But there was one hill that I hadn't forgotten. From it, on this road, one got his first view of the town. As we rose toward its crest a new sensation gripped my heart—a sensation that wasn't direct in itself, but was more a premonition of sensations to come. Something unexpected was going to happen to me, something rare, high, divine. My blood tingled, my fingers couldn't keep still. Soon I felt that we had stopped rising. Now . . . I drew a long breath, and leaned forward.

"Then I saw the town. It lay in a broad valley, surrounded on three sides by rising ground. On the fourth side an arm of the larger bay made in to form the harbor. Lights twinkled among the trees; village sounds rose through the still air. I looked once, shut my eyes, and opened them again suddenly. The vision persisted.

No words came to my lips now. I was trying to locate a certain house across the valley, trying to grasp, to comprehend. . . . Mother waited over among those trees. I had been allowed to return. A song broke out in my heart, and throbbed to the pounding of the horses' hoofs: '*Almost there! almost there! almost there!*'

"We descended the hill at a gallop, and entered the main street of the village. The bright lights of the stores illuminated our vehicle; men turned to scrutinize us; we heard our names go from mouth to mouth. This passed like a lantern-slide, and we went on to the eastward. By the Old Custom House, down into the Hollow, rising now on the opposite hill — '*Almost there! almost there!*' Our house stood at the top of the hill. Distances seemed unnaturally short. In the darkness we had reached the house before I could get my bearings. The hack stopped with a jolt. A spell had settled upon me; my mind was blank, my senses were numb. I found myself on the walk. Someone was moving inside the house—running. The door opened, a light flashed in my face. . . . '*Mother!*' . . . '*My boy! My boy!*' . . . I had come home."

Nichols paused. "Mother had expected me at the front door," he went on after a while. "But it was the back door that I'd gone to, the door that I'd always used as a boy. I went into the kitchen, took off my hat and coat, and stood in the center of the floor, looking around. Everything was the same—everything was the same. It seemed as if I had been out playing that afternoon, and had come back just in time for supper. Delicious odors filled the room. While mother took up the supper I hung about the stove. She said that I bothered her, and pushed me away. And when it transpired that she had forgotten to salt the biscuits, the blame fell upon me.

" 'Mother,' I said, 'the wind's coming up from the southward.' It had been one of our games to guess the direction of the wind from the different sounds that it made in the kitchen chimney.

"She was too preoccupied to catch my meaning; thought I was telling her a fact that I'd noticed on our drive. 'Is it?' she asked indifferently.

" 'Listen. Isn't that the southerly howl?'

"She made a faint sound, and suddenly burst into tears. 'You haven't forgotten, have you?' she cried.

" 'Don't cry, mother. You're the one who forgot, you know.'

" 'Yes, I forgot. I'm glad to have something to make me forget. I've been listening to that chimney every night for three years.'

"We sat at supper a long time. My younger brother was away at school; mother and I were alone. There was a roast chicken, with new vegetables—mashed potato, turnip, squash, boiled onions; there was a little dish of spiced gooseberry, my favorite condiment; there was one of mother's famous lemon pies. We talked of the voyage, and of the news of the town; a wide field lay before us. It wasn't brilliant conversation; no one else in the world would have been interested in it; but to us it was exciting, absorbing, the best of life—the story of ourselves and of our friends. Now and then, as we faced each other across the table, personalities interrupted the relation.

" 'Mother, you haven't grown any older.' She had, though; I trembled to see it.

" 'Haven't I, Bert? Look at my hair.' She knew, better than anyone else, how much older she had grown; but my remark had pleased her.

"Then it was her turn.

" 'Bert, how you have thickened up! You're going to be a big man like your father.' I knew very well that I would never be a big or a strong man; but she had pleased me just the same.

"Late that night I went up to my old room. I found it exactly as I had left it three years before. The pictures, the ornaments, the books—things that I'd forgotten, but that came back to me at a single glance, with all their buried associations. Suddenly I sat down. Everything the same—yet what a difference, what a great difference in *me*. God in Heaven, I'd been away three years!

"And she had been living here alone most of the time. Living and thinking. I hadn't had time for much of that. Some of my work, too—a good deal of it—had been in the nature of play. I had been unhappy—how unhappy? Did I comprehend what mature unhappiness might be? Empty days, an empty house; the dead at rest, a son far off on perilous waters. Shame on you, to call yourself a man! Why didn't you write her how happy you were, what playtime you had?

"Before she went to bed, mother came up to my room and found me sitting with my head in my hands. 'What is it, Bert?' she cried in a frightened voice.

" 'I was thinking of you.'

" 'Oh!' She laughed. 'I was afraid—'

" 'Afraid of what?'

" 'Will you promise not to be offended?'

" 'Of course, dear.'

" 'I was afraid that you were in love.'

" 'Nonsense! I haven't had a chance. Only in love with you.'

" 'Yes,' she said. 'I know. I'm glad. But it will be someone else some day.'

" 'I was thinking, mother,' I told her, 'that this lonely life is too hard for you.'

" 'Hard, Bert?' She laughed bravely. 'Why, you make it easy. Perhaps I'm not so lonely as you imagine. My neighbors are kind. I manage to keep busy. And then I have a Comfort.'. . . True— I'd forgotten that. It silenced me like a shock, like a bolt from the blue; it overturned the whole structure of my immature conceptions. She bowed her face on my knees, and prayed. Her faith reached me, she brought it down out of the sky. It came on the breath of joy, on the wings of love. . . . How strange, to think of to-day! I haven't heard a prayer for years.

" 'Mother, it's a long time since you've made my bed,' I said. 'I suppose you haven't come here much the last few years.'

" 'Every day,' she answered. 'Every morning, to dust your things and think of you. Warm afternoons I'd sit here at the window and read your letters over. I like to look out over the water from this window. But at night I couldn't bear to come.'

"We talked a long while. It was one of those close, deep talks, that stand like milestones along the life of a wanderer. Mother searched me for the record of my three years, and I found that I had no desire to hold anything back. Some of it must have pained her, though I doubt if my small misdeeds seemed so serious to her as they did at that moment to me. She didn't absolve me, however; she was far too wise.

"I awoke early the next morning—awoke into a town that never existed, into a light that never shone. In our latitude the real Indian summer had come. The first thing I noticed from my window was that the tide was out, so after breakfast I took a bucket and hoe and went to the shore for a mess of clams. My heart sang as I stooped above the hoe, pulling aside the rock-weed, inhaling the musky odor of the flats; each clam that I found was an adventure, a diamond, a nugget of pure gold. When I straightened up to ease my back, the past swept over me. There it lay, my earliest and best playground—mine still, after three momentous years. There I had tried my boats; there I had learned to swim; there I had won my memorable fight with Charlie Blake, the leader of the village gang. There, too, lay the old ship-yard, the center of boyhood aspirations. Three ships had been launched there since I'd last seen it. And I had been to China, I had rounded the Horn! A golden haze hung on the water; the fields along the margin of the bay had begun to wither and turn brown. The air was full of the smell of autumn fires. Home. My port of hail.

"When I'd filled my bucket with big clams, I left it at the head of the beach and wandered off to the eastward along the shore, toward the point that's been utterly and forever spoiled. I found rocks that I remembered, rocks with peculiar veins of quartz running through them. I paused at the waterfall, where long ago I'd helped to fill the casks of the ship *Talavera*, just off the stocks and sailing on her maiden voyage. Near the waterfall a long ledge of slate runs out from the bank. The Sunday before I had left home in the *Hudson* I'd spent an hour or two on that ledge; and while sitting there in a rather gloomy and miserable mood I'd employed my hands in driving an old spike into the rotting slate with a big flat stone. By Jove, I found that spike again, just where I'd left it sticking out of the ledge. It seemed a very wonderful thing to me, an event full of significance. I sat down, gazed at the rusty spike that my hands had driven home, that had weathered seasons and gales; and trembled before the profound and in-scrutable purposes of life. . . . I can't quite see the connection now. As I said, I have lost the charm.

"A little way farther I came across a boy sailing a boat in a landlocked pool among the rockweed. He looked up at my approach, and tried to hide his toy.

" 'Hello!' I cried. 'What's your name?'

" 'Sammy Curtis.'

" 'What are you doing there?'

"Without answer, he gathered his precious boat to his bosom and fled—actually fled, glancing over his shoulder with a sullen scowl. What had I done? I'd supposed that I was speaking kindly; I'd wanted to play with him. But it was impossible—the door between us was closed. I couldn't forget my ship-voice, my official dignity. I was too old, and I wasn't old enough; I was neither boy nor man. The child's condemnation startled me, smote me with vague alarm. He'd recognized so clearly what I had lost. Did he see, too, what I had won? Had I won anything, after all?

"In a little while I took my bucket of clams and went home. Mother was busy in the kitchen.

" 'Mother,' I said, 'it's hard, sometimes, to grow up.'

"She looked at me keenly, fathoming my trouble at a glance. 'That isn't the right way to feel about it,' she answered. 'It can't be helped. . . .' She trailed off into silence; I had a notion that, whatever she might profess, in secret she shared my vain regrets. 'Just don't forget,' she said suddenly. 'Don't forget!' Advice to solve the human quarrel, if we could hold it, if we would think it worth our while.

"But marvels were happening that morning; I couldn't bother long with a serious mood. I sat down by the north kitchen window, looking up the road. Who was this coming? could it be . . . ?

" 'Mother,' I cried, 'here's old Bill Co'son going by!'

" 'Yes?' she answered from the pantry. I wondered if she could have understood. I'd told her that old Bill Co'son was going by.

"Soon Manly Tripp, with his bow legs, waddled past; and after him stalked Marlboro Pike, as martial-looking as ever. I laughed to see them; I would have recognized them a mile away. When Josiah Harriman appeared with his lame horse—the horse that resembled the master, that walked so ridiculously like him—I couldn't contain myself.

" 'Mother, here's Josiah Harriman driving his old lame horse!'

"She came to the window, looked out, and smiled at me. 'It seems good to you, doesn't it?' she said.

"I caught her hand. 'Good?' I cried. We were happy . . . I'd come home.

"That afternoon I went to the village and renewed my acquaintance with the town. I saw the boys—I've forgotten many of their names. No doubt I bragged shamelessly, posed as a man of the world, swore, told silly stories, smoked big cigars. No doubt the men made fun of me; but I didn't mind it, wasn't aware of it. The younger fellows gave me their unstinted adulation. The dream brushed me; and all humanity appeared good, true, noble, to my eyes. Even old Ike Sloan, whom everyone knew as a useless cuss, revealed to me an unsuspected worth.

" 'Bert—Nichols?' he mumbled, thrusting out a palsied claw. 'Home—from—sea?' You remember how he used to speak in gasps. 'Home—from—sea—Bert? Think—you'll—like it? Going—to—keep it up? Better—stick—to it. Good—job.'

"I gave his hand a hearty shake. Poor old Ike—who should judge him? Perhaps he wasn't altogether to blame, wasn't such a bad sort, in the main.

"So the day went . . . a dream, a dream. For one day life disclosed itself to me. I saw beneath the surface, into the deep heart, into the secret places where truth and beauty hide. The eyes of faith were given me. And what I beheld there in the dream inspired me, purified me, filled me with messages of love. I might have done great things . . . in that dream.

"But I lost it. I went out into a world which is not the true world, into a life which is not the true life at all. Scene by scene the dream was taken from me; my trust was betrayed, my faith languished. I learned that love is not legal tender, that honor is no talisman. I learned that truth must fight hard for its own, win seldom, lose so often and so much that the heart fails looking back upon the disastrous field. Life would be fine, life aches to be true. But this thing we call the world, this thing that isn't life, that isn't truth—something artificial, something to conceal the truth, as clothes conceal our bodies: I hate it. It won't *let* us live, this world. It would run us all in a mold; it would take us, and melt us down. It *makes truth fight.* And we must earn our bread. Who will go out with me against the world? Who will cry aloud from a high mountain? . . . Nonsense! I hate it. It has denied what I loved, it has robbed me of my dream. I am not reconciled."

Nichols went to the rail. Suddenly he faced us. "But I have the memory," he said. "A prayer, a word or two—the old times, the old hard lessons, the sadness, the joy—home, and the dream of what life might have been. I haven't forgotten all of it. It's here—in a place so secret, so secure, that only God and I hold the key. The world hasn't been able to violate that place yet; though I suppose it will find a way, in the ages to come."

I WAS BORN IN A
STORM AT SEA

I was born at sea in the region of Cape Horn, in the cabin of a sailing ship. We had just rounded "the Horn" on the passage from Valparaiso to New York, deeply loaded with nitrates. It was midwinter in those latitudes, the 14th of August, 1883. A black southwester had been blowing for many days; before this gale the bark "Charlotte A. Littlefield," my father's first command, scudded under two lower topsails, laboring heavily in the mountainous running seas. Two days before the ship had sprung a leak. She was old, and the cargo was the hardest possible on a vessel.

Now the situation was growing serious. The water in the lower hold was gaining on the pumps, the gale had increased in the previous night; and at the particular hour when Fate decided to launch me in a world that looked more like an inferno than a place fit for human habitation, my father had grave doubts that the old craft under his feet would pull through the storm.

It was a bad time, but seafaring people expect bad times. Their training has largely been in the way of meeting emergencies. The matter of sinking could be put off for a while; there was more imperative business at hand. Father, forced to keep the deck constantly, was waiting for his call.

The Chinese steward rushed up the after companionway: "Cappen, Mississee wanchee!"

Mother lay below in the dim stateroom, listening to the roar of the gale and the crash of waters overhead, feeling the heavy pitching of the vessel, trying to steady herself in the bunk as the old bark lunged and wallowed.

There was another baby beside her, my sister, born eighteen months before off the island of New Caledonia, on the passage from Newcastle, South Wales, to Kobe, Japan. Mother must have recognized the condition of the ship. But perhaps she had no strength left to worry over secondary matters; or perhaps the danger that threatened them all helped her, in a way, by obscuring the nearer personal danger. Death is always close at such a time, hovering over birth like a morose and jealous rival. At any rate, she waited there in the tossing cabin for what might come, while the ship raced desperately before low black clouds across the face of tearing waters, an atom lost in the infinite violence of sea and sky.

"Cappen, Mississee wanchee!" The dread words must have struck fear to the heart of a man already burdened with the fate of a ship and her company—his own among the rest, the living as well as the unborn. He went below, and took off his dripping oilskin coat. These were the inhospitable auspices of my birth. It really was no place for a new-born child. Years afterward I once broached the subject to Father. "Wasn't it pretty tough, sir?" I asked. He gave a short laugh. "Tough things have to be done," he said. "The memory of them gets swamped by time." It was an epitome of the high creed of seamanship. I have never asked Mother about it. Perhaps it was not so much harder for her than birth is always hard.

But the old bark didn't sink, and nothing of moment happened. The child was born; the gale blew itself out; the open seams closed as the sea went down; Mother's health improved rapidly; and by the time they had reached the southeast trades she was able to be carried on deck in the shade of the spanker, her two babies beside her, to bask in the soft balmy air as the vessel slipped northward through kindly seas. The worst was over now, for the time being, an event already transmuted by the magic of memory, as soldiers soon learn to recall their battles and wounds.

They were nearing home again. These young people, just turned twenty, had been married one afternoon in the Maine coast town where their families had lived and followed the sea for five generations, and had started out the same evening on a three years' voyage in the little bark, taking up the life that had been cut out for them. From this voyage, a circumnavigation of the globe, they were returning with two children. My sister had been a mid-voyage gift of the joyous South Seas. I was the seal of their circumnavigation, a souvenir thrust on them roughly and in haste by the cruel masters of the Horn, as they thundered past in the grip of perilous waters.

Later I was to circumnavigate the globe in my own right under sail, on board another vessel, rounding the Horn this time in pleasant weather. It was January, the heart of summer, and we carried a light breeze with royals set over a gently heaving sea. I remember standing beside my mother at the rail, as she gazed on the placid face of that usually tempestuous region. Her arm went around me. "It doesn't seem possible!" she whispered. I was too young to appreciate what she meant—the vastness and terror of the scene that had suddenly opened up before her eyes.

This was the only time that I ever visited my birthplace. But I have a memento of it. In after years my father became master of a steamship, and died on board his vessel in a foreign port. Among the personal tokens that came home with his effects, things he had loved and treasured, there was a small pasteboard box containing a piece of shell-encrusted seaweed. On the box, in his handwriting, was this inscription:

> A bit of weed from Lincoln's birthplace, washed on board the American in 44° south latitude, South Atlantic Ocean, in the same kind of a southwest gale in which he was born; picked up and salted down by his father, this being the first that any of the family ever have seen of that country.

My bond with the sea goes back further than my birth. It is a family matter. The first Colcord landed in Portsmouth, New Hampshire, in the year 1635. I am in the tenth generation of direct descent from him. The family name, Colquitt, is still to be found in the south of England, through Devonshire and Cornwall. After the emigration to America, there were five generations of farmers and coastwise sailors in New Hampshire. Then a branch of the family moved to Maine, locating on the west shore of Penobscot Bay.

After the Revolution the sailors of this region began to go "deep water." In the course of time they made the town of Searsport famous throughout the shipping world. One of my great-great-grandfathers, Jeremiah Sweetser, commanded the first full-rigged ship built on the Penobscot, the "William B. Leeds," a little vessel of three hundred tons. Another great-great-grandfather built vessels in the old shipyard, now dropping into decay, that stands just below the house I live in. These were the days of the opening up of the China trade.

It was nothing unusual then for a child to be born at sea. I know a dozen such, out of this one shipping town. Some of the girls have geographical names. There is Fastnet, born off Fastnet Rock in the English Channel. There is Iona, born among the Ionian Isles. There is Mindoro, born in Mindoro Passage in the heart of the Malay Archipelago. At one time in its history, with seven shipyards building square-rigged vessels, the town of Searsport produced one tenth of the deep-water ship masters in the American merchant marine. These men frequently took their wives and families on long voyages. Many a child was brought home that had not gone away.

The question of citizenship involved in birth at sea used to be well understood by the authorities along the Atlantic seaboard. We who first saw the world out of sight of land were admitted to citizenship under the law providing for children born in American embassies abroad. Our ships, too, were "patches of American soil." The American flag flew over us, the craft was tax-paying American property, our parents were Americans of Americans. The flag raised over my birth, I believe, was immediately blown to ribbons and snatched away by the gale. But I am far from being a man without a country.

My first conscious memory is of the sea. It is one of those vivid pictures photographed on the mind of a young child which live with singular completeness and vitality in after years. I must have been about four years old. Mother had carried me to the head of the companionway, and set me on top of the after-house; with her arm around me and her face close to mine, she stood just inside the door.

The scene that lives in my mind is one of wild, stormy waters, heaving and bursting into foam, under the hard, brilliant sunlight of a cloudless gale. The ship was hove to and must have been light-loaded, for the decks were dry. I recall even the sensation this scene gave me—a sensation of boundless joy and exaltation, of pleasure in the deep blue color of the water streaked with foam, of delight at the rushing wind and the waves constantly in motion, of love for the straining ship and the bright ocean world of which she was a part. I flung my arms around my mother's neck, and shouted aloud in glee.

Then I noticed that her glasses were clouded with a whitish opaque substance. On childish impulse, I leaned forward and touched this substance with my tongue. It tasted salt. Years later, when I had to wear glasses myself at sea, I learned how they would collect the flying spindrift in a gale. But saltness, too, is part of this first sea recollection.

The memories that follow are mostly of the sea. I knew no other home than a ship's deck, except the distant home in Maine that we visited for a few weeks every year or two. My countryside was the ocean floor, where I could roam only with the spyglass; my sky line was the horizon, broken by the ghostly silhouettes of passing vessels, or at intervals by the coasts of many continents, as we sailed about the world. It was a varied life. But where everything was foreign, nothing was foreign, and it all happened as a matter of course, the only life I knew.

Once I went to a friend's wedding in Greenville, Pennsylvania. I left New York at midnight, and the next morning found me still traveling. As I looked out of the car window a strange feeling of loneliness and oppression came over me. I seemed hemmed in by the land. Then I realized that this was the third time in my life that I had ever been away from the world's seaboard. The first time had been on a trip from Mollendo, a port on the west coast of South America, to Arequipa, the old Spanish capital among the Andes of southern Peru. The second time had been on a trip from Port Natal to Johannesburg, in South Africa. All the rest of my days had been spent either on the sea or along the margin of the sea. So closely do we sailor folks cling to the sight and smell of salt water.

Ships were the best of my boyhood, and it is ships chiefly that I remember. There is something of simple and fundamental life about a ship that makes her a true companion for either boys or men. A ship was my constant playmate through boyhood, and all the ships we met joined the game. Unknown and mysterious, they appeared on the rim of the horizon like tokens of undiscovered worlds. If we approached them near enough, they had to be signalized, an operation of which I took full charge. The hoisting of flags, the reading of signals through the spyglass, the patient solving of the mystery by aid of the international code book— this was play of the finest sort, a game in full reality, as the two ships sped on their way with miles of blue water between.

I remember races that lasted for weeks on end. Day after day the ships would be in sight of each other. When morning dawned, perhaps your adversary would be hull down ahead; per- haps you had caught a slant of wind in the night and put her topsails under on the lee quarter. Or perhaps the ships would break company for several weeks, only to come together farther along the course, under different conditions of wind and weather, and fight it out once more in plain sight of each other.

No seaman likes to be outsailed. Happily for my peace of mind, my boyhood was spent on board a fast ship. She was the clipper bark "Harvard," a low black-painted craft of a thousand tons register, hailing from Boston. This handsome little vessel was a jewel of seaworthiness and sailing qualities. She would lay up within five points of the wind, and sail her best close-hauled; I have seen her beat to windward through a fleet of schooners. She was a marvel in light airs, rarely losing steerage way, slipping through the water at three knots in a breeze that could barely be felt, when other ships were turning around to look at themselves. Best of all, the "Harvard" would tack in a teacup, and never was known to miss stays. A ship that can beat through the narrow gut of Lymoon Pass is worthy of record, even though she were han- dled by a Chinaman.

With a vessel like this, and under a master like my father, it was impossible for a boy not to acquire the fine art of sailing. The feeling of the sea sank in my blood. I learned it as one learns the better part of love, through daily application. I could "take the sun" and "work a sight" at the age of ten. The instinctive parts of seamanship—judgment and caution, the sense of a vessel's con- dition, the subtle message communicated by the heave of the deck—were mine by virtue of a romantic comradeship. I was an expert helmsman.

How well I remember one morning under the lee of Princes Island, at the entrance to the Straits of Sunda. We were crossing the great threshold of the East after three months at sea. The afternoon before we had sighted Java Head; morning found us hugging the land to escape the strong current in the middle of the straits. A gentle but steady land breeze wafted off the hills, a breeze that seemed trying in wanton play to head us off and knock us out into the current. "Take the helm, my boy, and see what you can do," said my father in his short way.

My palms had been itching for the spokes. "Please ask Mr. Forsyth to brace the main royal a little flatter, sir," I said, "and flatten everything aft on the foremast as hard as he can." The shadow of a smile crossed my father's face, but he gave the order. This luffed her half a point. Under the land, there was scarcely a ripple on the water. The weather leech of the main royal lifted. I held her so, barely moving the spokes of the wheel from minute to minute; and the little bark seemed to eat her way bodily to windward, as if making an effort independent of the rudder. I verily believe she lay within four and a half points of the wind that morning, while the green palm-clad shore of Princes Island, close aboard, slipped by at a steady five-knot gait. In ways like this, going to sea was fine.

I was allowed to climb the masts at will, to the royal yard, the highest point I could reach. I submit this as a test of my mother's character. Few women, I believe, would have been wise and brave enough to give a boy his freedom among a ship's swaying spars, walking the man-ropes a hundred feet above the deck, or overhanging the deep sea. I like to think that I repaid this great gift in the coin of prudence and heedfulness. I never came to accident aloft; I was safe because I was careful and free.

I used to love the royal yard when the ship heeled quietly at a constant angle, or lay at rest in the heart of a calm at sea. From that height the ocean assumes a wider, distant look, the aspect of a background. The deck is far away; the plan of the ship lies spread out before the eye. In a light, airy solitude, out of the ship yet in her, above the belly of the topmost sail, I used to sit by the hour astride the yard, one arm around the royal backstay, the only inhabitant of a world all my own. It was on the main royal yard, crossing the Indian Ocean, that I first read "Pickwick Papers." I have sighted many a sail from that perch, and examined many a landfall with eager eyes.

There was another place, more perilous still, that used to attract me in a sterner mood. This was the tip of the jib boom. I am not sure that my mother knew I went there. On a vessel of the "Harvard's" size, the jib boom extended some forty feet beyond the knight heads, hanging clear above the water in the path of the ship's progress. It was a stupid place in light weather, except for fishing. But when an eight-knot breeze was blowing, the jib boom became a seat of inspiration. Looking back, the narrow bows of the vessel lay directly before the eye. You saw her rushing toward you, dipping and plunging, tossing the spray to windward, rolling a broad wave-curl off the fine curve of the lee bow, her cutwater racing with eager and passionate intensity through the ocean that slipped with the steady motion of a panorama under your perch, the whole beautiful body advancing with power and purpose, as if alive. This was the place to see and know a ship's vitality.

Every boy reaches an age when he struggles with the problem of a personal God. A deep experience of this sort is associated in my mind with the jib boom. We were rolling lazily in a light air. All forenoon I had been on the jib boom, watching a pair of porpoises play around the bows. At length they finished their play, and settled down to lead the ship for a while, as they have a habit of doing.

The longer I watched them, the more I began to fear for their safety. Two days before, the mate had harpooned a porpoise, and the horror of it was still fresh in my mind. A porpoise is a mammal. It has warm blood by the bucketful; it squeaks and groans when it is hurt. A good-sized specimen will weigh three hundred pounds. To see such a creature harpooned and hauled out of the water on the end of the iron—the blood and struggle of it, the dumb sounds of the victim—had caused a sudden revulsion in my whole nature. I could not eat a mouthful of that porpoise. Now here were two more, placing themselves in prime position to be slaughtered. And as if in answer to my worst fears, at that moment the mate mounted the forecastle head and peered over the buffalo.

"Hello—porpoises!" he cried in great excitement, sighting them and me together. "Why didn't you sing out?"

"They just arrived, sir," I lied glibly.

"Well, keep them there. I'll run and get the harpoon."

Keep them there! What could I do? I had nothing to throw at them; porpoises are not easily frightened. Surely, I cried in agony, God will not permit this awful thing to happen again. And suddenly I realized that this was a test of Him. While sounds of running broke out along the deck, I burst into fervent prayer.

"O God," I prayed, "if there really is a God, and if You have power to do things, send these porpoises away. Send them away quick, before the mate gets the harpoon rigged. It depends on this, whether I will believe in You or not. If I don't want these porpoises killed, it seems to me You ought to feel the same way. Warn them, God! You must have the power. Give me a sign."

There was no time for more. The mate had rigged the harpoon, and now stood at the knight heads poising it in his right hand. A row of grinning faces leaned over the buffalo. The porpoises had not moved. A moment passed while the mate shifted his stand, so that the stroke would go clear of the bobstays. My heart sank like lead. But at that instant a wonderful thing happened. As if in obedience to a sudden command, the two dun-colored bodies turned abruptly to starboard, gathered quick headway, and left the path of the vessel. I could scarcely believe my eyes.

"Shoot, sir! They're going!" cried a dozen voices.

The mate flung the harpoon, but it fell far short. The men hauled in the empty iron; after a while they all went away. I sat on the jib boom, motionless and overwhelmed. I had seen a miracle. Why, I had caused it—it had been sent to me! That awed me, yet I felt wonderfully safe and secure. I had proved God's presence, had almost heard His voice. I tried to imagine the nature of the divine command that I had seen obeyed. God could hear, then; He was close at hand. The emptiness of the ocean surrounding me was His, the wind and the wave, and the fishes of the deep. How could I doubt that I was His also?

That voyage was a deeply religious one for me; before it was over God gave me another sign. We were lying beside the wharf in the basin of Port Natal. One morning after breakfast, I missed my dog Pint. He was nowhere on the ship. I called and whistled, but he had disappeared from the locality. This dog, an overgrown puppy, a sort of mongrel mastiff, had no acquaintance with the land. I was frantic, for I loved him dearly. I rushed ashore and started up the road toward the city of Durban. There were dogs everywhere—dogs playing in the gutter, dogs fighting, dogs running up the side lanes, my memory of the broad paved highway connecting Durban with its port, is of a street of dogs. I had provided myself with a pair of binoculars, for I was near-sighted.

While I searched, I prayed; after the experience of the porpoises, I purposed to leave God no excuse for overlooking this predicament. But at noon I had to give up the search and come back alone to the ship. Pint couldn't be found.

I ate my dinner in silence. For a couple of hours I moped at the gangway, keeping a sharp lookout along the water front. The deck seemed empty and desolate. I would never see Pint again. At last I could stand it no longer. I had to take my sorrow out of the ship, to a place I knew of fit for thinking problems through.

This place was an immense ocean beach, fronting the seas that stretched from Africa to the Antarctic. It lay on the outside of the long arm forming the natural sea wall of the basin of Port Natal. To reach it from our berth I followed a roadway leveled through a ridge of rocks, where the roar of the surf echoed and thundered among the ledges, till suddenly I emerged on a vast view of sand and broken water, with the wreck of a steel bark in the foreground that had dragged ashore in some southerly blow, and ships and steamers at anchor, waiting for the tide to pass in over the bar.

The beach was bleak and bare that afternoon. A strong gale was blowing off the southern ocean; the air had a keen cutting edge. The sea was a dark lead color; the sky and sand were a dull, lifeless gray. The scene fitted my gloomy mood. I went down to the surf, thinking the grim and logical thoughts of boyhood. The worst of it was that God had forsaken me. My dog was as well worth saving as a couple of porpoises. What had I done, to make Him withhold His hand?

After a while the mood softened; memories of my dear lost dog returned, bringing a flood of tears. At such times, I am always easier if I break into a run. It was while running at top speed in a westerly direction toward the lighthouse that I came pointblank against a venerable old man seated on a curved piece of timber cast ashore from another wrecked vessel. His back was to the wind, and he was reading a book. He had on a brown ulster; a tweed hat was pulled low over his ears. The ends of a woolen scarf about his neck snapped in the breeze. He closed the book, and looked up at me with twinkling eyes.

"What are you crying for, my boy?" he asked in a kindly way.

"I've lost my dog, sir," I sniffled.

He laughed as if struck by a sudden thought. Then he raised his hand and pointed dramatically along the beach.

"There is your dog," he said. "Go fetch him."

In that instant of speech, I knew that I stood on the threshold of another revelation. I looked where he pointed. A little distance off lay something that resembled a pile of sand. I ran toward it, calling Pint by name. The pile became animated, the sand upheaved and flew about; the long legs uncoiled themselves, the thick ropy tail began to swing, the familiar ungainly form bounded like a young camel across the beach. We fell upon each other and sank together in the sand. Even as I hugged Pint tight, I felt the wonder of it. Unworthy boy, I had doubted—I had failed the test. Yet God had forgiven me. What a marvelous chain of slender chances! How easily I might have run east instead of west when the tears began to come. Or if I had seen the old man in time, I wouldn't have approached him. . . .

The old man—where had he gone? I found myself gazing at the piece of curved and weather-beaten timber; but the brown ulster and tweed hat had disappeared. Yes, disappeared. I suppose the wind had grown too chilly, or he had conveniently reached the end of a chapter. I suppose Pint and I had been lying in the sand longer than I realized. It seemed only a minute. And I was frightened; for on all that broad beach there was not a living soul in sight. The old man had delivered his message, and vanished whence he came.

My nondescript dog had sailed from New York with the distinguished name of Prince, but the Chinese cook could not negotiate the word. "Pint, Pint, fool!" he would call explosively, setting a plate of food on the waterway beside the galley door. As the dog developed, we came to recognize the fitness of the pidgin English; he was more a "Pint" than a "Prince," and Pint he soon became to everyone. The cook, my bosom friend, never addressed the dog except in terms of violent imprecation—and never failed to feed him twice as much as he should have had.

This assumption of violent temper was Ah-li's chief design. A diminutive, wizened Chinaman with bloodshot eyes and a skin like parchment, he delighted in a peppery truculence which no one by any chance paid the least attention to. I had sailed with him a long while; he loved me with a devotion next to my father's. We used to hold curious conversation in the galley, he snapping and snarling as he kneaded the bread or rattled the pots and pans, I sitting on the bench with my knees under my chin, calmly disregarding the tone but answering the words. We understood each other; we "got along." I had the freedom of his hard, clean bunk, to read in when I chose. Sputtering and fuming, he spent much time in cooking little dainties for my private consumption. "Ha, Linkin, what for you come? All-time eat, eat!" he would cry with a ferocious expression, thrusting into my hands a cookie or a tart. If I failed to go to the galley during the day, he would be morose and unhappy; I had to placate him with a serious explanation of my absence. I never teased him; but I suppose, like any boy in association with a true heart, I failed to recognize all the sweetness and generosity of his nature. Love's greatest gifts to youth are taken for granted.

Father trusted Ah-li implicitly. Every day, when the galley had been cleaned up after dinner, the old Chinaman would smoke his tiny pipeful of opium. If I happened to be using the bunk I gave it up to him and went into the galley. This was a matter we had never spoken of, yet the understanding was perfect. I was never to touch the opium things, or comment on the occasion; the assumption being that nothing unusual was going on. I could not stay in the little room; but the door stood open and I could watch from the galley.

After arranging his pillow, Ah-li would sink back with a sigh and light the pipe. The faint fumes of opium would begin to steal through the door. Little by little a change would come on the old Chinaman's face, a look of peace and meditation. His eyes would remain open. The hand holding the pipe would sink to his breast; a quiet immobility would settle on his form. This lasted exactly half an hour. Then without warning he would sit up, put the pipe on the shelf, and wind his queue about his head. Father carried several sticks of opium in the medicine chest, in case the old cook's supply ran short at sea. He respected the character that held this habit in such perfect control.

It was Ah-li's generosity that finally sealed Pint's fate, a year later and on the other side of the world. Rich food drove the dog mad. The sad event happened near the equator in the Pacific, on the passage from Mollendo to Puget Sound. Pint had been snappish and excited all the morning. While we were sitting at dinner, a cry arose on deck. In a moment we knew the worst. The ship's company had taken to the rigging. The cabin doors were shut. Father went up to see that someone remained at the wheel.

My sister and I sat on the sofa holding each other's hands, listening in horror to the frantic sounds above as the mad dog rushed fore and aft the vessel.

Then silence fell, and after a while Father came below to tell us the story. Pint, dashing against the rail in a frenzy of madness, had flung himself overboard. "I wouldn't go up yet," said Father. But I was bound to drink my cup of grief. I took the long glass to the stern rail, and scanned the wake astern. There I caught sight of Pint in the midst of his death flurry, thrashing the water into foam. It was almost too much for me. I fled to the cabin and shut myself in my room.

Storms and dangers came in the natural course of events, for going to sea was not all plain sailing. But, taken all in all, it cannot be said that a seafaring life, under a competent commander, was any more unsafe than life ashore. It is dangerous to be alive. For my part, I have been afraid of the land many times, but never of the sea. Fear is the product of ignorance and lack of confidence. I knew a ship, and had full confidence in my father. But ashore I have had to be my own commander, and I have never learned the land.

I have passed through a typhoon on shipboard, and seen all kinds of bad weather; but I never have felt the margin of safety disappear. The ship was always in prime condition aloft. My father was a careful and expert navigator; he did not get into tight places, because he knew how to avoid them. I would not be understood as claiming that the sea affords nothing to fear. There are times when the elements will not be appeased, when a ship's margin of safety is swallowed up in the wrath of heaven, when even the best seaman finds himself caught in a net that cannot be broken. But these occasions come seldom. In an astonishing number of cases of maritime disaster, the ultimate fault lies with the judgment of men.

Once I fell overboard in harbor, and passed through the first stages of death. It was an interesting experience. We were lying in the open roadstead of Santa Rosalia, a small port half way up the Gulf of Lower California. I had jumped for a boat in which my sister was drifting away from the ship, and had fallen short of the gunwale. I could not swim; the seas I knew had been too deep for me to learn. When I found myself overboard for the first time in my life I began to thrash out wildly with my arms. But I was careful not to swallow any water. I began to count the times that I went under. Suddenly I realized that I had counted six or seven. "Well," said I to myself, as I came to the surface once more, "here is another theory gone to smash, at any rate. I never believed that the third time a person went down, he stayed down."

Another thing that interested me, while I struggled for breath, was that none of my past life was passing before my eyes in a flash, as the story books write the scene. I had always felt this to be one of those artificial notions that authors like to bring forward as strokes of realism. As a matter of fact, I wasn't thinking of anything in particular, except to wish that Father would hurry up and save me. I still had confidence.

I had lost the edge of consciousness when they reached me: Father, the mate, and one of the sailors, had all jumped at the same time. But I was able to put my hands on their shoulders, in the way I had been instructed to do if I ever were being saved. It was all over in a few minutes. Once in the boat, I quickly regained my senses. I walked up the gangway when we came alongside the ship. My mother hugged me tight—but I broke away and ran aft, struck by a sudden thought. There under the stern swam my school of pet sharks, thirty-footers, blotched and hideous, curling their bodies like whips and cutting the water with their sharp dorsal fins. Where they had been while we were overboard, I can't imagine. They were always around the vessel in Santa Rosalia. But, strange to say, in the process of drowning I had not once thought of them.

Up to high-school age I had my education at sea. Father taught me mathematics and seamanship, Mother taught English and history. I cannot remember learning to read. Geography came as part of life to a boy who studied charts for amusement, found his own position by the sun, and circumnavigated the globe. My parents' method of teaching was remarkable. In this, too, they gave me complete freedom. I was assigned a lesson and told to work it out for myself. I could take what time I wanted. In this way, I recall the day when I was to graduate from arithmetic and tackle the new conceptions of algebra. No explanation was given. I was handed a Wells College Algebra, with orders to report to Father when I had got the idea. It took me a whole forenoon to fathom the rudiments of the new mathematical technique; but when I had reasoned it through I knew it in a way that no amount of explanation could have imparted.

A question that has often arisen in my own mind may well occur to others here: where did a boy with this upbringing fit into the life of the land? The answer is, of course, that he didn't properly fit in anywhere. When I came ashore, I left my heart moored, I think, in the fairway of the Straits of Sunda, the gateway of the East, the portal of the dawn, where any ships that passed into the China Sea would sight my mooring buoy. It lies there yet, for all I know, unless it has broken adrift and started on one of those long sea journeys in the march of ocean currents. I have a notion that it will never drift ashore.

For my part, I pass the days like a man between ships, paid off but not yet signed up, waiting for the next voyage to come along. I love to watch the faces and manners of shore people; the things they do amuse and puzzle me, I am curious and appreciative, I enjoy looking on at the show; but shore life, the strange, complicated, urgent business of the land, will never seem quite real to me. My feelings and aspirations were built on other foundations—on foundations that, along with the ship of my birth, have sunk in the tide of time. When I grew up there was no sea career for me. The day of sailing ships was done; and I did not give a thought to steam.

But man, even without his heart, is an adaptable creature. I went to college, and became a civil engineer. For five years I helped to locate and construct railroads, build bridges, fill in swamps, and carry forward all the absorbing enterprises of a field engineer. There are points of resemblance between engineering and seafaring. I liked the work. But all the while, at long intervals, letters were arriving from my family on the other side of the world, from Anjer, Singapore, Hong-Kong, Amoy, Foochow. Father had another and bigger ship, and was making his last China voyages. Each letter brought me news of boyhood scenes; in a tent in the Maine woods, with the day's notes plotted and the evening game of poker with the axmen wound up, I would lie awake by the hour, bringing the ship through Gaspar Straits or Lymoon Pass to the tune of the wind in the pines overhead, or wondering if at that moment my family might not be going ashore in the sampan across the dancing bright waters of Singapore Bay. The pine trees were a great comfort; I think the Northern forest is a sister to the sea. It was while in the Maine woods, on railroad construction, that I sold and published my first sea story.

The longer I live, the more clearly I recognize the profound and subtle truth hidden in my parents' educational method. It was a truth derived, I suppose, from an elemental view of life, from the daily spectacle of man's audacious energy pitted against the majestic indifference of the universe. This was a matter too deep and hard for explanation. Eras and cultures, schools and philosophies, had made no appreciable headway against the strong current of human destiny. They had settled nothing; they had only served as starting points for new eras and schools. These two devoted seamen who had sailed so long together, who knew the earth and the heavens, had found no formula adequate to solve the plain things that had come to them in the guise of life, no lesson that could impart the strength to meet emergencies on the high seas of time.

Only the formula of seamanship, the lesson of integrity. Life brings its own education, and the life of the sea permits no truancy. It says to man, learn to be a seaman, or die. It takes no slurring answer, it gives no immunity. A man must get one hundred in that examination, or he is thrown out of school. If he is a poor navigator, he runs ashore. If he uses poor judgment in handling his ship, he loses her. If he is reckless, he meets disaster. If he neglects his watch at night, he has collision. If he slights his duty, something carries away. If he does not know his ship, to understand her voice, he takes the masts out of her. Even though he be apt in all these ways, yet if he lacks courage and quickness of action, the instinct and ability to meet a situation that never has risen before, the emergency will find him out some day, and he will pay the price of incapacity. The ocean cannot be cheated. It stands as the ultimate test of life. It may not be crossed except by those who know the stars.

PREFACE

In making another selection of stories for publication, I have been led to inquire more closely than ever before into the essential nature of nautical fiction. It was the sub-title to the present volume which, as it were, brought me up with a round turn. " . . . And Other Stories of the Sea" —the caption went down naturally, almost without thought. Why, certainly, stories of the sea! What else, if you please? I am accustomed to regard myself as a sailor, and what I write as being more or less directly the product of seafaring. The sea is my ground and origin; I have no other point of departure. I am a native of a latitude and longitude. The other day in the attic, overhauling a chest of old letters, I ran across a small pasteboard box containing a piece of shell-encrusted seaweed; it was one of the mementoes that came home among my father's effects when he died on board his vessel in Bremerhaven the year before the war. On the box, in his handwriting, was this inscription: "A bit of weed from L——'s birthplace, washed on board the S.S. *American* on June 2nd, 1905, in 44° south latitude, South Atlantic Ocean, in the same kind of a S.W. gale in which he was born; picked up and salted down by his father, this being the first that any of the family ever have seen of that country."

This selection first appeared as the preface in Lincoln Colcord's second volume of short stories, *An Instrument of the Gods and Other Stories of the Sea*, which was published by Macmillan in 1922. Colcord's knowledge of the sea and of literature of the sea makes the article a valuable statement about the sea story as a literary genre. Here he also gives the reader very telling glimpses of his own philosophy and of what he learned from his years at sea.

Thus, although I live ashore, ostensibly engaged in terrene projects and relations, I find that in all matters which seem to me of importance I am sailing still. I measure conduct in terms of seamanship; I pass my days in the condition of a man waiting for the next voyage to begin. The land seems alien to me, and fixed life an enigma, strangely complicated by motives which I lack, strangely barren of what intrigues and sustains me. "We live in manhood," says Thoreau, "to fulfil the dreams of our boyhood." He meant more. We live in manhood to explore and circumnavigate our boyhood; it is the only world we ever know.

But when I scanned my table of contents, it occurred to me to wonder if I were playing fair with my readers in the promise of the sub-title. What constitutes a sea story? Because I was born in a gale of wind in the region of Cape Horn, because I was brought up on the quarter-deck of a sailing ship, am I at liberty to call anything I may choose to write a sea story? Hardly. Yet, on the other hand, may it not be possible that certain pieces extraneous to the sea derive a nautical aspect from the very hopelessness of my maritime preoccupation? Is it no licence that a man views the world through sailor's eyes?

Sailors themselves have strict ideas of the legality of nautical fiction; they might be among the first to call some of my stories before the bar. Yet, all else being equal, I would rest my case on the factor of nautical verisimilitude. In sea literature, as in the kindred matter of the nautical painting, it is this question of the accuracy of the picture which above all others concerns the sailor. Life has overwhelmed him with lessons of the value of spiritual integrity; the dominating note of sea experience is that inaccuracy, incompetency, insincerity, spell danger, ruin, defeat, and even death. All slipshod work at sea is inartistic; the inexorable criticism of the free-spirited ocean affords no margin of safety. Thus seamanship, to those who understand it, acquires, like engineering, an application beyond the technical field. It means the attitude and way of life which faces facts, which deals in realities without evasion, which knows that the only failure is dishonesty and that error is truth betrayed.

In the matter of reading, then, the sailor is well aware that the stalls are filled with sea books written by landlubbers. Rarely, indeed, does he find a work which bears the authentic stamp of seamanship. How vividly I recall my father's scorn at an incident in one of the novels of a famous writer of nautical fiction. He was reading the book aloud one evening, on board the bark *Harvard*, going up the China Sea. The tale had arrived at the point of love-making; the scene was set on the quarter-deck of a sixteen hundred ton sailing packet. The heroine reclined in a deck-chair against the lee rail; a gentle air from the spanker wafted down upon her, for they were sailing sunny seas. The hero whispered his message; and while she listened, turning her face away, she trailed her hand idly in the water. "Ha!" snorted my father, when he reached this passage. "That fellow had better look out for himself—she has long arms." An incident like this will ruin a book for a sailor. And why not? The distance from the rail of a sixteen hundred ton packet to the water would be something like twenty feet. The author obviously was thinking of punting on the Thames. He had confessed himself a landlubber. How, then, could anything he had to say of the sea be taken seriously? This particular writer had produced a formidable array of sea volumes, some of them regarded as classics by a landlubber standard; the whole set thereafter was damned and doubly damned in my father's eyes.

I must confess that I entirely sympathize with this point of view. The landlubberly sea story is an inartistic product; no man can tell a true tale of something which he does not know. The high degree of specialization in the craftsmanship of the sea, and of differentiation between it and anything to be found on land, alike make the writing of true nautical literature a task for seamen alone. For only through a knowledge of the craftsmanship may one arrive at a sense and appraisement of the underlying values, the secret urgent sentiments, which are the unique characteristics of seafaring—all that we mean when we speak of the "feeling of the sea."

On the score of nautical verisimilitude, also, the sailor has a criticism of the daily press which, to my mind, cuts well below the surface. The press, as everyone must recognize, has developed a distinctive style for handling news with a sea flavor, a style compounded of equal parts of mild facetiousness and smart romanticism. It carries a great deal of this material, the most of it topical or feature stuff; tales of strange happenings beyond the horizon, tales of terror or crime or mutiny, tales of trivial humor, tales of disaster or miraculous escape. To the landsman, these may serve their ostensible purpose of entertainment; but the sailor writhes and curses as he reads them, for almost invariably they are nautical monstrosities. They are untrue to the sea; and this, to him, is sacrilege. Even when a straightforward news report of some maritime event needs to be written, it suffers from the same fatal injection of landlubberism.

Every sailor, at some time in his career, has met with the experience of participating in such an event, and of reading the newspaper accounts of it afterward. Oftentimes he was the man who gave the story at first hand to the reporter, who pointed out the facts, who explained the technical situation, who warned against certain obvious pitfalls. And when he sees the story in print, a bitter laugh is all that remains to him. Every pitfall has been tumbled into; the technical situation has been rendered unintelligible to a seaman; the facts have been juggled to suit an imaginery taste, to conform to a professional technique; everything about the job serves only to confirm a strong impression which this sailor has acquired through a lifetime of observation— an impression of the general incompetency of the press in his own special field. He makes a saying of it, a saying known to seamen everywhere about the world. He says: "If the newspapers so badly misrepresent this event in which I participated, and so ignorantly treat of this life which I know, what shall I think of their report and treatment of things which I do not know?"

The sailor's demand for accuracy, however, like any other virtue, may easily be driven too far. Indeed, it cannot be denied that the constant pressure of this demand, coupled with an arbitrary superiority of special knowledge, tends to create in him an attitude of extreme literalness, if not of rigidity, toward the broader problems of literary creation. I prize, in this connection, an incident of my first reading of Conrad's "Lord Jim." I was fresh from the sea at the time, fresh from Singapore and China waters as well; and the book, as was to have been expected, struck me flat aback. (I still maintain that "Lord Jim," when all is said and done, will live as Conrad's masterpiece.) In the fervor of my enthusiasm, after that first reading, I forwarded the book at once to a shipmaster with whom I was in close relation. He sent it back, after some months, with a criticism and a comment. The criticism ran: "This man Conrad backs and fills too much." The comment said: "He has tried to tell the story of W——, but has made a poor job of it. I know W——; his wheels don't go around that way. He didn't give a damn."

It is necessary to explain this comment at some length. The original of Conrad's character, Lord Jim—that is to say, the fellow who did go mate of an old steamer carrying native pilgrims from Singapore to Mecca, who did, along with the rest of her officers, abandon this steamer somewhere in the Indian Ocean, leaving the pilgrims to their fate, and who did return from this despicable adventure to become a runner in the ship-chandlery business on the China coast—this fellow is, or was, an individual well known to all seafaring men whose courses used to lead them to Eastern waters. His name is W——, if he is still alive.

This man actually did, as I have stated, undergo the initial set of experiences out of which Conrad developed the story of "Lord Jim"; but there the resemblance ends. For the sentient and palpable W—— was not in any degree the sort of chap to follow Jim's romantic and tragic destiny. In the phrase of my shipmaster friend, he didn't give a damn for the loss of reputation involved in the abandonment of the steamer; he used to treat the matter as a broad joke. As I recall him twenty-five years ago, located in the cosmopolitan center of the East as runner for the firm of McA——'s, living the life of a European renegade, he was a man of gross and materialistic parts, a man without conscience, I should say, and with very little principle. He lacked every quality which brought to Lord Jim the refinement of life's cruelty; he was everything in life that Jim would have abhorred. In short, W—— himself was more like the man Brown, who finally drove fate home to Jim in Patusan, than he was like the character reared on a foundation of his own experience.

Knowing the facts, it is plain to see what Conrad did. The incidents of W——'s story, familiar to everyone in the East, kindled his creative imagination; he saw in them a powerful motive for a tale of human weakness and divine fatalism. W——, he felt acutely, ought to have suffered, his conscience ought to have driven him from the world, his life ought to have sunk in retribution. The next step was to make things as they should be; that is, to create a character with the proper temperament, and put him in W——'s shoes. That W—— himself lacked a conscience, of course made no difference; from the point of view of creative genius he had lived inartistically, and had wasted marvellous romantic opportunities. But the literalness of my seafaring friend would not permit him to bridge the gap of literary creation. This book, "Lord Jim," by one Conrad, was nothing but W——'s story in much-garbled form; he knew W——, who wasn't that sort of a character at all. In fact, I think he loathed W——, and took this as an effort to whitewash the rascal. He never could forgive Conrad for what seemed to him a lapse in veracity.

But we have not yet defined the sea story. The loose popular definition, I take it, would be a story of the sea, about the sea, or situated on the sea. This is at the same time too broad and too narrow a ruling. It admits, on the one hand, that vast body of landlubberly sea fiction which I have instanced; for this material is just as truly of the sea, about the sea, or situated on the sea, as that of the most legitimate nautical production. On the other hand, it would exclude the authentic works of sea fiction primarily concerned with the development of character, perhaps with the character of landsmen, but presented through a nautical atmosphere; those land books in short, which have suffered a sea change. It would exclude "Lord Jim," for instance, or "Captain Macedoine's Daughter." Neither of these books is primarily of the sea, or about the sea, or situated on the sea; both are studies in human psychology, thrown against a background of sea experience—they are life looked at through sailor's eyes. As such, they are works of unimpeachable nautical realism.

It is this matter of characterization, I believe, which more than any other leads to confusion in the real measure of the sea story. The sea in fiction has been looked upon almost exclusively in the past as a source of romantic plot material; and the great reading public ashore has become thoroughly familiarized with, if not educated to, this aspect of nautical literature. It expects unusual and exciting happenings in its sea tales, scenes of elemental struggle, of broad comedy or tragedy. It scarcely realizes that it has formed the habit of regarding the sea too narrowly with a plot motive, and that its estimate of the sea story is unconsciously cast in this plane.

But the sailor himself, the native of the wilderness of waters, quite as unconsciously thinks of the sea in the plane of characterization. He thinks of it as a place where life goes on. He thinks of it as he knows it, and wins his way across it, and freights on its broad bosom the precious cargo of his own particular life problem, the simple and universal problem of human enterprise and aspiration. To him, in consequence, a sea story is a story of life touched by the influence of the sea; and a true sea story is such a story told by one who understands.

For my own part, the definition must forever be paradoxical; there are no categories. This work is authentic, that is spurious; the ruling is wholly arbitrary. I must submit each case to my own judgment, with the candor and responsibility of a man alone on the quarter-deck, bringing his ship through perilous waters. The integrity of true criticism is no less than the integrity of creative art, its nearest point of reckoning the sun and the stars.

The sea herself is a character in a stirring tale. As a child, I knew that she lived about me. I was taught at my father's knee that, notwithstanding the countless disasters of the deep, the gruesome record of maritime adventure, the sea had no harm or terror for those who loved her—for those who found it in their hearts to be faithful to her stern but generous decrees. I have been afraid of the land many times, but never of the sea. The dangers of life ashore are insidious; afloat, one sees what comes and reaches where one steers. We who have come up to the land cannot in nature think of the sea alone as wind and water, silence and solitude, the materials for romanticists to make their tales a little more romantic; rather, we think of her always as part and symbol of our better selves, a creature of light and color, of pain and joy and love, a spirit of proud endeavor and conscious humanity. We have learned from her the meaning of truth. We know no aim but that of fidelity to her character.

Lincoln Colcord.

Searsport, Maine,
  March, 1922.

THE BOGIE HOLE

When I was a boy, at sea with my father, we went one voyage to
Newcastle, New South Wales. There I became acquainted with
a chap of about my own age, the son of the American Consul.
One day soon after our arrival he took me home with him. They
lived far back from the harbor, on rising ground; my sense of
direction, added to the study which I had made of the chart of
Newcastle, told me that we were heading towards the ocean
outside the point, but a street was not my natural element, and
I felt that I must be mistaken. The sights of the land were strange
and confusing. Later, as I sat on the broad veranda, my eyes were
agreeably surprised to catch a distant glimpse of the Pacific horizon. The road ascended a gentle grade in that direction, and
seemed to end abruptly some distance beyond the house; I wondered if the brink of the cliff might be there—if the ocean might
be close at hand, concealed by the shoulder of the land. At
length I put the question; my friend jumped up.

"Come on!" he cried. "You haven't seen the Bogie Hole!"

We started on the run, and came out suddenly on the brink of
a high precipice, hanging above the sea like the bows of a
tremendous ship. The outlook was magnificent; a wide arc of
horizon, a brilliant panorama of ocean thick with arriving and
departing sails. Far below, the surf thundered with a steady voice;
the noonday sun flooded the scene with that dazzling brightness
which seems to belong more to the sea than to the land. Through
the clear, quiet, air, and from such an altitude, vessels appeared
much nearer than they were. One could scarcely realize that on
those distant decks men were shouting their orders, and the
clamor of their work was going on; even the steamers, trailing
their smoke on the water, stole by without a sound. The long

Pacific swell seemed as insignificant as a ripple on a pond. I was reminded of a picture from my child's geography, illustrating the commerce of the world; a broad ocean shown from continent to continent, its surface dotted with every kind of craft in magnified proportion.

Following the margin of the cliff a little way, we came to a course of steps hewn in the solid rock. They dropped diagonally down the face of the precipice, and seemed to vanish in a cave-like shadow at the base of the cliff. My friend dashed forward and ran down the steps without a word, leaving me to follow at my discretion. I reached the top step, and hesitated; then I made out a group of naked boys disporting themselves on a ledge of rock below, apparently in peril of the bursting swell. The scene opened before me as I descended; at the foot of the steps I paused again, dumb with delight and incredulity, beholding for the first time the wonder of the Bogie Hole.

This swimming pool lies close under the towering cliff, directly facing the Pacific, entirely cut off from any other view; the most remarkable, the most utterly romantic haven that ever boy enjoyed. It owes its situation to a mighty geological formation. Along that section of the coast of New South Wales runs a stupendous upturned stratum of rock; the sea for many miles is confronted by a series of massive fortifications. Huge buttresses, supporting the upper works, extend boldly into the ocean. On reefs and ledges the powerful swell breaks incessantly in swirling undertow, flinging its spray in sheets against the impregnable bulwark of the land. Above the Bogie Hole the precipice leans seaward; and here, before the hand of man had changed it, lay a table of rock at least a hundred feet in width towards the sea, some several hundred feet in length alongshore, and high enough above sea-level to escape the body of the swell.

The pool itself is blasted from the living rock, to a depth of six feet and more. Its only possible approach is by the course of hewn steps down which we had come; ragged ledges flank it on either side. A wall of the natural rock guards the seaward side of the pool, topped by a row of iron stanchions and festooned by a heavy chain-rail. Crests of green seas burst constantly through this open protection, swinging and rattling the chain, and falling into the enclosed basin. No other supply is necessary; the shelf lies at a perfect elevation for the purpose; and all day long the top of the booming swell launches itself across the rocky barrier, renewing the water from the exhaustless reservoir of the Pacific, sluicing down the surrounding ledges, flecking the pool with foam. Clouds of spray fly singing through the air. The steady roar of the sea, at first a tumult to stun the senses, soon comes to be the natural sound of that heroic place; the view of the ocean is intermittently obscured by breakers, rearing and vanishing in the same instant of majestic beauty. During heavy storms, when bathing is forbidden and the Pacific reigns in terrible and solitary supremacy, the surf has been known to fling live sharks into the Bogie Hole.

Withal, the pool is as safe a place for bathing as any strip of sheltered beach. The danger in the air serves but to heighten its attraction. Of the same alluring nature is the absolute seclusion of the spot; the port of Newcastle lies hidden around the point to northward; to southward, stretches of rock-fronted uninhabitable coast; the lighthouse on the Nobbys is the only sign of man in sight, except the enchanted vessels passing to seaward. These lend the place its final charm. Tired of swimming or other play, a boy may crawl out on the rocks and sun himself awhile, watching the ships through half-closed eyes. They nose out past the Nobbys; they turn to port or starboard, setting their magic sails; they vanish up the coast, they pass close by, they dwindle and are soon hull-down on the clear horizon, sinking one by one along the mysterious reaches of the sea.

I have wondered who first called it the Bogie Hole; the name is significant. I have been there late of an afternoon, when the sun was dropping behind the cliff; and looking around me at such a time, have felt the grip of terror on my young heart. Shadows enveloped the black rock ledges; the spouting foam of breakers, no longer touched by the brilliant sunlight, took on a tone of sombre, chilly grey. The air grew cold; the voice of the sea had acquired a threatening note. Fear crept about the ledges. Boys grimly taking their last dip glanced up in apprehension as the sharp spray lashed their faces, and suddenly losing courage, made for the shelter of the dressing-ledge before the next wave could reach its hand into the pool. The spirit of play quickly died out; and we who had been brave and careless in the sun fell back, as better men than we had done, before the menace of a dark-ening sea. At that hour we used to dress quietly and steal away;

shuddering, perhaps, as we regained the daylight of the upper steps and glanced back at the gathering gloom of the Bogie Hole.

The time to see the pool in all its glory was in the morning, when the sun stood high over the sea. Boys gathered there as if by magic, playing naked the whole forenoon. The rocks were warm, and slippery with salt spray. By that time the chill was burned out of the water; crowds of young urchins ducked and ran screaming before the onslaught of each wave from the heart of the Pacific. Great games were carried on among the breakers; certain daring boys climbed out along the sea-wall, hanging there by the chain-rail, and holding their breath as the crests of rollers passed over them in a smother of foam. The hot sun streaming into the caves among the upper ledges made pleasant retreats for the exercise of confidence and speculation. The waters of the pool sparkled with ocean clearness and purity. Lithe white bodies gleamed in the dark ground of the rock in statuesque and charm-ing attitudes. The deep blue color of the ocean filled the eye. Flocks of dazzling sea-birds wheeled above the outlying reefs. The noise of the surf mingled happily with the clamor and shrill cries of boyhood at play. From that sacred spot a native, tireless paean of youth, high spirits, and the urge of life, went up to the gods. And hour by hour, as we played, ships passed on the face of the sea in stately procession, under the steady glow of the sun.

I cannot say that the boys of Newcastle are different from other boys about the world, but I feel sure that in some vital, unseen part they must acquire a priceless gift from the Bogie Hole. That free, romantic prospect of ocean must stir and swell their better dreams; that air charged with wind-blown spray must clear their hearts of many moods and influences. They meet the sea like sailors; they come to know its sounding voice; a manly boldness surges in their blood as they play naked at the feet of nature and the elements. In moments of repose they see the ships of nations pass before them, freighted with fancies, off on long, adventurous voyages, bound for foreign lands. Perhaps few who play as boys in the Bogie Hole will follow either adventure or the sea; but all will have their memories, and all, I trust, their high adventures of the armchair. It is seldom given to men to remember such a play-ground, in the days of their bondage and infelicity.

EASTERN NAMES

What's in a name? If the heart has atrophied, having attained that wisdom which is mainly disillusion, a name is nothing much; but if the heart keep young, a name's the world and all. What man of parts, choosing a book at random, would hesitate between Paolo and Francesca and Peter Simple, or spend his money for "Martin Chuzzlewit" if his eye fell on "The Last of the Mohicans" or "The Master of Ballantrae" in the next row of the stall? And, of all right-spirited young sprouts of sensibility and good romantic proclivities, who would not rather love a girl named Eleanor than one named Mary Jane; who would not rather follow a commander named Nelson than one named Henry Simpkins; who would not rather go to sea in a ship named the Talavera than in one named the Codfish; who would not rather sight the land in the Straits of Sunda than at Brackett Bay?

Even though Tristan d' Acunha is a bleak and uninhabitable island, and though the full-rigged ship Henry B. Hyde was one of the swiftest and most beautiful vessels that ever spread a sail, yet the sailor's heart refutes the prose of knowledge, and still believes in delectable and sounding names. He dreams of capes and islands whose appellations are music and a song, of lands that echo their delightful syllables, of mountains that shout the grandeur of their crowned and stately realms; and if by any chance a ship were given him again and he were told to sail in search of treasure and romance, he would lay his course for Eastern waters, where squalls hang in the shadow of Sumatra-side, where the North Watcher stands like a sentinel at the head of the Thousand Isles, where the land breeze drops at evening from the Java hills.

The track towards the East is marked with singing names. No sooner is the voyage well under way, than Fernando de Noronha heaves in sight; that island of the tall black Pinnacle, a pencil of rock, a mighty spire above the mountain roof, known to every sailor who has crossed the Line in the Atlantic. It appears, rises, stands on the horizon pale and wonderfully green in the shimmering tropic air, a jewel set on a still and silver sea. It vanishes astern, as the ship picks up the southeast trades.

In the height of the trades another island, Trinidad (not Port of Spain) breaks the horizon, a dark lump of barren rock in the midst of sparkling waters, quickly passed in the hurry of the constant breeze. Soon afterwards the Cape of Good Hope stands abeam: the Cape of Good Hope, first called Cabo Tormentoso, Cape of Storms. Vasco de Gama, the Portuguese, first rounded it. And then the Indian Ocean, past Algoa Bay, Natal, and Madagascar. And past the Keeling Islands, that bold piratical group, where blood and mutiny abound, and treasure caskets lie buried under burning sands.

The first big land sighted on the outward passage is at Java Head; beside it stands Cape Sangian Sira, with its name like a battle-cry. We are in the Straits of Sunda: name charged with the heady languor of the Orient, bringing to mind pictures of palm-fringed shores and native villages, of the dark-skinned men of Java clad in bright sarongs, clamoring from their black-painted dugouts, selling fruit and brilliant birds. These waters are rich in names that stir the blood, like Krakatoa, Gunong Delam, or Lambuan; or finer, more sounding than all the rest, Telok Betong and Rajah Bassa, a town and a mountain—Telok Betong at the head of Lampong Bay and Rajah Bassa, grand old bulwark on the Sumatra shore, the cradle of fierce and sudden squalls.

How shall we cross the China Sea—through Banka, Gaspar, or Caramata Straits? It all depends on the monsoon. In Banka, we are fairly launched among the smooth Malayan names. We pass the Lucipara Islands, we take a bearing on Tobo Ali Lama and the Karang Brom-Brom. But Gaspar is the main highway. How often have we picked up the light on Shoalwater Island, made the coast of Billiton, and passed close under Southwest Point, where the white lighthouse stands above the palms. Navigation in these channels was a constant menace to the old-time navigator. Many a vessel driving home on a clipper passage touched a point of coral that showed no breakers, and found herself wrecked beneath calm and tropic skies. She left her name along with her bones. Hippogriffe Shoal, and Hillsborough Rock, Actaeon and Severn Reefs and many more, each mark the grave of some fine ship. We think of them as we pass by. The waters of Caramata touch the shores of Borneo, inscrutable and lovely island of the East. We hail the town of Banjarmassin, and sail on.

Perhaps the two most beautiful names in all the East are given to the waters lying along the opposite coasts of Borneo—Palawan Passage, and Macassar Strait. Palawan skirts the Borneo shore in the China Sea, running between Palawan, Labuan, and the group of shoals to westward in open water, named mostly for ships or captains of the past. South of Palawan, Balbac Strait leads into the Sulu Sea; to the northward lies Mindoro Strait. The names along these coasts are divided between the English and the native tongues; Triple-Top Island, Treacherous Bay, Boat Rock, and Conflagration Hill alternate with such names as Appurawan, Bahelee, Inlulutoc, and Malampaya. Spanish names, too, begin to appear: Santa Monica is a town on the north of Palawan, and Punto de San Tomas, on the island of Mindanao, is the site of a remarkable Spanish ruin.

Along the coast of the Philippines, Spanish, English, and native names are equally divided. Beside the island of Popototan lies Isla Verde, and next to that, the Haycock. Off to the westward we find another group of shoals and dangers named for clipper ships: Diana Reef, Elphinstone Rock, Rifleman Bank, Investigator Shoal. Out on the middle track, the track of fair monsoons, lie the Anamba Islands, Amboyna, and Seluan. And farther still to the westward, in the Gulf of Siam, are many well known names of fine romantic flavor: Saigon, Bangkok, Cambodia, Pulo Condore, and Cape Padaran.

But if the northeast monsoon is at its height, we would better turn aside from Sunda and the China Sea, and take the Eastern Passages to the Pacific. These waters have seen stirring times. Here, in days when great fleets of sailing ships traversed the eastern seas, when coasts were carelessly charted, the captain lived in constant fear of hidden dangers. Winds were baffling, tides confusing and strong; the channels were so narrow and tortuous that often it was a difficult operation to work a ship through without striking on the outlying shoals. Many a man has looked down through the clear waters of Macassar Strait or Ombay Pass, and seen the white coral rising to his keel when he thought he had twenty fathoms to spare. But on they drove, for tea and silk and spices, across the Flores Sea through Ombay Pass, across the Bania and Arafura Seas, up through Molucca Passage, past Amboina and the rich Spice Islands, out at last through the Straits of Jillolo to the open Pacific. Then northward and in by Bashee Channel, where in the fairway lies Botel Tobago, an island named for a boy's wildest dream.

And on to the ports of China, so familiar that we seldom try to remember how they used to sound. Hong Kong, Amoy, Canton, Foochow, Shanghai—these speak a secret language to the sailor, a tale of ardent adventure in the old clipper tea-trade, and bring to mind the long procession of ships that have passed away. Romance. He likes to repeat the names that once were part of every day in port: Stonecutter's Island, Lymoon Pass, the Great Ladrones, and Kowloon-side. With joy in each syllable, he tells of Pratas Reef, and Pedro Blanco, and the Pescadores, which used to lead him in from sea. And he remembers, too, another place called Happy Valley, lying amid the palms and blossoms of Wanchi.

OUTWARD BOUND

WINDLASS CHANTY

Oh, soon she'll bite the swell—the breeze is singing;
Sandy Hook is dropping fast astern!
Come, walk her up, my boys—the pawls are ringing;
And the long low coast goes down.
Then it's good-bye, and a year we'll be a-sailing;
Sandy Hook is dropping fast astern!
So sheet your topsails home—the dawn is paling;
And the long low coast goes down.

LOSING THE LAND

The sea seemed very blue and wide
After the muddy harbor tide;
The slender masts looked strange and high,
Towering with canvas to the sky;
The deck became the scene of tales
Under the shadow of the sails.
A new life entered in the ship;
We watched the main-truck wheel and dip,
And felt her lift beneath our feet
With able lunge and motion sweet.
She slipped along with scarce a sound;
The broad horizon hemmed us round;
Over the ocean's floor appeared
The lonely spirit never feared;
To us who knew and loved the sea,
It seemed like home—and we were free.

TRADE WINDS

Northeast trade winds bore us south,
    Southeast drew us on;
We met the ships from every port
    For Good Hope or the Horn.

Seas so quiet, skies so blue,
    Little squalls of rain;
The winds that blew about the world
    Filled our hearts again.

FERNANDO DE NORONHA

We lay becalmed; the white-hot sun
    Beat down above an even swell;
And, clear upon our starboard bow
    Stood out your spar-like Pinnacle.

THE WESTERLIES

Cold winds, dead aft, and heavy running seas
That swung us onward faster than the breeze;
Bleak day, and lurid sunsets, and wild skies,
And lonesomeness that broods as the day dies.
Abandoned course, below the happy world;
A staggering ship, with upper canvas furled,
Flooded by crashing seas, day after day,
In the Roaring Forties, where the wind has its way.

CHRISTMAS ISLAND

One day we raised your lonely hills
    Like clouds against the sky,
And proved our course, and kept our faith,
    And passed you by.

Java Head

Ships of all nations and all venturing times
Have passed and left you on the starboard lee,
Dark headland, guardian of strange Eastern climes,
Above the shimmering purple Indian sea.

The North Watcher

What poet named you, setting your beacon there
On a lone island, lighting all the miles
Of dangers, pointing for ships your channel fair,
North Watcher, heading the Thousand Isles?

Gaspar Straits

We passed the Watcher at night,
And dawn put out its sinking light;
All day we held the fair monsoon,
All night we ran beneath the moon;
And in the early morning hours
We smelled the near land and the flowers,
And saw, abeam, the hillsides on
The southwest point of Billiton.
A little lighthouse, white as snow,
Looked out upon the strait below;
Each garden was a tiny square,
Terraced and blooming everywhere;
Toy cows were grazing on the grass,
Toy men ran down to see us pass;
It must have been a pleasant place,
To wear that glad and smiling face;
But we held such a steady breeze,
The village soon was lost in trees.

The Fishing Fleet

Brown sails of fishing boats
On a sea of jade,
Startled at early dawn,
Fleeing afraid.

Far as the eye can see
    Into the sun,
Count we their endless fleet
    One by one.

Dim foreign hills in sight
    There on the beam;
Voices, now close aboard —
    Like ghosts they seem.

Brown sails of fishing boats
    On a sea of jade,
Leaving on either hand
    The wake we made.

Yellow foam of breaking waves
    On a jade-green sea;
Brown junks and brown sails
    Windward and lee.

HONG KONG

In Lymoon Pass we felt the land
Grow near and high on either hand;
Strange voices shouted through the night,
Strange junks flashed out a signal light;
And soon we reached the land-locked bay
Where all the quiet vessels lay,
And felt the touch of life again,
And smelled the fresh land after rain;
While out from ships and hill and shore
There stole a voice we knew before.

CAPTAIN
ROBERT BELKNAP
GOES WEST

———————◆———————

In which one of the vanishing Americans speaks his honest mind
about the corruption and malfeasance in government which the
present-day citizen so spinelessly condones.

Hello! Come in. I'm damned glad to see you.
Well, here I am . . . hell of a place for a man to be.
Bed's made for better pidgin. Ha! I feel
Like some old hulk that wants to keep on sailing:
Stranded . . . I guess the sand has made around me.
Is anything more useless than a wreck?
I can remember coming up through Ombay Pass
In the northeast monsoon in the ship *Wandering Jew.*
You know how the tide runs there like a mill-race,
With green water to mark the coral patches;
A nasty place when the wind heads you off.
And there was a big wooden ship perched on a reef,
Sticking her snags of teeth up to the sun;
We went right by her—she'd been there a long time.
It made me shiver to look at her; I always hated
Dead things and broken things and things gone by.

What's that? Outside the window! . . . Nothing, I guess.
I have these spells, my head don't seem to work;
I keep hearing strange sounds to windward.
Funny how life goes back on you at last;

You aren't so able as you thought you were.
Well, what can you expect? Who's growling? Why
Should anyone want to hang around, roost on a reef,
With spars broken and bare ribs showing through?
I'd rather sink at sea and have it over.
I've lived a long life and am tired of it,
And any day death wants to she can come.
Wait—let me fold my arms the way they do:
Now won't I make a God-damned handsome corpse?
Ha! What are you jumping for? You can't dodge death.
Haven't you lived? Then aren't you glad to die?
It's death that gives the breeze of life an edge.

II

Has it ever struck you how we spend our lives
Sailing around the world and carrying cargo,
Seeing how trade goes on, and seeing how
Nations are all alike, and men the same
In China or in Russia or at home,
And trade the same, that makes the nations live;
And then we quit the sea and settle down
To watch them make a monkey of the show?

Politics! God, it seems to be the art
Of doing everything wrong for the devil of it,
Just to make work in cleaning up the mess;
The trick of never arriving where you are bound.
Set your course for the rocks and let her go!
Heave her to in a calm, and crack on sail
When one of those black squalls shows up to windward!
And if you take the masts out of her, all the better;
They'll make you President for that, the next election.

Or Congress, there—a forecastle five-hundred strong,
With every man his own sea-lawyer. Ha!
As if speeches could fill a vessel's sails,
Or law trim weather braces; who's to go
Aloft to furl the courses off the Horn,
Or man the pumps in silence? All they know

Is how to bring their grub aft in a gale of wind,
Because the salt-beef hash has rope yarns in it,
Yammering about their rights with the ship in danger.

The ablest politician is the man
Who spends the nation's money needlessly,
But makes the people think it is important;
The more he fails, the more they talk about him,
And talk is what he wants to build his name.
The lubberly fools! They ask to be misgoverned;
They wouldn't know what seamanship was for.
They like to sail her wild in any weather,
Never a look at the chart, never a question
Of how she heads or where she's going to fetch,
Driving along with only the wind for master.

You couldn't run a ship the way they run
The nations. . . . No, by God, we had to lay
A course, and trim our sails to use the wind,
And figure our position without error,
And beat the sea with judgment, and make a landfall;
Or take our medicine—not be excused.

God defend us! Foolish and blind! Foolish and blind!
Do you think the fog brings safety, do you think
The rocks aren't there because you don't see them?
Do you think a nation can't strike and go down?
For Christ's sake, haul your wind! Shake out the topsails!
You're on a lee shore now, in company
With other ships that couldn't navigate,
And other men who tried to lead by following.

There's something up aloft that makes me nervous.
Hear it? Something loose and flying adrift.
Listen! What is it, what is it? Call the mate!
Let me get up. I want to go on deck.
There she cracks! I knew it! The fore topmast!
Send me the mate, I say. I told the bastard
To call me when it breezed on. . . . So help me God,
Give me a hand . . . the masts are coming down!

III

What was I saying? . . . Well, it doesn't matter.
I never liked the land: a place where men
Can't seem to work life out; they'll never learn
That truth is only common sense and reason,
Like a straight course, or like an honest answer,
And that you can't run anything on lies.

Nothing tidy or shipshape about the land,
Ropes leading wrong and gear all tangled up,
Yards cock-billed and Irish pennants flying,
Men spoiling the beauty that God gave them,
No one in charge to straighten out the deck,
And no one aft to be responsible.

A crazy, mean performance; all the values
Seem end-for-end; the things that landsmen go by
Would lose a ship before she gained her offing;
The life ashore seems mainly given up
To building strong defenses against error.
No one seems glad, as when a man sets out
To handle his own ship, meet his own fortune,
And pay his price for what he fails to win.
The landsman seems to have but one ambition:
To find a quiet, safe, and shallow harbor,
And never lift his anchors from the mud.

The only men ashore I'd trust my ship to
Are failures, men who laughed at the wrong time
Because they couldn't stand the make-believe.
They are the only happy landsmen I've noticed,
The ones who dared to call their souls their own.

IV

Whenever I came in from the sea, in the old days,
I'd feel something closing in around me;
I wasn't free, I couldn't speak my mind,
I had to be careful or I'd lose a dollar.

Something hung on the land like a fever,
Fear and doubt, cutting the soul of action,
Sharpening everything false, blunting everything true.

But when I sailed again, and felt the sea
Up through my own ship's deck, and saw her beauty,
And looked aloft at her tall spars and canvas
Against the sky, I'd shake myself and breathe
The ocean air, and let it sink down deep
Into my blood, and know that I'd come back
To something braver in the scheme of things.
Now I was whole again; now I was all myself;
Myself against the ocean and the sky;
And that was all I asked for—no protection:
Nothing beyond the open right to fail.

God, let me go to sea again! My guts are heavy
With all this holding back and dragging down;
Work that is only time-serving; ideas
That land us nowhere; loud high-sounding words,
Empty of meaning, raised to drown out truth
And stop the sound of voices calling order.

I think death must be more like the sea,
Clean and pure and deep, no muddiness,
Open and wide, a dangerous place for fools,
But safe enough for men who know their way.
Blue water! Shining skies! The endless days!
Wind and sail, and the reaches of the dawn!
Work to be done—no rotting among the worms;
Another voyage to make, another landfall,
A new coast and a new line of trade.
By God, you'll have to keep your weather-eye peeled
Among the dangers there beyond the grave!
And after that, who cares? I'm looking forward
To sight that land and bring it close aboard,
Smell the air, and watch the hills grow nearer,
See what the people look like when they come off,
Taste of their fruit, and hear the latest news.
I'd like to meet this God they talk about;

He strikes me as a square sort of fellow.
You can't blame Him for the mutinies and disasters;
He's done His best, an able and faithful shipmaster
With a damned unmanageable crew on his hands.

V

Who sung out? Yes, I'm coming! Wait a minute. . . .
Hell, what's the matter with me? No one called.
Only the wind around the southern windows.

One trip we met a Tartar off the Horn,
Bucking westerly gales for thirty days.
I had a fine young fellow mate with me,
Ben Stinson, from the back part of the town;
But between getting hurt and being young
He lost his nerve; one night he came and begged me
To give it up and run for the Indian Ocean.
Why should I see his face now? A handsome devil;
He died of fever aboard his first command.
I laughed at him and said, "When you are master
You won't quit with all your spars aloft."
He hung his head and stood thinking it over.
"Yes, sir, I see the difference," he said.
"Why do they always make the right things hard?"

I wish the boys today could learn that lesson;
It helps to face it—life will be the same.
Machines can't run the world, or save mankind
From stress that only seamanship could cover.
Each generation has to round the Horn.
I wish men would be braver, or would remember
From age to age, or would put something down
As proved, and not depart from it thereafter;
I wish we could find out our own misfortune,
Or see that fate is only what we ask for,
And leave life plain and simple, as it comes.

What is this brightness all around? Is the day breaking?
Go up and take a look. . . . I want to know.

It seems so still. . . . Look out! It's times like this
That catch you. Oh, be careful! Take no chances.
I hear a breeze coming across the water,
And there she heels to it! Look out, I say!
It's making up too fast. . . . Take in the royals!
We're in for a shift of wind . . . a sudden change. . . .